SCRIBBLINGS
by Tom Kennar
with selected cartoons by Dave Walker

ISBN 978-1-913663-13-1

To John and Lindie
with many thanks for
all your love and support

Tom Kennar

© 2020, Tom Kennar

Published by:
Rev'd Canon Tom Kennar, The Rectory, Havant, PO9 2RP, UK.
www.tomkennar.com

Contents

169. Stories

Short stories to fire imagination

190. Ghana and Togo Journal

A little armchair travelling...

239 The Last Word

Pithy reflections from weekly news sheets

THE SERMON

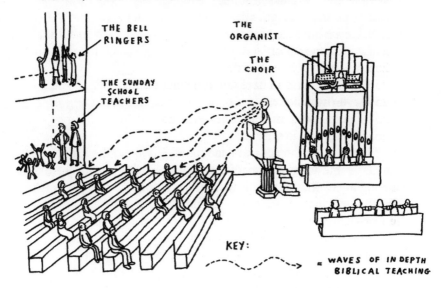

THESE PEOPLE SHOULD BE VISITED REGULARLY FOR
A CHAT ABOUT RECENT SERMON TOPICS

Preface

One of the huge privileges of being a priest is to be able to speak, on a regular basis, to congregations. Whenever I do so, I find myself conscious that a church service is not usually the best place to have a debate – however contentious the ideas are that I may be trying to get across.

Being conscious of these challenges, I have for some years been publishing a large portion of my sermons, meditations, stories and other thoughts online (at www.tomkennar.com). Often that has led my listeners to engage with the thoughts being expressed. Sometimes we've argued and debated online. Sometimes my own thinking has been shaped by the contributions or responses of others. Sometimes, I hope I have been able to do the same for them.

However, it has become increasingly clear in recent years that easy access to the Internet is a luxury that not many members of my congregations have. I have therefore endeavoured to make this collection of assorted scribblings available in book form – in the sincere hope that it might enable others who don't (or can't) use the Internet, to be able to participate in the ongoing conversation about God. (More information about how to converse with me is available in the Epilogue.)

The collection of scribblings included here span a period of about eleven years – from around 2009 to the beginning of 2020. They include stories, meditations, sermons and a travel-log of one of my recent forays into Ghana.

First, under the general heading of 'Living in the Light', I have included some talks and meditations which I hope will get readers thinking about what it means to be today's followers of Jesus Christ. These also include various sermons preached at key turning-points of the Christian year, in the hope that readers will have the chance to reflect on some of the possible meanings of these great events.

The second section of the book includes some original stories. I am a great believer in the power of story to open our minds up to new possibilities. They are often more helpful than a polemical blast from a pulpit.

The third section is a journal I made during my 2012 visit to Ghana. I hope that the arm-chair travellers among my readers will enjoy spending time with me in Africa, and gain some insights not just into my own mind, but also the challenges of the very much missionary faith of the Church in Ghana.

Finally, I have included a few pages of 'last words' – these are 'thoughts for the week' which I have published from time to time in our parish newsletter (over the last couple of years).

My hope is that these 'scribblings' will offer food for thought, no more than that. I claim no expertise as a theologian (except in the sense that we are all called to be those who at least try to think about God). Some of my more erudite colleagues will doubtless find errors of theology here, and I certainly don't insist that anyone should take my own ruminations as authoritative. I am a parish priest who tries to speak into the lives of the people he serves; nothing more. But, by presenting these thoughts in this format, I hope that those who find them will think about them. And perhaps make a personal journey a step closer to God.

A few words of thanks are certainly in order. First, my most sincere gratitude must go to my ever-patient wife and daughter, Clare and Emily. They have had to sit through many of these talks and meditations when they were delivered orally, and they are sometimes the butt of humorous anecdotes (it's part of the sacrifice of being a priest's family!). Without their loving encouragement, and the time they have generously allowed me away from family duties of all kinds, most of the thoughts I have had about God and God's world would simply have been lost to the ether. Their gifts of time and encouragement to me are more appreciated than they can imagine.

Secondly I want to thank the people of the two parishes I have served in the last decade, the North End Portsmouth Team Ministry, and my present parish of Havant, St Faith with St Nicholas, Langstone. By listening and responding to these thoughts over the years we've been together, they have shaped my thinking and honed my ideas. I hope I have done a little shaping in return.

Finally, it is only right to acknowledge that many of the thoughts in these pages have been inspired or suggested by the writings of others. In terms of living authors, I owe a debt of gratitude to the minds of Rowan Williams, Richard Rohr, Rob Bell, Jonathan Sacks, Tom Wright, Brian McLaren, Rosalind Brown, Alistair Begg, and the contributors to the many biblical commentaries on my shelves.

Sermons and meditations are not generally the place to make academic references to where ideas have come from. When possible, I have tried to do so, without unduly altering the rhythm of the speaking-moment. But the occasional resonant phrase or idea, originating from one or more of these authors has often crept into a sermon or meditation without such acknowledgement being overtly made. Often I have no memory from whence they came – only that their resonance spoke to me, stayed with me, so that my own thinking was nourished by them. For such occasions as I have failed to give due acknowledgement in the following pages, I apologise to their authors, and humbly beg forgiveness.

Tom Kennar.
May 2020

A collection of sermons, meditations and talks about being a Christian today.

THE PARISH SYSTEM

THE ENTIRE COUNTRY IS DIVIDED INTO PARISHES. EACH ONE HAS ITS OWN CHURCH. EVERYBODY GOES TO THEIR LOCAL PARISH CHURCH*

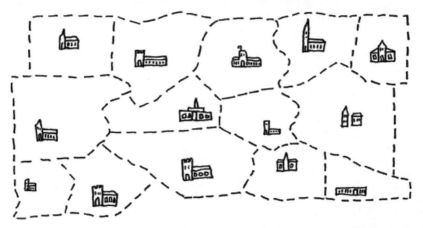

*UNLESS IT IS TOO HIGH, TOO LOW, TOO LIBERAL, TOO EVANGELICAL, TOO CATHOLIC, TOO MIDDLE OF THE ROAD, TOO UNBIBLICAL, HAS TOO MANY BELLS AND SMELLS, HAS TOO MANY SMELLS, HAS SERMONS THAT ARE TOO LONG, HAS TOO MANY CHILDREN, HAS NOT ENOUGH CHILDREN, HAS NO SUNDAY SCHOOL, HAS MUSIC THAT IS TOO OLD FASHIONED, HAS MUSIC THAT IS TOO HAPPY CLAPPY, HAS A VICAR WHO IS A WOMAN, HAS A VICAR WHO IS A MAN, HAS A VICAR WHO IS A BIT ODD, HAS SERVICES THAT START TOO EARLY IN THE MORNING, HAS REALLY BAD COFFEE AFTER THE SERVICES, HAS PARTICULARLY UNCOMFORTABLE PEWS, HAS SERVICES THAT CLASH WITH SUNDAY LUNCH PREPARATION TIME, HAS SERVICES THAT DON'T USE THE BOOK OF COMMON PRAYER, HAS SERVICES THAT DO USE THE BOOK OF COMMON PRAYER OR ISN'T THE CHURCH ASSOCIATED WITH THE PRIMARY SCHOOL THEY HAD IN MIND

Just ordinary, spiritual people.

Reading: John 11.17-44. First preached in 2009

One of the joys of having a computer is the receiving of 'round robin' emails, which people constantly send me. One particular email which arrives routinely, every few weeks or so, is one which lists alleged bloopers from Parish Magazines. I have to admit, some bloopers from parish magazines are priceless. Here's a small selection of my favourites:

- "Ladies, don't forget the rummage sale. It's a chance to get rid of those things not worth keeping around the house. Don't forget your husbands".
- "Today the Vicar will preach his farewell sermon after which the choir will sing 'Break Forth into Joy' "
- Notice in the kitchen of a Church Hall: "Ladies, when you have emptied the teapot, please stand upside down in the sink".
- And here's a special favourite of mine: "During the Easter Sunday service, Mrs Williams of the Mother's Union will lay an egg on the Altar"

Speaking of eggs - it's nearly Easter, so this seems as good a time as any to think about them. Eggs, of course, remind us of new life...and Jesus rose from the tomb in a similar way that new born chicks emerge from an egg. This year, there has been a campaign to produce a Real Easter Egg - chocolate eggs which actually have the story of the Resurrection printed on the side...to try to help an uneducated public make the connection between chocolate eggs and Jesus.

But there is another way in which we can use the image of the egg to contemplate Easter.

In a book called 'Hope Against Darkness', the Franciscan priest Richard Rohr invites us to use the egg to understand something perhaps even more profound than the image of an empty tomb. He suggests that these three elements of the egg - yolk, white and shell, can provide an image for our growth as children of God. The three elements can be thought of as three stories...there is my story, then there is our story, then there is the story. Rohr suggests that true, biblical religion (and especially true, biblical Christianity) honours

9

and integrates these three stories. He calls that process of integration a 'Cosmic Egg of Meaning'.

Let me try to explain Rohr's ideas, especially in relation to our life together as a parish.

The first level at which we all exist is at the level of the individual. This is my story...the essential being that I am. At this level, I live as a private individual - I make my own choices. I decide what I will believe, about God, or about the world. I am the one who has the free will to live a creative life, or to vegetate my days away in front of the television. This is the level of individualism - which is a concept that has really taken hold in recent years... especially in the Western world. This is the level at which we embrace concepts like celebrity... where we become fascinated with the intricate detail of individual lives. Hello Magazine is the herald of the individual. Consumerism is its life-blood. Strictly Come Dancing and the X-Factor are all about the small life of individuals, raised for a moment of fame above the normal boredom of human, individualism.

But on its own, being an individual is a very small stage indeed. It's the little stage where I do my own dance and where the sort of questions we ask ourselves are "Who is watching me? How do I feel? What do I believe? What makes me unique?"

Each of us is, of course, an individual - a loved, beautifully created, individual child of God. But doing 'life' by ourselves is not the solution to a happy and fulfilled existence. Unless we draw from something greater than our mere selves, we are doomed to an endless self-critical, or self-deluding individualism... and we will wither and die. Jesus calls us to something greater, something bigger than mere individualism. In John 15, verse 5, he warns that 'the branch which is cut off from the Vine is useless'. And in today's Gospel, he reminds us that he is both the Resurrection and the Life. Life, in all its fullness cannot be attained by an individual alone.

And so we move to the second part of the egg...to the 'white' if you like. If the yolk symbolises 'my story', the white symbolises 'our story'. This is where the life of the individual becomes integrated into the life of a community. 'I' becomes 'we'. This is where we find our group... our community, perhaps, or our country, perhaps our nationality, or our ethnic group. For many people, the concept of 'us' is often caught up with the kind of music they listen to, or what gang they belong to. We feel protected inside the group. We might be members of a Rotary club, or a jam-making club. We might be supporters of a football team - and gain a sense of purpose by waving flags and signs around. Now we no longer have to be great by ourselves; our greatness is found by belonging to a larger group, whose greatness 'rubs off' on us.

All of us belong to many groups. It is necessary for our growth as human beings to move beyond the yolk, into the 'white' - beyond individualism, and into the group. For Christians, of course, one of the groups that we choose to belong to is the 'Christian Club' - or as we call it, the Church. Here, with other Christians, we find group identity, and group purpose. Together we identify what we need to fight for, and fight against.

For us, in this parish, our mission is enshrined in our Five Year Plan. In that plan, we committed ourselves together, as a group, to being a praying, learning, serving, visible church that is diverse and all-inclusive. That is, in a nutshell... or an egg-shell! It's our group identity.

In that endeavour, we have been prolific together. We have ministered to the sick, and to the lonely, to the bereaved, and to the families of baptised children, and to couples preparing for marriage. We have provided community activities for our neighbours to meet one another (and to migrate from being individuals to being members of a life-giving group). We have maintained our church buildings, so that the Kingdom is seen in bricks and mortar... as well as in lives. We have raised funds, and supported mission in other places. We have sung, we have prayed, we have laughed and we have celebrated. We have danced. We've been together in pubs, and in schools, at quiz nights and concerts.

But we need to go broader and deeper still. If all we are is a group who like doing things together... then we've missed the point entirely. Groups can be wonderfully nurturing places... essential for our growth away from the smallness of individualism. But groups can also be dangerous places. Just think how many people have thrown away their lives for causes which were all about 'group identity'...everyone from the Crusaders to the Nazis. If we are not careful, our group can become our God. We can end up worshipping the Vine, instead of the source of the Vine's life. We can end up worshipping our Church, rather than the God who gives his life to the Church, just as Jesus gave life to Lazarus.

How can we escape from that trap? How can we go deeper and broader, beyond the life of our group, our parish, into the very heart of God?

That is the third part of the egg...the shell. If the yolk is 'my Story' and the white is 'our Story'...then the shell, which binds it all together is 'the Story'.... the sacred story of a God who creates all life and all possibilities, and holds them in his hands. The way to avoid our group becoming the reason for our existence is to go deeper... into the Divine Life, into that which transcends our individualism and our particular group - and which opens us up to the incredible potential of life to the full...or 'eternal life' as Jesus called it.

"I am the Resurrection and the Life....and everyone who believes in me will never die". Or as Jesus is quoted in John 4.14, he is the Living Water: "anyone who drinks of me will never be thirsty again."

The challenge of Richard Rohr's Cosmic Egg is that we should learn to live with all three of its parts. Not content with individualism, we embrace the group. Not content with the group, we embrace the whole... the transcendent reality which is God, in Jesus Christ. Richard Rohr gives some examples of the kind of people who have managed to become like that… people whose sense of themselves and the groups they belong to are enlarged by their connection to the Divine Life. He lists people like Mahatma Gandhi, and Martin Luther King, Mothers Teresa and Julian of Norwich.

But how? How do we do this?

I used to get a great deal of ribbing as I drove around our Diocese and Deanery. I got teased mercilessly by my colleagues in clerical collars because, for a while, I insisted on driving around in a car which had stickers on the door. One of my colleague vicars kept turning my stickers upside down, from the day he discovered that they were magnetic!

What did those stickers say? Basically, just four simple words...words we agreed some time ago would be our motto as a parish..."Just Ordinary, Spiritual People".

Because that's what we are...or at least, what we aspire to be. On the one hand, we are ordinary people. We are individuals, who like many individuals have discovered something of the joy and the challenge of living together in community. In our case, we live as part of a group we call our Parish. Like other ordinary people, we care about our buildings, and our social programmes. Like other ordinary people, who belong to other ordinary clubs, we sing in choirs and bands, we run table top sales and fayres, we paint, we dig, we polish, we maintain.

But that is all, basically, the stuff of ordinary people. Essentially, on that level, there is little difference between what we do and what most community clubs do. Go into the local Community Centre, or the local community choir, or any charity shop and you will find people who are just as committed, just as passionate about what their organisation, their group, is doing for the community around them. And rightly so. And many of our members are members of these other clubs and groups too.

But we aspire to more. We are ordinary yet spiritual people. That's what we claim about ourselves. We claim that our inspiration comes from a greater, wider, deeper, broader root than pure group identity. We claim to be people who are spiritual. We are those whose lives are caught up not just with each other, but with the source of all life...the transcendent reality of God. By our simple claim to be 'just ordinary spiritual people' we claim to be in touch with the whole of the Cosmic Egg...yolk, white, and shell. We claim to be people whose lives are rooted in the Lord who is the Resurrection and the Life.

So here is our challenge for years ahead. We have laid some strong foundations together in the last few years. Our buildings are better maintained than they have been for some time. Our congregation numbers are rising, and our income is holding steady, despite the economic hardships of our age. But now, we need to go deeper. Now we need to discover more of what it means to be people who are spiritual beings – those in whom the Holy Spirit makes His dwelling.

What would it mean for us to be truly spiritual people? Could there come a time when anyone who visits any of our churches finds only unconditional love and acceptance? Sometimes I think we're nearly there. Could there come a time when we truly begin to see ourselves as intimately connected not just with each other and God, but with a whole world outside our doors...a world which is desperately lost in the lies of consumerism and individualism? Could there come a time when we give as much money to alleviate poverty as we currently give to maintain our church buildings?

That's the kind of vision that I want to hold before you today. It's just not enough for us to be just three churches who happen to have a presence in this area. God calls us to something greater, wider, deeper, and much more spiritual. God calls us to be salt and light to our neighbours. God calls us to become the spiritual heart of this community...the first place that anyone turns, when they begin to glimpse that there is more to life than just individualism alone.

We are called to be those who understand the full implications of the Cosmic Egg. We are called to be those who model what it means to be ordinary, yet deeply spiritual people.

BEHIND THE SCENES

THERE IS MORE TO THE LIFE OF A CHURCH THAN THE GOINGS ON THAT ONE CAN OBSERVE ON A SUNDAY. MUCH OF THIS ACTIVITY TAKES PLACE IN A SECRET LABYRINTH OF SUBTERRANEAN TUNNELS

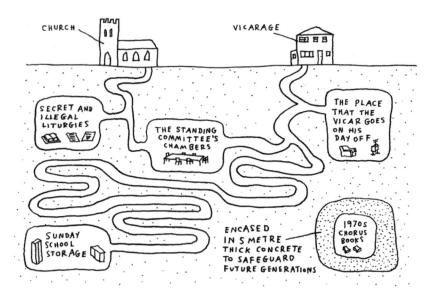

Walker under water

Reading: Matthew 14.22-36. First preached 2011.

Have you ever heard of William Walker? Walker was a diver, who was born in the 1800s. He was one of the first divers of the Royal Navy, training in 1887 at Portsmouth Dockyard. As one the nation's earliest divers, he had many exciting adventures. On one occasion, he was called to Wales, to rescue drowning miners from a pit collapse. He was one of the divers who worked on the Blackwall Tunnel, and he held the distinction of being the diving instructor for King George V. However, the achievement for which he is most famous was something rather more local to us.

Between 1906–1911, working in water up to a depth of 20, he shored up Winchester Cathedral, using more than 25,000 bags of concrete, 115,000 concrete blocks, and 900,000 bricks.

Winchester Cathedral, you see, had been built about 800 years before by the Normans. At the time, the land all around the Cathedral was essentially a peat bog. So, with their typically cunning engineering, the Normans built their cathedral on a giant raft. For 800 years, the Cathedral had essentially floated on top of the peat bog. But by the end of the 19th Century, with the peat bog drained away to create the town of Winchester, the cathedral had been in imminent danger of collapse as it sank slowly into the ground. William Walker was responsible for shoring up the walls by putting concrete underneath them. He worked six hours a day, in complete darkness, because the peat sediment suspended in the water was impenetrable to light.

It's a wonderful story, isn't it? I love the idea of a church floating on water for so many years. And yet, this is actually a very old image. Matthew's story of Jesus walking on the water begins with a very similar metaphor. Water, for the Israelites, was a symbol of chaos, and challenge. It was over the chaotic waters that the Spirit of God had brooded, in Genesis, before God spoke and brought forth the land. It was through the dangerous waters that God brought the Israelites out of Egypt. Jonah and the Whale. Noah and the Flood. Over and over again, water is a symbol of chaos, difficulty and challenge.

So, to a first century reader of Matthew's gospel, the idea of Jesus sending all his disciples off in a boat would have been instantly recognised as another story of challenge on the ocean. The boat in this story can very easily be pictured as the church, containing all the disciples of Jesus (who were, then, the Church!). In fact, Matthew goes still further, to make his point. Where our English translation describes the little boat as being battered by the waves, Matthew's original word, in Greek, was 'tortured'...the little boat was being 'tortured' by the waves, just as the church in Matthew's own day was being tortured by the Authorities.

This then is Matthew's picture of the church. Jesus sends out his followers into a leaky tub, into an ocean of challenge, difficulty and chaos. This is not a church which rides above the difficulties of life, but a church which finds itself in the middle of everything life can throw. Buffeted, even tortured, by the world around it, church members look to the shore, desperate for a word of encouragement from Jesus, wondering why he is not in the boat with them.

Because, you see, the little boat on the Sea of Galilee has left Jesus behind on the shore, just as the church left Jesus behind in history. It seems impossible that Jesus could be with us. And yet, as the morning dawns, the disciples in the boat see Jesus striding towards them, over the chaos of the sea. He calls to them, over the storm, "Take heart! It is I! Do not be afraid".

But like us, Peter still wonders. Can this really be Jesus? He proposes a little test. "If it is you, Lord, command me to come to you on the water". Jesus replies with a single word, "Come". Peter - the first disciple, the archetype for all disciples, steps out of the boat, walking towards Jesus on top of the water! He does what Jesus does. He copies him, and for a while, he succeeds. But as he looks at the storm all around him, he becomes frightened, and starts to sink.

Jesus reaches out his hand, and rescues Peter. He helps him into the boat, commenting sadly, that Peter is of little faith. "How could you doubt?" Jesus asks, sadly.

I wonder how many times you have heard this story. And I wonder how many times, like me, you have been told that this is a story about faith. Certainly all the preachers I heard as a youngster used to tell me that Peter's problem was his lack of faith. "If only Peter had had more faith, he could have overcome his fear and conquered the act of walking on the water". The message to us is often read as "If only we had more faith, we could conquer all our problems in spectacular ways".

But I wonder…

I have a problem with that interpretation. Can it really be that God wants us to believe that bad things happen to us because we don't have enough faith? Can it be that God wants us to feel guilty when we are sick, or when accidents happen, or when people persecute us - guilty that these things are happening because we don't have enough faith? I'm not sure I can believe that.

Faith is not about being able to walk on the water. Only God can do that. Faith is about believing, in the midst of the storm and the chaos of life, that Jesus is in the boat with us. In spite of all the evidence, faith is the act of believing that God is in the boat with us, sharing our pain, sharing in our weakness. God is made real in the community of faith as it makes its way through the storm, battered, tortured, by the waves.

Do you struggle to respond to all the challenges of your community, your building, the starving world?

"It is I: do not be afraid"

Are you feeling ill or depressed?

"It is I: do not be afraid".

Are you doubting the reality of God in your life?

"It is I: do not be afraid"

Are you nearing the end of life?

"It is I: do not be afraid"

This too is the message of the Cross. On the Cross, all the chaos of the world was brought together in one sustained attack on the goodness of God. Christ, the one who mediates between God and Man, is overpowered by the chaos of humanity, which punishes him, tortures him and kills him. Jesus shares in the suffering of all human beings on the cross and yet manages to overcome them. He walks on the water, above the chaos. He rises from the dead, above the chaos.

Peter's mistake in the boat was to fail to recognise the transforming power of God. Instead, he tried to do it himself. "Let me walk on the water" was his cry.

I remember my daughter, when she was very small, struggling with a jigsaw puzzle. I got frustrated at her lack of progress, and bent

17

down to help her - and was astonished at her reply. "Do it myself!" she said.

Isn't that what we all do, from time to time, to God? In spite of all that God has taught us about how to live, we still try to 'do it myself'. We try to walk on the water, instead of letting Jesus come and sit beside us in the boat.

Jesus says to us: "Live simply. Do not worry about what tomorrow will bring".

We say "Do it myself!" and hoard our possessions and savings in case of the coming storm.

Jesus says to us: "You are members of one body, fruit on the vine of the church"

We say "Do it myself" and decide that we don't need the hassle of coming to church.

Jesus says: "Blessed are the peacemakers, the children of God"

We say "Do it myself" and harbour our hatreds and our lack of forgiveness for decades

Peter's problem was that he didn't understand that Jesus comes to us through the chaos of life. Peter didn't have enough faith in the God who walks beside us on the road, or who comes to sit beside us in the boat. He wanted to get to Jesus, through the chaos - instead of letting Jesus come to him.

We yearn for instant answers, instant solutions. We want to walk on the water too! But Jesus wants to sit beside us in the boat, going through all the challenges of life, sharing them and helping us to learn through them. There are two storm stories in the Gospel. In one of them, Jesus says to the waves, "Quiet, be still". In the other, Jesus strides above the storm, through the storm. You see, Jesus doesn't always still the storm...sometimes he uses the storm for greater purposes.

If I am poor, Jesus can show me how rich I truly am. If I am sick, Jesus can show me how well I really am. On the other hand, if I am rich, Jesus can show me my poverty. If I am healthy, Jesus can point me to where my sickness lays. In every circumstance of life, there is something to learn, some new growth for our souls to embrace. Life - the storm, the ocean, - is the proving ground for our souls. It is here that Jesus prepares us for life which goes on forever. It is here that he sits beside us in the boat.

So, let me ask you. What is Jesus teaching you today? As he sits beside you in the boat, in the middle of your own particular storm, what is he saying to you?

Can you hear him?

If you can't, then seek him out.

How? Here are some suggestions:

First, try speaking to another Christian - listen for the voice of Jesus through the voices of other believers. Chat with Christian friends. Seek out a priest, or a deacon, and share what's on your heart. Listen, together, to what God is saying.

Secondly - and here's a really radical thought...why not read Jesus' words? Try actually opening the Bible you keep on your shelf at home. Start with the Gospels, and work through the New Testament (leave the Old Testament until you've got some practice at hearing God's voice).

Thirdly - give yourself some space to think, and to pray. Switch off the TV or the radio from time to time. Spend time in quietness, mulling over the circumstances of your life. Ask God to teach you what God wants to teach you Reflect on all that is happening and how God is growing your soul today.

Fourthly - why not buy a book? Try one of the many challenging, encouraging books which will lead you to think more about what God is saying to you, each day.

And finally - be diligent about meeting with the rest of us. Don't stop being together in church. Don't try to get out of the boat and walk on the water by yourself. We are in this boat together - and together we will hear Jesus calling over the waves:

"It is I: do not be afraid".

Rituals

Reading: Mark 1.4-11 (The Baptism of Jesus). First preached 2009

When I first came to North End, one of my greatest fears was that I would mess up, when performing the rituals that you have traditionally used around here. My background churchmanship was very low, very low indeed.

In fact, the Anglican Church I attended during the 1990s was so 'low', that we only celebrated Holy Communion about once every three months...and that was in the evening. We never lit candles (because our priest thought them to be rather too 'Roman'), and the Lord's Table was never dressed in fine linen. We drank from a normal wine glass, and we ate chunks of real bread, scattering crumbs everywhere (instead of the crumb-less wafers that are used here). Our minister (who never referred to himself as a priest) almost never wore a clerical collar, and almost never wore robes either. Robes were reserved for weddings and funerals; never for a Sunday service.

The church in which I served as a Curate was somewhat less closed to ritual. While I was there, I learned a great deal about the power of symbols, and the value of certain rituals. But I was still a long way from the kind of Catholic tradition you have developed here in North End, over the years.

So I came here in fear and trembling! Would I get it right? Would I bow in all the right places? Would I know when to do things, and how to do them, in the 'right' way? But I was willing to give it a go - to see what I could learn from participating. This is why I now carry the gospel high and proud above my head as we process into church. It's why I willingly go through the motions of carrying the same gospel out into the body of the church, when we read it. It's why I symbolically wash my hands before celebrating the Eucharist. And it's why we had incense during Midnight Mass, just a couple of weeks ago. (Although the more observant of you will have noticed that I was too scared to do the 'wafting' myself...I got our Head Server to do it!)

This morning's gospel reading confronts us with a truth that some people find uncomfortable - especially those who would like to rid the church of all symbolism and ritual. That uncomfortable truth is this: Jesus was into ritual. By submitting to the practice of baptism, by allowing himself to be submerged under water in a symbolic action of cleansing, Jesus opened himself to letting the ritual speak to him and to those around him. The result of his willingness was that voice of God, from heaven, announcing "You are my Son, whom I love; with you I am well pleased".

And baptism wasn't the only ritual that Jesus engaged with. He worshipped in the synagogue and temple thereby subjecting himself to all the rituals that would have gone on there. He celebrated the Passover - a ritualistic feast, with a thousand-year history. He instituted new rituals for his followers, like the symbolic washing of feet, and the Lord's Supper - the very Eucharist which we will soon celebrate together.

Of course, every church, even the least obviously-ritualistic, has its rituals. Just the act of gathering together at a set time, is a ritual of a sort. Choosing to start every service with half an hour of singing is a ritual. Having coffee and fellowship after the service is a ritual.

And of course, our whole lives are full of ritual. My morning ritual, for example, is very important to me. I wake up, pray briefly, then stagger down the stairs for my first infusion of super-strength caffeine. My family will tell you that unless I'm allowed half an hour to come to, on my back porch, then I just won't be human. I need my morning ritual. It's part of who I am.

So I completely understand why some of you tell me that you need your church rituals as well. Sometimes, when you tell me you want certain things to happen, I confess that I'm a bit naughty with you. Some of you have already heard my question, "Why? Why do you want to do such and such? What does it mean?"

There's a reason why I ask that question. You see, for me, religion should never be about ritual - it should be about relationship. Unless a certain ritual serves to deepen our relationship with God and with each other, then, frankly, it should not be used. Let me tell you why I think that.

Remember the story of Moses and the Burning Bush. At the end of his conversation with God, Moses asks God what his name is. "Whom shall I say has sent me?" is the question that Moses has for God. Moses is after God's name. He wants a word which will sum up what God is. He wants a noun for God.

But God doesn't give Moses a noun; a simple naming word, like 'The Creator', or 'The Lord' or Eric. No, God gives Moses a verb, a doing word. God says that his name is Yahweh, which translates as "I am that I am", or "I will be what I will be".

A verb is an active word: living, crying, loving, laughing, sighing, moaning, being - these are all verbs. God wanted Moses (and us) to understand that in his very nature, at the very core of who God was and is there is the concept of being. This is a God who is active and at work. This is not the God who simply 'created', but the God who goes on creating. This is not the God once loved the world, but the God who goes on loving us, second by second, minute by minute, day by day.

Just think about that for a moment. Perhaps it might help to think of a light bulb. A light bulb will only keep on shining as long as there is electricity flowing through the filament. We are like that. The Universe is like that. We only exist, and continue to exist, because God continues to give us life. St Paul, writing to the Colossians said about Jesus that 'in Him all things now hold together'. (Col 1.17)

So we don't worship a dead God, a God of the past, a God who can be named, and put in a box. We worship a living God, an ever-creating God, a God who wants to flow into us, through us, and out of us.

So our rituals need to reflect that reality. Dead ritual only speaks of how things were. Dead ritual is done because 'that's the way we've always done it'. Living ritual is ritual that is connected to our common belief; the belief that God is alive among us and that Jesus calls us to be his brothers and sisters.

So I hold the gospel high because I want to point to the importance of the words it contains. I carry the gospel out to you, when it is read, because these words point us towards life. They need to be shared with all the people. I bow to you, the congregation, because in you I see and experience God, and because I want you to know that I am your servant. I celebrate the Eucharist, or the Mass, or the Holy Communion (or whatever you want to call it) because I believe that Jesus offers us his life, as well as his death. By eating and drinking of that life, we ritualistically and symbolically say 'yes' to living with God at our core. God as our Lord. God as the source of our own lives.

Ritual mattered to Jesus. Signs and Sacraments (like the Baptism he submitted to and the meal he instituted) were living, visual images of the life that Jesus called us to. By his baptism, Jesus calls us to repent, to 'return' to God, the source of our life. By his last supper, Jesus invites us to drink deeply, and eat heartily, of the life he offers us.

By these rituals, Jesus points us to and reminds us of what it means to be a child of the living God.

THE SERVICE
WHERE THE VICAR GOES

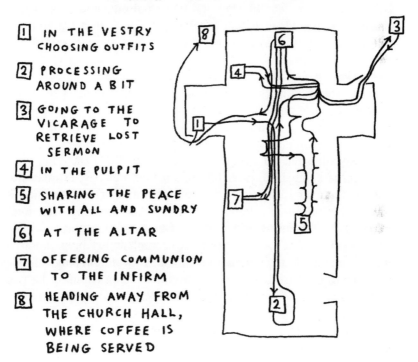

1. IN THE VESTRY CHOOSING OUTFITS
2. PROCESSING AROUND A BIT
3. GOING TO THE VICARAGE TO RETRIEVE LOST SERMON
4. IN THE PULPIT
5. SHARING THE PEACE WITH ALL AND SUNDRY
6. AT THE ALTAR
7. OFFERING COMMUNION TO THE INFIRM
8. HEADING AWAY FROM THE CHURCH HALL, WHERE COFFEE IS BEING SERVED

Bread and Circuses

Reading: Luke 4.1-13: The Temptation of Jesus

A Meditation for Lent 2010 – the year of the London Olympics

Here we are in Lent, again! What, already? It seems like only last week we were celebrating Christmas! But here we are; entering that great period of preparation for the Festival of Easter.

Preparation is everything. Athletes who are competing in the Olympics have been preparing for the last four years for this very event. Four years of early mornings, strict diets, punishing exercise routines. I guess all that is why I will never be an Olympic athlete!

School teachers will tell you how vital preparation is. Unless you have prepared what you are going to do with a classroom of children, the class will be chaotic and a waste of time for everyone.

It's the same for us in the church too. Preparation undergirds everything that we do. Sermon-writing, music selection, choir practice, rota-fixing, Sunday school teaching, maintenance, flower arranging, counting the collection, writing-up the service-register, writing, printing, folding and distributing the pew news, paying the bills so that the lights come on. A massive amount of preparation goes into every time that we meet, by a small army of dedicated people.

Jesus believed in preparation. In fact, our best estimates are that he took over 30 years to prepare for his ministry. He studied, he prayed, he observed life and finally, when he was completely prepared, he set out to be baptised. But even then, there was still preparation to do. Jesus needed to complete his preparation by opening himself to the temptations that he knew might plague him as he began to exercise his ministry. So, after being baptised, he went off for 40 days, into the desert to be, in Luke's words, 'tempted by the devil'.

Now before we go any further into this story, I need to say a few words about the devil. I have to tell you that I'm not a great believer in the idea of an actual, real, demonic person called the devil, or Satan, or Beelzebub. I personally think it is rather too easy to blame a distant, un-seen person for all the evil in the world that is, in the main, caused by simple human greed. I also have theological

24

problems with the idea of a loving heavenly Father, who creates children for his delight, and even sends his son to die for them and then at the same time lets an evil little demon among them to tempt them away from his love. It just doesn't make sense to me. It would be like an earthly parent who says to their children "I love you - with all my heart, soul, mind and strength. But I'm going to let an axe-wielding, drug-addicted, child-beating murderer come and live in the house to constantly tempt you away from my love". We believe God to be all-powerful. He could deal with such a devil with the snap of his fingers! The idea that God would permit such an evil force to have free reign over his children on earth is, frankly abhorrent.

I believe that the devil, therefore, is a metaphor; a 'personification' of the idea of evil. The devil represents the idea of anything that is not pure, good and holy. So, when Luke says that Jesus went into the wilderness and was tempted by the devil, I prefer to think that Jesus was tempted by the same human instincts that we all have. He had the same human instinct to dominate, the instinct to use our power, or our intelligence, or our cunning to get what we want. Talk about the devil is intended to sum all that base human instinct up into one word.

But you are perfectly entitled to believe in a real, personal devil if you need to. Just, please, don't blame him for everything that is wrong with the world. Human beings are quite capable of messing up their lives without any help from a guy with blood-shot bananas on his head!

So, if you will allow me, I'll use the language of metaphor. Let's talk about the devil as if he were an actual person, just for the sake of the story. So - what happens next?

The devil - Jesus' human instincts - begins to make some suggestions for how his ministry might play out.

Here comes the first challenge: "Why don't you turn those stones into bread?"

You see, Jesus was being tempted to use his power to provide food for himself. He was starving-hungry. He had not eaten for 40 days. He must have been as thin as a rake, and as hungry as an ox. But why bread? Why is the temptation limited to bread? Why not a steaming bowl of stroganoff? Or a nice Tikka Masala?

25

Let's think about the context of this story. Remember that Jesus lived during the time of the Roman Empire - the most politically and militarily powerful empires there had ever been. A few years ago, my family and I went to Italy for a few days, and we visited the Coliseum in Rome. We were amazed at what we saw - a HUGE arena in which the citizens of Rome would watch gladiators fighting each other, and Christians being fed to the lions. The Coliseum was also the place where the Emperors of Rome would distribute free food to the crowd.

The Emperors were clever politicians. They understood that simple people needed just two basic things to keep them happy (and to stop them complaining about the way the Emperor spent their taxes). The solution was simple: entertainment, and food. Or, as the Roman expression went, "Bread and Circuses". The Kingdom of Rome was based on Bread, Circuses and political power. But Jesus had come to proclaim another Kingdom. Not the Kingdom of Rome, but the Kingdom of God, which he also called the Kingdom of Heaven.

When Jesus was challenged to turn stones into bread, we could say he was being tempted to follow the Roman way: "provide food for people, and they will follow you".

But Jesus said no. "It is written: Man does not live on bread alone, but on every word that comes from the mouth of God."

Jesus knew that food alone is not enough. If you feed someone, you only put off the time when they will ultimately die. But if you can change their heart, help them to tune themselves to the words of God, then you open up the opportunity of eternal life with God. Jesus wanted his ministry to count for ever, not just until the next meal.

So, our metaphorical devil tried a new tack. Effectively: "Why don't you throw yourself off the temple and let the angels catch you?"

Bread and Circuses. The old Roman trick. The devil was tempting Jesus to use his power to do amazing miracles that would wow the crowd. I'm pretty sure that if I threw myself off the top of St Mark's after this service, and some angels rescued me, you'd all think I was pretty fantastic. Word would soon spread around the City of the amazing flying Rector!

But again, Jesus knew that amazing miracles would not turn people towards God. He knew that the changes we need to make take place on the inside, not on the outside. Faith is not about asking God to do amazing feats of supernatural wonder. It's about trusting that God is in control, and is with us through every circumstance of life...the high circus-type experiences, yes. But also when the chips are down, and the going gets tough.

So Jesus rebuked his 'devil' - the darker potentials of his human nature: "Do not put the Lord your God to the test."

So the devil tried for the last time. He took Jesus to the top of a very high mountain and showed him the kingdoms of the world laid out before him. (Incidentally, that's another reason to look for metaphor in this story. Even from the top of Everest, all the kingdoms of the world could not be seen. The world is just too round for that!)

"Why don't you worship me?" says the devil, "then I will give you all this!"

Bread, circuses...and political power. The old Roman trick again. The devil was tempting Jesus to establish a kingdom of political power. To use his power from heaven to defeat the Romans by the sword, and to raise up an army which would conquer the world. Many people expected that this was exactly what the Messiah would do.

But again, Jesus wasn't interested. He knew that all the political power in the world would not create the circumstances that he wanted. God sent Jesus into the world because God loves people. God loves us. God has great passion for the poor.

God hates war and poverty and slavery and injustice and global warming. It's right that we fight to improve the world in which we live. But after 2000 more years of human beings trying to solve their conflicts through ever more ingenious weapons, perhaps the time is coming when we might try another way. God's way.

George Bush and Tony Blair famously began what they called the War on Terror. A decade and more later, Afghanistan is still a terrorist stronghold; Iraq is a political mess, and terrorists still set off bombs around the world. Violence has not defeated violence. It rarely does. The circumstances which created 9/11 are still there. The Western World still seeks to dominate the rest of the world, and to control the oil supplies. The West still seeks to export its way of life around the world and closes its ears to the idea that there might be other ways of living. Dialogue and cross-cultural exchange is drowned out by the ugly voices of exclusivism and nationalism.

God's way is the way of turning the other cheek, of forgiveness to your brother, and of carrying your brother's burden. The way of the Cross is the way that initially submits to evil, and then overcomes it through love. Jesus could have taken political power. He could have raised an army to smite the Romans and every other political force in the world at that time. But unless the hearts of the people were changed, any political solution would only be temporary.

There's another question for us here too. What system of political power does each of us willingly submit to, day by day? Is it Liberalism or Socialism, Marxism or Materialism, Conservatism or Consumerism? All of us, in different ways, submit to a political viewpoint, or a way of acting that we think will make the world a better place. But the message of Jesus is this: submit, first to God. Submit, first, to the Lord of the Universe, and to his simple message of loving our neighbour. That is the way to happiness. That is the way to peace. Seek ye first the Kingdom of God, and his righteousness and all these things will be added unto you. Halleluiah!

So what was Jesus' response? "Away from me Satan! For it is written 'Worship the Lord your God, and serve him only!'"

In other words, we need to put God first. Not bread, not circuses, not earthly power systems, but God. God who made us. God who sustains us. God who has saved us, and continues to save us through Jesus Christ.

So in this period of Lent, let me invite you to take some time to ask yourself what you are putting first in your life. What is it that you trust, and base your life on? What is the most important thing in your life?

Do you crave material possessions? Do you long to own more stuff? Are you filling your house with things? It's all just Bread.

Do you seek new and exciting experiences? Is another holiday all that you live for? Are you in desperate need to catch the latest episode of Big Brother, or Strictly Come Dancing? These are just circuses: which switch off our brains, and dull our senses. Instead of being people who are alive for God, working for a just, loving world, we can so easily become sofa-fodder. Sunk into our comfy cushions, we can be those who never raise a finger or reach out a hand to another human being. I'm as guilty as anyone of that. It's so easy to give-in to the one-eyed god in the corner of my living room when there are relationships to be made and sustained - real people, not ghosts in the machine in front of me.

Do you place your hope in a political system? Capitalism, Communism, Consumerism? They represent only earthly power. Temporary, and doomed to fail.

To each of us, the invitation of Jesus rings loud and clear: "Come to me. Seek first the Kingdom of God, and trust in me. I am the faithful one, unchanging, the rock who will be your anchor through all the storms of life."

Scripture constantly throws a question at us: 'how are you going to spend your days?'. Are you going to spend them accumulating wealth that you can't take with you, or soaking up the TV and the next adrenaline fix? Or are you going to spend your days building community, creating relationships, caring about others, and worshipping God for whose pleasure you were made.

Will it be bread and circuses and the vain promises of political power? Or will it be life, to the full, through a total dedication to loving God and loving our neighbour.

The choice is ours to make.

May you find, during these 40 days of lent, a new light for your path, a new sense of the exciting call of God on your life. May you be drawn to a life that is made full by a focus on God and neighbour, in which the needs of self recede into the back-ground. May you say 'no' to the demonic temptation to bury yourself in bread and circuses, closing your eyes to the reality of life around you. May you say 'yes' to the call of life, the call of God, the call of eternity.

Sex and Seduction

Reading: Mark 6.14-29. Preached 2009

One Friday night, at an end of term party for the choir, I happened to mention that I was going to be preaching about sex on Sunday. One of the choir (who shall remain nameless) immediately responded, "Oh no! I've been doing that all day!" After everyone had a good laugh, and the lady in question had a wonderful blush, she explained that the children at her school had been doing 'Personal and Social Development' all day, and that they had been learning about sex!

This story of the beheading of John the Baptist is one of the more gruesome stories in the Bible; not just because of the hideous notion of presenting a man's head on a platter. I think it's even more gruesome than that because of what it says about the power of seduction, and the allure of sex.

Picture the scene. The daughter of Herodias (the niece of the King) was asked to dance for Herod and his guests at a banquet. Her dance is known as the dance of the seven veils and has been repeated throughout history in ballets and operas. It's a seductive dance, from which other famous Middle Eastern dances sprang like the alluring 'belly dance'. It no doubt contained lots of shaking hips, and wobbling mammary glands! By tradition, the dance involved the successive removal of seven veils; each one showing a little bit more of the dancer and her face. It was a tease; literally the fore-runner of the strip-tease. It was designed to titillate, and to drive the male audience into a frenzy of desire.

Well, it certainly worked on Herod. He didn't worry too much about the fact that this was his niece. After-all, he had already married his dead brother's wife (for which John the Baptist had already condemned him). Ruling families in those days quite often married their family members as a way, they thought, of keeping the royal blood-line pure. (Of course, madness was often the result).

So Herod paid no attention to the fact that the dancing girl was his niece. What he saw was simply an alluring young woman, slowly and deliberately removing layer after layer of clothing. We can easily imagine him clapping his hands, sighing and mooning over the girl.

At the end of her dance, captivated by her beauty, and letting his royal guard down for a moment, he said, "Ask me for whatever you want, and I'll give it to you - up to half of my kingdom!"

That was it! The girl rushed back to her mother who seems to have been a rather manipulative sort. Half of Herod's kingdom didn't really amount to much. Herod was only a vassal King, who ruled with the permission of the Romans (who actually owned the land). Herodias knew that even half a kingdom of goats and desert wasn't worth much. But she did see her chance to rid herself of the prophet, John, who had been a thorn in her side for a long time. "Ask him for the head of John the Baptist", she said.

And so, because he couldn't go back on his royal word in front of his guests, Herod reluctantly ordered John to be executed, and had his head brought in on a platter.

Herod had weakened. The power of the sexual urge is very strong. Throughout history, great men have often been brought down by it. Helen of Troy - over whom two great nations went to war. Cleopatra. Delilah. Greek myth is laden with men who have gone to their deaths for beautiful women. Sex-starved sailors have often been lured to rocks because of the mere possibility of glimpsing a mermaid.

In our own time, marketing professionals know the power of seduction. We've all seen the perfume adverts, and the car commercials. I wonder. Do you think I drive a Renault because an advert once told me to 'shake a little ass'?!

At the darker end of seduction, we all know stories of people who have been drawn into obsessions with sex. We've all heard the stories of people who have given into their primal urges at all sorts of levels - from pornography, all the way down through wife-swapping and orgies, as far as the great evil of paedophilia.

We might well ask what this is all about. How has this sexual urge within us come to be so fundamental to us? Why is it so strong? If our picture of God is of one who designs the world with intricate care, what (we might wonder) is God doing when he makes us to be such powerfully sexual people?

Well, at one level it's a relatively simple answer. According to the Hebrew Bible, God's command to creation and to humans in particular, was "Be fruitful, and multiply". The sexual desire is ultimately rooted in the desire to pro-create. We need to pass on our genes to the next generation (as Richard Dawkins so eloquently explained in 'The Selfish Gene'). And let's face it, the sexual urge is a powerful tool in that act of pro-creation. For one thing, it helps us to overcome our more natural urge to sit on the sofa, on our own, with a bar of chocolate, or a huge tub of ice-cream!

But there's more to it than that. As men and women who are made in the image of God, we are sexual beings. We relate to each other in all sorts of ways that are coloured by our sexuality. I was recently reading some guidance for people involved in one-to-one counselling situations, from a book of 'Ethics in Pastoral Ministry' by Richard Gula. The guidance was essentially focused on creating safe, non-threatening situations - avoiding the possibility of inappropriate sexual behaviour. Gula says that it is important to acknowledge the place of our sexuality in such relationships.

Counsellors (whether they be church ministers, or psycho-therapists) of course need to be aware of the potential for the exploitation of vulnerable people who seek their help. Body language, or the way that chairs are placed, having someone else around in another room - all need to be carefully considered in order to give protection to everyone involved. But while all of that is vital, Gula suggests that we need to acknowledge, and even celebrate the fact that our sexuality is a resource for ministry. That is because our sexuality is "a relational power, supplying energy for creativity, responsiveness, passion and commitment. It is also a means of being present to those who are hurting as well as being passionately devoted to setting relationships right...our sexuality is the ordinary medium through which God's love moves to touch, to create, to heal."

Our sexuality, then, is one of the God-given ways in which we relate to each other. It has sometimes been suggested that one of the reasons that some parts of the Church has resisted the ordination of women is because many women find that they can relate more easily to a male priest. If they are heterosexual, women can find it easier to connect with someone of the opposite gender. That's because issues of sexuality come into play.

Our sexuality then is a gift from God that enables us to connect with other people. When two people are in love, we are not at all surprised when one of them is able to sense at a deep level how the other is feeling. But that ability to sense and have compassion for others isn't just something which manifests itself through romance. It is something that is in us all. In many senses, it waits to be fanned into desire for one particular person, but it's always there, subliminally, in the way in which we feel, and love, and care for all people.

But, like all of God's gifts, our sexuality needs to be carefully and properly managed. There are clear boundaries which the writers of the Bible have set for us. Our sexuality, while always with us, and always part of us, should only be allowed its most unfettered expression within the bounds of faithful, committed relationships. Anytime that we allow ourselves to be seduced by the lure of sex in the marketplace, on the street, in the magazine or on the internet - then we let our sexuality get out of balance. Instead of being a force for love, care, compassion and commitment to others, it can be twisted into a morbid, self-satisfying desire for personal gratification.

The Bible teaches us that we find our fullest expression of our humanity through loving God, and loving our neighbour. But when we start to seek our own gratification first, we get out of balance. We can become obsessive, wrapped up in our desire for the next sexual experience. We can quickly forget the higher purpose and calling for which we were made. We are called towards the love of others, including God, before ourselves - and called to be changed from glory into glory. We are called to become ever more like the self-giving God in whose image we are made.

Of course it isn't only sex that can seduce us. The world is full of many seductive temptations. We can be seduced into believing that wealth will make us happy, or that a new set of clothes, or that new car, will fulfil our deepest desire. We can be seduced into believing that another cigarette is all we need, or that another pint of beer will bring us happiness. But how are we to be able to judge? How can we stay in balance when so many seductions are around us? There are so many metaphorical dances of the seven veils being danced around us.

Jesus gave us a piece of advice that may perhaps guide us. "Where your treasure is, there will your heart be also" (Matthew 6:21). You see, the way we choose to spend our money, or our time, says a great deal about which seductions we have given in to. I want to suggest to you that this is, again, a question of balance.

Let's try a little exercise together. Let me invite you to think about what you spend your money on, week by week. Leave aside all the essential stuff - the rent, the mortgage, the petrol, the council tax, the weekly food-bill. The question I want you to ask yourself is "what do I spend my disposable income on? How do I use the money that is left over after the bills are paid?" Then, ask yourself "what is the largest single expenditure that I make from my disposable income?"

Just think about that for a moment.

What do you spend your cash on?

Is it life-affirming? Does it reflect your (and my) calling to be people who love God and love our neighbour?

How does the amount you spend on that one item, or one luxury, compare to the amount of money you give to relieve poverty or sickness? How much is given for the work of God in this church or around the world?

"Where your treasure is, there will your heart be also."

We can, of course, do precisely the same exercise with our time. We all have at least some spare time. How much of it is used up doing things that are life-affirming and love-sharing? How much is used up in things that we have been seduced into doing by marketing managers and television producers?

"Where your treasure is, there will your heart be also."

Please don't misunderstand me. I don't want you to go forward from here feeling miserable and guilt-ridden! I simply want to invite us all, in the light of the story of Herodias' daughter, to become alert to this question: "What am I seduced by?" Maybe it's sex. Maybe it's alcohol. Maybe it's TV or computer games. Maybe it's food. Maybe it's consumerism. Maybe it's the desire to gossip. There are very few of us who are not, at one time or another, seduced by something.

Our task (as people who are striving to be more like our creator) is to recognise what seduces us; and then to learn from the story of Herod. Our task is to lay aside our personal seduction, before it consumes us or leads us into real difficulty - as it did for Herod. Our task is to re-distribute our time, and our money, into spending and tasks that are life-affirming, and life-enhancing.

For where our treasure is, there will our hearts be also.

Healing (Simon's Mother-in-Law)

Reading: Mark 1.29-31. First preached 2012

A gospel reading with the title 'Simon's Mother-in-Law' is very tempting isn't it? It's very tempting to quote some of those old mother-in-law jokes from the likes of Les Dawson. (You know the sort I mean: 'We always know when mother-in-law is coming up the path, because the mice start throwing themselves at the traps!'.) But I'm going to resist, not least because these ten verses of Mark's Gospel have, apparently, a rather different attitude to mothers-in-law.

Did you notice, during the reading that after Jesus healed her, Simon's mother-in-law set about serving her guests? Reading that with modern eyes, we might wonder what's going on. It's almost as though Jesus healed the poor woman so that she would go and get him a cup of tea!

But of course, nothing could be further from the truth. In the first century, the privilege of serving an honoured guest was one which was given to the senior woman of the house. It was counted a right, an honour and a privilege. Simon's wife might have served the guests, especially after her mother had been so ill. But clearly, serving guests was what her mother wanted to do, as soon as she was well. It was a matter of honour, not servitude.

Have you noticed how often Jesus' healing miracles are about more than just restoring someone to health? As soon as she is healed, Simon's mother in law is immediately restored to her position of honour in the house. When Jesus heals someone, the healing doesn't just deal with physical symptoms. It also, invariably, has the effect of bringing people from one state of being in society to another. Jesus seeks to restore not just health, but to life in all its fullness (John 10.10).

In the first century, sick people were often treated as though their illness was their fault. The Hebrew Scriptures led some people to believe that illness was the result of sin; either something done by the sick person, or perhaps by their parents. Sickness was seen as a punishment for sin...and sinners needed to be shunned and excluded from society. They were kept on the margins, often reduced to begging for their very existence.

Jesus, however, confronted that idea head-on. He understood the causes of sickness to be far more complex. In the story of the paralysed man, let down through the roof to be healed (Luke 5.17-26) Jesus plays with these ideas in public.

First, we notice that he says to the paralysed man "Your sins are forgiven" (demonstrating that he had the divine power to forgive sins). But the man still lies on his stretcher, while Jesus disputes with the religious leaders whether or not it makes any difference to forgive sins, or to give healing. Then, Jesus turns to the man "I tell you...get up, pick up your stretcher, and go home". It was Jesus' words of healing which restored the man to health, not the forgiveness of sins (although that was freely offered too).

Jesus clearly did not believe that sickness arose out of sin. Sickness is not a punishment for sin, although it can certainly arise out of human sin in general (such as human greed, or the human refusal to pursue wisdom, science and medicine). After being healed by Jesus, all those he healed have the chance to be restored to human society. Simon's mother-in-law is restored to her position as the senior woman of her household, and given the high privilege of serving her important guest. Lepers are restored to their friends and family. The blind are no longer reduced to begging at the side of the road. This, for Jesus, is one of the signs of the Kingdom. It's an echo of the words of his Mother in the Magnificat..."he has filled the hungry with good things...he has exalted the humble and meek".

Sadly, in these days when we are far more aware of some of the causes of disease, we are in danger of giving-in to the same blame-culture that Jesus tried to combat. Now that medical science has given us reason to believe that low weight, moderate exercise, and the eating of 'five a day' are the cure for all ailments, we still tend to blame people for their illnesses.

How often do we hear people say "it must be her fault -she hasn't looked after herself"? "I told her she should have stopped drinking, or smoking, or eating, or going out without a coat on (or whatever!)." We quickly blame people for their illness; attributing it to a sin on their part. Health authorities routinely threaten to with-hold treatment from those who have 'brought about their own illness' through poor diet or a lack of exercise. When we do that, we fail to understand, unlike Jesus, that the causes of sickness are far more complex.

Our society is driven by massive marketing, campaigns and the easy availability of sugar, alcohol and fat. We live highly pressurised, stressed-out lives as we desperately to keep up with everyone around us. How easy it is for us to point to someone else's illness and say, "It's their fault!". We seem to take a perverse delight in blaming people for their sickness. Shouldn't we rather try to understand that human life is messy, and living that way helps humans to cope?

Jesus' response to the messiness of human suffering was profound. First, he turned over the idea that sickness was linked to personal sin. But secondly, he also embraced human suffering itself. By taking all that the society of his day could throw at him, even to the point of death on a Roman instrument of torture, Jesus entered fully into the messiness of human life. This is, I think, part of what it means to say that Jesus took the sins of the world onto himself. He took the messiness of human suffering onto the Cross. He allowed human messiness to overwhelm him to the point of dying because of it. Human messiness, human weirdness, human suffering, human pride, human greed...all of it was nailed onto the Cross with Jesus.

And then?

And then Jesus transcended it. The story of the Resurrection is the story of how God has the power to transcend and overcome all human messiness. Through the Resurrection, God offers us a powerful symbol of the way life can be. New life - life lived to the full - puts suffering and messiness in the past.

Notice how in the days after the resurrection, Jesus offered forgiveness even to Peter who had denied him three times. There is no room for blame and finger-pointing in the Resurrection Kingdom. Instead, blame and finger-pointing give way to forgiveness and understanding. Peter who had denied Jesus (and therefore contributed to his suffering) was offered forgiveness, and a job to do ("Feed my sheep"). Like his own mother-in-law, Peter finds himself restored through healing and forgiveness to his proper role in society.

So what might we take from this story, and from Jesus' attitudes towards sickness, and from his attitude towards the messiness of human lives?

Of all people, Christians should understand that sin - human messiness - is endemic.

Of all people, Christians, like Christ, should be willing to offer forgiveness and healing, whenever sin is encountered.

Of all people, Christians should understand that everyone messes up - because we ourselves mess up, all the time.

I love this church, and I love its people. I love the commitment you have to supporting each other when you are sick, or to fundraising, or to working in the Cafe, or singing in the choir. I love the way that many of you reach out to those who struggle to make sense of their lives in our community. I want us to be the kind of community which accepts, unreservedly, without any surprise whatsoever, that all human beings are messy. Like Jesus, I want us to be those who simply understand that none of us is perfect. Every single one of us is striving to be better, but we will often fall, often stumble, often mess up. I want us to be the kind of community which says to itself "before I criticise that person, I need to walk mile in their shoes".

I want us to be the kind of community which continually, constantly, offers forgiveness, healing and understanding to each.

We can be the kind of community which offers understanding to those whose choices in life lead them to make, what seem to us to be strange decisions.

We can be those who, when we find someone falling over, reach down and pick them up. We can be those who get on with being the kind of loving, understanding community that Christ calls us to be.

There is no room in Jesus' Kingdom for blame. Jesus didn't blame Simon's mother-in-law for her illness. He offered her healing, and restoration to the role she was called to play in life.

And he calls us to do the same.

Changing Water into Wine

Reading: John 2.1-11. First preached 2012

So, there's this old priest, who over the years has become a bit of an alcoholic, right? It's an occupational hazard, given all the wine we are supposed to finish up after communion! Well, this old priest had to go on a long journey, and he couldn't face the prospect without a little tipple now and then along the road. So, as he was driving along, he kept taking little nips from a bottle of gin on the passenger seat. Unfortunately, after a few hours, his driving started to deteriorate and he began swerving from side to side down the road, until he was pulled over by a policeman. The priest wound down his window...

"What's the matter Ocifer?"

"Father, I believe you are drunk at the wheel"

"Imposhible" said the priest. Then the policeman pointed to the bottle on the passenger seat.

"What's in that bottle, Father?" he asked.

"Itsh water, Ocifer. Just water"

"Let me have a look" said the policeman, and the priest reluctantly passed him the bottle. The policeman sniffed, and exclaimed,

"That's not water, Father, its alcohol!" at which the Priest crossed himself, looked up to heaven and said,

"Jesus, you've done it again!"

I must ask you to forgive me. Alcoholism is no joke. As the members of Alcoholics Anonymous who are members of our congregation will tell you, it's a vicious disease, which has the capacity to take away everything of real value from one's life. In that context, the story of Jesus turning water into wine - towards the end of a wedding feast - can be a little problematic! After all, by the time that the wine already provided by the host had run out, it's a fairly good bet that most of the guests would already have been very nicely oiled. What on earth was Jesus doing making even more wine? Was Jesus into drunkenness? Or was Jesus perhaps pre-figuring the advice of St Paul so beloved by churchgoers who enjoy a visit to the pub at Sunday lunchtime..."thirst after righteousness"?!

This is where we have to be careful. Frankly, we are on dangerous ground when we attempt to take many (if not most) biblical stories literally. I have even heard stories of abstinence-advocating preachers who, convinced that every story must be taken literally, insist that Jesus must have turned the water into grape-juice just so that they can continue to hold on to the story as a literal fact.

Instead, as intelligent readers of Scripture, we are invited to go deeper, to seek to understand the meaning behind the story. It particularly helps if we remember who wrote this story. John clearly had a remarkable imagination. Just a quick delve into the imagery of Revelation (his other great book) will tell you that! Even more so, we need to remember John's purpose in writing his Gospel. More than any of the other three Gospels, John goes to great length to tell us what Jesus' life and death means; what the core message is really all about. To read the Gospel of John is to enter a world of symbols and rich, deep meaning.

Interestingly, none of the other Gospel writers bothered to record the miracle at Cana. They were much more interested in healings and exorcisms. But something in John's imagination resonated with Cana. He saw, in Cana, a sign that pointed to the very purpose for which Christ had come into the world. The wedding guests saw water turned into the best wine. John saw a man who, in this first sign, revealed the very purposes of God.

It's perhaps worth remembering that only John records Jesus as saying, "I have come that they might have life and have it more abundantly." (John 10.10) This is what the miracle at Cana is all about. Water, the basic necessity of life, is changed into wine--the symbol not just of life, but of abundant, joyous, and extravagant life.

Think about it. Water is good. There is nothing wrong with water. There is nothing which needed fixing in the water. Why then should Jesus need to change it into wine? The message of Cana is that Jesus doesn't only transform the bad into the good (like when he heals the sick or casts out a demon). The message of Cana is that Jesus has the capacity to make the good even better! That is one of most persistent themes of John's gospel. Jesus hasn't only come to give life, but to give life 'abundantly'.

This, then, is the promise for those whose lives are already pretty good. The transformation at Cana is the promise for those who are already heading in the right direction. This message is for those who have a basic trust in God, who already look out for their neighbour, who do what they can, when they can, to be good Samaritans. This is the message for those whose life is already like good, fresh water - nourishing, and life-sustaining.

There's a message here: "enjoy the water...but taste the wine!" God doesn't call us to only live lives of duty and charity, as right as they are. Yes, we should live by the commandments - but there's more to following Jesus than simple obedience. Remember what he said? "I came that they might have life, and have it more abundantly." Not just life, but abundant life, joyous life; life lived in celebration and exuberance.

This doesn't mean that God promises us each a Rolls Royce. Neither does it mean that we will never experience pain and suffering. But it does mean that the good clean water of our lives can be transformed into the best wine through the love of God. Then even the worst circumstances that life can offer can have a richness and depth that they never had before. If we will only drink of the new wine of the Kingdom, Love can transform us, and bring meaning and richness to every human moment.

As we begin to taste the new wine of the Kingdom, we begin to look for God's capacity to transform and elevate even the most apparently awful of circumstances. Sometimes I sit with sick and elderly people who despair of the fact that they now need others to do things for them. Understandably, they mourn the loss of their independence and resent the fact that they can do nothing on their own any more. But then, I ask them,

"Tell me. You have spent your entire life caring for others - your children, your friends in the church, your neighbours. How did that feel?" Invariably, the sick or housebound person will tell me, in so many words, that their service to others made them feel needed, wanted, and that they had a role in life.

"So," I tell them (in so many words) "isn't it time that you gave the gift of your incapacity to others? Isn't it time that you let others feel needed and wanted - by caring for you?"

That's just a tiny example - but I think it's a real example of how, if we will let it, Love has a way of pouring new wine even into difficult and tragic situations. Love has a way of helping us find new

41

meaning, richer meaning, better, deeper taste. The trick is to taste the wine.

Sometimes, we get fixed on a particular idea in life, don't we? We make up our minds that we want a certain thing, a certain job perhaps, or a certain possession. And when we don't get that job, or possess that thing, we can become listless, dry, even depressed - believing that our life will only be complete when we have achieved our goal. But a Christian's joy is not found in achieving anything. A Christian's joy is not found in the winning of a job, or the possession of any one thing. A Christian finds their joy by learning that God is at work in every circumstance of life, changing water into wine. Christians find their joy by declaring that 'our God reigns' whatever befalls us. Christians find their joy in the exuberant celebration of each moment of life, trusting that God is present now, that Love is at work now.

What do people see when they look at our lives? Do they see that we have access to living water? I hope so and I pray that those who are thirsty will be drawn to the water of life by observing us. But there are many who simply don't feel thirsty. I watch them walk past our doors every day. They are living decent, even happy lives. They are perfectly content. So, what about the extra dimension? Do our lives look like those of the servants of a God who turns water into the best wine? Is the way we practice our faith something that turns water into wine. Or can it sometimes look more like we are turning wine into water?

I wonder. What would our lives look like, what would our church look like, if we let Jesus turn our water into wine?

The State we are in

Sermon for the Patronal Festival of St Saviours Church, Stamshaw - on the Feast of Christ the King (21st November 2010)

Readings: 2 Samuel 5:1-3, Colossians 1:12-20, Luke 23:35-43

Note: A substantial portion of this sermon is derived from the thinking of Archbishop Rowan Williams, and especially from his book 'Christ on Trial' (published in 2000). He has a brain the size of a planet. This sermon is an attempt to distil his thinking into something which could be preached. I have not always marked William's words in direct quotation, and have weaved them into my own thoughts. But, the substantial core of this sermon is his, and he rightly deserves the credit.

I'm sure you've heard the quote from Shakespeare's Hamlet: "Something is wrong in the state of Denmark". Shakespeare invites us, as he so often does, to hold up a mirror to our own society. He challenges us to ask ourselves whether there is anything rotten in the state that we live in too. Is there something wrong with the State of our World? Is there something wrong, for example, with a world which, in the last century, slaughtered one hundred and fifty million people in wars? That's more than have died in all the preceding centuries put together. Is there something wrong with a world in which one billion people survive on less than a dollar a day, scratching round in rubbish tips for something to eat?

Have you ever wondered how many people is a billion people? Let me give you some idea of the scale. Imagine, if you can, a line of one billion people, standing one yard apart. If I were to get in my car, and drive along the line of people at sixty miles per hour for one hour, I would pass just over one hundred and five thousand people. Do you know how long I would have to drive at sixty miles per hour, all day, all night, without stopping, to pass by one billion people? One year and twenty-nine days.

That's how many people live on this planet in abject poverty. That's how many live in refugee camps, reliant entirely on aid agencies or other hand-outs just to survive from one day to the next.

Yes, there is something wrong with the State we are in.

In a little while, as bread and wine are consecrated, we will remind ourselves that Christ claims dominion over all creation. We will remind ourselves what His Kingdom is like: a kingdom of truth and life, a kingdom of holiness and grace, a kingdom of justice, love and peace. How very different that Kingdom is from the one which was in place in the time of Jesus.

The Romans believed that they had a duty to conquer and then rule the known world. Not through ideas, not through love and generosity; but through violence. They brought many good innovations with them - as the 'Judaean Popular People's Front' had to acknowledge in Monty Python's movie 'Life of Brian'. "What have the Romans done for us...apart from the roads and the schools and the hospitals and the sewerage systems?" But Roman rule was ultimately based on the idea of 'redemptive violence' - the idea that society, and life in general, can only be improved through conquest and coercion.

That had terrifying consequences for the people of Jesus' day. There were two ways, primarily, that local people used to resist the Romans' violent oppression. The first was the reaction of the Zealots. They were a small group of revolutionaries, who believed in defeating Rome by Rome's own methods of violence. They ran small scale attacks on Roman installations, and Roman people, trying to drive out the Romans through a campaign of fear. Today, we would call the Zealots 'terrorists'. They were people who use the fear of attack to change the mind or policy of a ruling power.

The other reaction to the Romans was religious fundamentalism. The Pharisees, in particular, had established a system of religious law, and believed in a fundamental religious principle. They believed that if every Jewish person would follow all the Laws of God for just one day, then the Messiah would come to liberate them from their oppressors. There were other fundamentalist religious reactions too, like that of the Essenes (who escaped to the desert in an attempt to flee the violence of Rome).

So, we have terrorism and religious Fundamentalism. They sound very familiar don't they? The ancient world was so much like our world. In fact, apart from the fact that we have electricity and fast transport systems, there is actually very little that has changed. The world is still ruled by powerful men. Poor people still starve every day. And ordinary people still lose their lives in pointless wars and conflicts. Power, imposed from above, is so endemic that we all know what is meant by that old joke: "What's the difference between God and the President of the United States? Answer: God doesn't think he's the President of the United States."

That one little joke opens up a whole wealth of meaning because it assumes that we know exactly what Presidents are like. We assume that they are power-mad, and so we get the joke. But it's a worrisome joke too, because it assumes that we also think of God like some kind of brutal power-monger as well.

Our view of God is shaped by the society in which we live. We tend to paint a picture of God in our heads as a sort of bigger, stronger Prime Minister or King. Or perhaps we see him as a sort of super-Headmaster, who will either punish us or reward us at the end of term. We treat God like some distant Emperor who will be cross with us if we don't behave, and who stands ready to punish us if we don't believe the right things, or do the right actions.

Saint Luke was very conscious of the kind of political and religious world into which Jesus came. He frames his entire narrative in terms of Kingship, as we shall hear again through Advent and Christmas. Chapter one: "In the days of King Herod of Judaea...". Chapter two: "...at this time Caesar Augustus issued a decree". Chapter three: "In the fifteenth year of Tiberius Caesar's reign". Luke framed his story by reference to three rulers...but then, at the end, as we heard in today's Gospel reading, he places Jesus on his cross with the massively ironic sign 'King of the Jews' over his head.

But Luke also contrasts the three great rulers with three simple people. In his first three chapters, the references to Herod, Augustus and Tiberius are contrasted with Mary, Zechariah and Simeon: all of whom proclaim a different kind of Kingdom. These are people who, as Rowan Williams says, are "lifted up by a God who snubs and turns away the powerful". In Jesus, God has "turned upside down the assumptions of the world". Jesus presents us with a God who is nothing like the God of our power-corrupted imaginations.

It is perhaps during his trial that we get the clearest sense of what Jesus believed about power. Throughout the Gospel of Mark, for example, Jesus steadfastly resists any attempt to be named as God's Son, or the Messiah - let alone the King of Kings. He silences the demoniacs, the healed leper, and even Simon Peter when they identify him. But, there does come a point, a crucial point, where he permits himself to be revealed. During his trial, the High Priest invites the prisoner to incriminate himself: "Are you the Christ", he asks, "the Son of the Blessed One?". Jesus answers with the plainest of plain words: "I am".

Why then? Why at that point?

Here I turn again to Rowan Williams for help. In 'Christ on Trial', Williams comments that "Jesus before the High Priest has no leverage in the world; he is denuded of whatever power he might have had. Stripped and bound before the court, he has no stake in how the world organises itself. He is definitively outside the system of the world's power and the language of power. He is going to die, because that is what the world has decided. It is at this moment and this moment only that he speaks plainly about who he is. He names himself with the name of the God of Israel, 'I am'..."

Christ the King is nothing like the Kings we have known. He is much more after the pattern of the gentle Shepherd which David was challenged to pre-figure, in our first reading. According to St Paul's letter to the Colossians, Jesus is the firstborn of all creation, through which everything was made...including even "thrones, dominations, sovereignties and powers" ...but his task is to reconcile all that he has made (not dominate it) bringing it together in him, through him and for him by his peace-making death on the cross.

Jesus death on the cross has many layers of meaning, of course. But, as Williams says, "one of them that we must not miss is that by his death, Jesus unmasks the Kingdoms of this world. He demonstrates that the notion of redemptive violence, practiced by the Romans and the Priests, is nothing but a mask for unadulterated evil. By his death, Jesus shows Emperors and High Priests in their true light. They are bully-boys, whose ultimate achievement through violence is the death of a simple, loving man, and the nailing of God himself onto a cross". It's as though Jesus says, "this is what happens when you live with the lie of redemptive violence...you end up squeezing God out, onto the margins, onto a hill outside the City."

But, as Williams teaches us, Jesus redeems even such marginalisation. There, outside the City wall, pushed away by the State, he is still at work. He still works to redeem creation. To the thief beside him he turns and promises "Today you will be with me in Paradise". It's as though having failed to persuade the State to embrace a different way, Jesus switches tactics. If the State will not bow to the love and just mercy of God, then Jesus will start from a different point. He will carry out his redemption one thief at a time, one person at a time.

And that finally is where we come in to this story. There is not much that you and I can hope to achieve in changing the State we are in. We can't hope to halt the armies of the world, as they pound each other to dust. We can't hope to shift the priorities of a world economic system which can find £100 billion dollars to bail out the banks, but which can't help those billion people in a line outside our door.

But like Jesus, with the thief on the Cross, it turns out that we can do something, after all. One person at a time. One life at a time. We can love our neighbour. We can sponsor a child - just talk to World Vision. We can give the gift of life to a family in the two-thirds world - just 'Send a Cow'. We can choose to live in love and reconciliation with our neighbours, whether they are local or global, next-door neighbours, or religious neighbours.

We can continue to live with the false myth that the State we are in can be improved through violence and coercion - the 'myth of redemptive violence' - or we can wake up to the call of Christ the King, and embrace a different kind of kingship altogether.

The End of the World?

Revelation 21.1-14. First preached 2011

I guess you've all probably heard by now that according to Pastor Harold Camping of California, none of us should be now. Pastor Camping is a retired Civil Engineer, not a trained priest, but he conducted his own research into the Bible's prophecies about the end of the world, and confidently predicted that the world was going to end on May 21st 2011.

He was so convinced that he had got his calculations right that he has been running major advertising campaigns across the USA and other part of the world, warning us that May the 21st was judgement day. Massive advertising hoardings were erected, in English and Arabic announcing 'the great the terrible day of the Lord'. Scandalously, followers of Mr Camping have been selling their homes, and cashing in their investments to pay for all this nonsense.

Oh dear. I bet he feels a bit of a silly-billy now. Worryingly, Harold Camping is not the first person to have predicted the end of the world. John of Toledo thought it would happen on the 23rd of September 1186. William Bell predicted the 5th of April 1761. Nothing apocalyptic happened on the 28th of April 1843, or on 21st of September 1945. Jehovah's Witnesses have predicted the end of the world 10 times in the last century!

It's easy to mock. Actually it's very easy to mock, especially when one considers where these predictions tend to come from. They have never been made by any of the mainstream churches. None of the main churches, neither Orthodoxy, Catholicism, or Anglicanism has ever tried to predict the end of the world. Instead, usually part-time bible scholars, especially those with a mathematical brain, attempt to mine the Bible for hints and clues, usually based on numbers. We call this 'numerology' - the study of mystical numbers.

That was how Mr Camping arrived at his date for the end of the world. He mixed up all sorts of number assumptions - including an assumed date of the Great Flood, probably based on the calculations of the seventeenth century Irish scholar and Bishop, James Ussher. He then examined texts like those of St Peter. In his second letter, for example, Peter says that one day to the Lord is as a thousand years, and a thousand years is as one day. Most Christians would take that to mean that God is not bounded by time in the way that we are. But for Mr Camping, it was a code which meant he could predict that the end of the world would happen precisely 7,000 years after the Great Flood (because God had said to Noah that he had seven days to warn people of the end of the world).

Numerology is a popular pastime for certain people. Even Isaac Newton had a go at it...and predicted the end of the world would happen in 2060. We'll have to wait and see if he was right!

But frankly, numerology is a very silly way to spend your time. The Bible simply does not contain secret codes for the end of the world. Neither, generally, should one text from the Bible be used to add meaning to another text – certainly not for the purposes of prediction. I'm surprised that none of our numerologist friends have caught on to that yet, given the present failure rate of their predictions!

But that is not to say that the Bible fails to ponder what the end of all things might be like. The writers of the Bible were, almost exclusively, people who lived under oppression. They were occupied or enslaved people – having been subjugated by the Egyptians, the Babylonians, the Greeks, the Assyrians, the Persians and the Romans - to name just a few! It is no surprise that people who were under such occupation and oppression should begin to tell one another stories about what the world might be like when the oppression was over. It's not surprise that they would dream of a time when the oppressors would be over-thrown and when, from a Jewish perspective, the world would be remade.

This was no different for the early Christians. By the time that John was writing his 'Book of Revelation' on the Island of Patmos, Christianity, and Judaism, were all going through dark days indeed. The Temple in Jerusalem had been demolished by the Romans. Jews were scattered across the known world. Christians were being persecuted by a Roman political system which insisted that everyone must worship the Divine Emperor, and were hiding in the Roman catacombs or private houses. Peter had probably been executed by that date, along with Paul and - tradition tells us - most of the other first followers of Jesus. It was a dark time, an uncertain time. Faith was being tested and challenged.

In the middle of this turmoil, St John had a vision. Some less-than-charitable scholars have suggested that the Island of Patmos was a great place for growing hallucinogenic mushrooms - but we have no idea whether John was a mushroom eater! What we do have, as the last book of our New Testament, is an astounding, poetic, troubling, magnificent vision. It's a vision of what the world might be like, when all the enemies of God have been dealt with.

But it's not a prediction. It's a series of complex images. It's a dream-like catalogue of angels and demons and great beasts and cities and lakes of fire and multi-headed beasts and anti-Christs. Many is the Christian who has tried to read the book of Revelation, and ended up giving the whole project up, just out of sheer confusion. Many of the complex, beautiful and terrible images of Revelation mean very little to us. We don't live in the same world as John. Many of the images he uses have no modern equivalent. For us to truly understand the book of Revelation would be as difficult as it would be for John to understand a story of blind-dating via the internet. Our cultures are worlds apart.

And yet, the Church believes that the Spirit has preserved this book for us. More than that, we believe that this book contains truth; truth which will repay careful study and reflection. Like all the books of the Bible which the church has so carefully preserved, the Book of Revelation seeks to answer some of the most important questions of life. Where did we come from? Where are we going? Is God involved in our past, present and future?

The book of Revelation's answer to this last question is an emphatic 'yes!'. The whole thrust of Revelation is an assurance that God is caught up the in messy business of this world. God is battling against anti-Christs and multi-headed beasts. God is sending out angels and blowing trumpets. God is calling the people of God to battle the forces of evil. The Word of God rides out on a white horse...and has a metaphorical sword coming out of his mouth. Crucially, he is promises, in the final chapters, that none of this effort will be in vain.

John's final great vision is of a holy city. He calls is the New Jerusalem, and it is seen coming down out of heaven from God. Interestingly he says that the City is prepared as a bride, adorned for her husband...which is another strange metaphor. How exactly does a City dress up as a bride? Maybe the City wears some kind of enormous veil? Maybe there's a blue garter wrapped around a tower?

But let's not get hung up on the details! An evangelical Bible - teacher called Alistair Begg once taught me that the key to understanding the book of Revelation is this: "what is plain, is main. And what is main, is plain". And the plain message of chapter 21 is this:

"I heard a loud voice from the throne saying 'Behold, the home of God is among mortals. He will dwell with them; they will be his peoples and God himself will be with them; he will wipe every tear from their eyes. Death will be no more; mourning and crying and pain will be no more, for the first things have passed away." (Rev 21.3-4)

This is a resurrection message. This is a hopeful, passionate, declaration that God is indeed involved with our world, and with our lives. This is a declaration that God himself will restore the relationship which we human beings have messed up. He will take away mourning and crying and pain...and will defeat even death itself.

The people who search the Scriptures for an actual date for Judgement Day are looking for something. They are hoping, perhaps a little too desperately, that among all the awfulness and chaos of this world (in so many places), someone, somewhere, has got things under control. The point of the book of Revelation is two-fold: it is to assure us that indeed, someone has got the whole of history (His Story) under control. But secondly, John writes to seven churches, on behalf of Jesus. He encourages them, he corrects them, he warns them, and he praises them. He essentially says to them, through the whole of Revelation that yes, God is in control. But he chooses to bring about his purposes for the world through us, through me and you and through the Church which bears his name.

And, as both Jesus and Paul reminded us, whether or not the actual world is going to come to an actual end, we are expected to act, always, as if it is about to finish. Harold Camping may be a numerological crackpot, but he has at least at least reminded us that God calls us to something greater, higher, deeper, broader than the humdrum round of every-day human existence. The Holy City, the new Jerusalem, the Bride of Christ - these are all explicit metaphors for the Church. We are the people of God who are called to work with

God, and in God and through God, for the building of God's kingdom on earth.

Will there ever be a Universal Judgement Day? I don't know. I suspect not, frankly - not in the sense of a Day when Jesus comes riding on a cloud and winds up human history. I might well be wrong (and won't be at all disappointed if I am).

But, rather, I tend to believe that Jesus comes again every time that there is peace and justice in the world. Jesus comes again every time a hungry child is fed. Jesus comes again every time one of us reaches out to our brother or sister with love. Bit by bit, person by person, day by day...Jesus comes again.

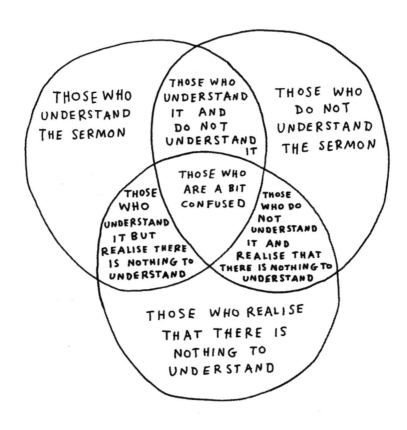

Will the real St Nicholas stand up?

A sermon for the Feast of St Nicholas (6th December - during Advent).

(First preached 2011, at St Nicholas North End, and since then a few times at St Nicholas, Langstone with minor alterations and cuts)

I wonder if everyone knows what name St Nicholas is also known by? What are some of the names that he is called? Here's a clue – for those who don't already know. In some countries, he is known as "Santa Niclaus" (Santa is a Spanish form of the word Saint). Sometimes Santa Niclaus gets shortened to "Santa 'Claus". Yes, St Nicholas is the person we know as Father Christmas! And this is Father Christmas' Church!

There are lots and lots of traditions concerning St Nicholas – and I'm sure you've heard many of them here over the years.

It's fascinating to see how St Nicholas is celebrated differently, in different parts of the world. In many places St. Nicholas is the main gift-giver. His feast day, St. Nicholas Day, is December 6, which falls early in the Advent season. In some places he arrives in the middle of November and moves about the countryside, visiting schools and homes to find out if children have been good. In other places he comes in the night and finds carrots and hay for his horse or donkey along with children's wish lists. Small treats are left in shoes or stockings so the children will know he has come.

Where St. Nicholas is prominent, his day, not Christmas, is the primary gift-giving day. Instead of gathering to give presents on Christmas Day, like we do in the UK, parties are held on St Nicholas' Eve, December 5th. Shoes or stockings are left for St. Nicholas to fill during the night. Children then find treats of small gifts, fruit or nuts, and special Nicholas candies and cookies.

One vital difference between the way we receive gifts, in England, and the way that others do it, is that St. Nicholas gifts are meant to be shared, not hoarded for oneself. Whatever little treats St Nicholas brings – sweets, nuts, fruit, candies – these are to be shared, around the whole family.

In Romania, St Nicholas' Day is a very great festival. On the night of December 5th, boots are cleaned and carefully polished to be put by the door or on the windowsill to wait for St. Nicholas' (Sfantul Nicolae's) visit. He is generous to adults as well as children, putting a little present in each boot—usually nuts, tangerines, sweets and small items, like new socks. In some areas a walnut branch or thin twigs with gold, silver, or bronze gilded walnuts are left as a warning that behaviour needs to improve. On the sixth of December, gifts are given to friends, children, and those in need. It is one of the most important Romanian holidays.

More than eight hundred thousand Romanians are called Nicholas, Nicolae or Nicola – or other variations of his name. Remember Nicolae Ceausescu, the infamous Romanian Dictator? They all celebrate their name day on St. Nicholas day, December 6th. Over 1000 churches are dedicated to St. Nicholas in Romania; at least 23 are in Bucharest.

It's worth knowing about some of these traditions, because they help us to see our own traditions in a new light. Perhaps they might even make us think a little about the way we have celebrated Christmas, for the last few decades.

Everyone I meet agrees that we have become far too obsessed with presents, and that Christmas has become too expensive. And yet, no-one seems to be able to stop. We all feel under pressure to keep up with everyone else's idea of what Christmas should be. The stories about St Nicholas from other countries encourage us to see Christmas as something a little simpler. A small gift, here and there – a bar of chocolate, a bag of nuts. Nothing too elaborate. Just enough to send a message of love.

Of course we all know what it's like. You go to the toy shop, and you buy the biggest present you can find. On Christmas morning, you watch the eyes of your child go wide at the possibilities of what might be inside. Then, the wrapping is torn off, and the child is encouraged to explore the contents. "Look", says you, "There's a complete play-kitchen in here. There's a cooker, and some saucepans, and some pretend fruit. Look, there's a pretend iron and ironing board…so you can do the ironing….just like Daddy!"

But the child has other ideas. "Look", says the child, "There's a great big empty box! It could be a house, or a castle, or a motorboat, or a car, or a bed. It's fantastic." So for the rest of the day, Daddy spends his time assembling small pieces of plastic which his child will never play with, while his child is happily sitting in the box, going "Brummm....brummm".

St Nicholas invites us to use our imaginations. St Nicholas himself became famous because he was known as a generous giver. He understood how much God had given to him – life, health, friends, a community to live in. And out of his gratitude, St Nicholas wanted to give something back.

There are many famous stories about St Nicholas. The most famous tells of a poor man with three daughters. In those days a young woman's father had to offer prospective husbands something of value, called a dowry. The larger the dowry, the better the chance that a young woman would find a good husband. Without a dowry, a woman was unlikely to marry. This poor man's daughters, without dowries, were therefore destined to be sold into slavery. Mysteriously, on three different occasions, a bag of gold appeared in their home-providing the needed dowries. The bags of gold, tossed through an open window, are said to have landed in stockings or shoes left before the fire to dry. This led to the custom of children hanging stockings or putting out shoes, eagerly awaiting gifts from Saint Nicholas. Sometimes the story is told with gold balls instead of bags of gold. That is why three gold balls, sometimes represented as oranges, are one of the symbols for St. Nicholas. And so St. Nicholas is known as a gift-giver.

In France the story is told of three small children, wandering in their play until lost, who were lured and captured by an evil butcher. St. Nicholas appears and appeals to God to return them to life and to their families. And so St. Nicholas is the patron and protector of children.

Several stories tell of Nicholas and the sea. For example, when he was young, Nicholas is said to have made a pilgrimage to the Holy Land. There as he walked where Jesus walked, he sought to more deeply experience Jesus' life, passion, and resurrection. Returning by sea, a mighty storm threatened to wreck the ship. Nicholas calmly prayed. The terrified sailors were amazed when the wind and waves suddenly calmed, sparing them all. And so St. Nicholas is the patron of sailors and voyagers – which makes him a pretty good Saint to have in a town like Portsmouth! That's why one of his symbols is a ship.

Something that is consistent about all these stories is that Nicholas was someone who constantly looked for ways to help and encourage other people. Responding to God's love, Nicholas wanted to share that love wherever he could. He was constantly on the look-out for ways to help other people. And his stories encourage us to think in similar ways.

Let me encourage you to think like St Nicholas, this Christmas. In a short while, many of us are going to give gifts which will be given to children throughout the City who otherwise wouldn't get a present this year. For that, I am very grateful – and I'm sure that St Nicholas is too. But there is one gift that every single one of us can give this year, a gift which can be given and received all through the year. It's the gift of a question…

Here's the question: "What can I do for you?". Mummy, you've been cooking all day. What can I do for you? Daddy, you've been ironing all morning…what can I do for you? Neighbour, you haven't spoken to anyone today, what can I do for you? Homeless person, sitting in the shop doorway - what can I do for you? Starving person I've seen on the TV, whose crops have failed or been washed away - what can I do for you?

There's another little thing that St Nicholas can teach us. St Nicholas is never seen. If we try to stay awake, to see him coming down the chimney, he won't come. St Nicholas always gives his gifts in secret. He gives what we might call 'random acts of kindness'. He gives in secret, without expecting any reward (though I know he's always grateful for a glass of brandy and a mince pie for the reindeer!) But he gives without looking for thanks, he spreads a little happiness as he goes by.

There are some lovely stories out there about Random Acts of Kindness. There's the story of a woman in America who was going through a drive-in restaurant, on her way to work. It was a cold, grey morning, and she really didn't want to go to work. When she got to the window, a little bit of sunshine broke out when the assistant gave her a cup of coffee, and said "It's paid for, already". It turned out that the taxi driver in front of her had paid for her coffee. The assistant explained "He does it every day, for one person".

There are lots of random acts of kindness done in this parish too. Those of you who have brought presents today get my thanks for your act of kindness. Those of you who are buying vouchers for the homeless – for people you will never meet - thank you for the random act of kindness. Those of you who filled up Shoeboxes for the annual shoebox appeal - I thank you! Those who gave to the Harvest appeal for food, or money for the church in Ghana – thank you. Those of you who give regularly, sacrificially, to the work of the church; St Nicholas would be proud of all of you.

And doesn't it feel good? Doesn't it feel great to know that today, your life counted for something? Today, you helped another human being a little further along their journey – however tough that journey has been.

Jesus taught us that it is giving that we receive. By giving out, we receive back a thousand fold – especially in that deep sense that today, we know we have made a difference.

St Nicholas stands as an example. According to all the legends, he is the giver who is never seen and who is yet loved by all.

That's not a bad example for any of us to follow.

ACTIVITIES THAT ARE FROWNED UPON

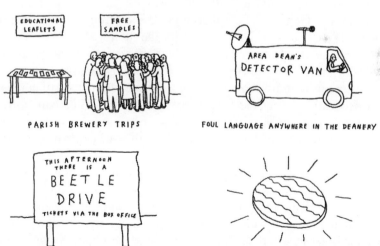

All Souls

Readings: Romans 13.8-10 and Luke 14.25-33. First preached 2011

This is a strange time of year, isn't it? With the feasts of All Saints, All Souls and Remembrance all coming so close together, it can feel just a little bit sad. Through these feasts though, we are encouraged to think about the difficult topic of death.

First, inevitably, we think about the death of those we have loved. Through these services, we re-member them...that is, we re-connect them, in our minds. We put their 'members' - their arms, legs, and faces, - back together in our minds. We re-member them. And that is good. It is an opportunity to thank God for all that our loved ones meant to us, and still mean to us. We might think about what they contributed to our lives. We might thank God for the love that they shared with us. That love is itself a sign, and a mirror, of the love of God itself.

For some of us, of course, some of the memories we have might be more complicated. All human beings are complicated, and human relationships are the most complicated of all. Some people even feel relieved when certain relationships are ended by death. Let's be honest, not every relationship is positive and life-giving. But that's alright too. We give those relationships to God, just as we give all our loved ones to God. We trust that in God, and through God, there is healing of past hurts, as well as hope for the future.

Interestingly, however, today's lectionary readings have little to say about the death of those we have known. Instead, the lectionary encourages us to think about our own lives, and ultimately, of course, our own deaths. For as the old saying goes, 'nothing is certain in life, except death and taxes'.

St Augustine of Hippo enlarged on this idea, when he wrote this:

"It is necessary to die, but nobody wants to; you don't want to, but you are going to, whether you like it or not. It is hard not to want something which cannot be avoided. If it could be managed, we would much rather not die; we would like to become like the angels by some other means than death. We want to reach the Kingdom of

God, but we don't want to travel by way of death. And yet, there stands Mr Necessity saying 'This way, please!' "

CS Lewis, writer of the Narnia books, was even more blunt. He said this:

"It is hard to have patience with people who say 'there is no death,' or 'death doesn't matter'. There is death. And whatever is, matters. And whatever happens has consequences, and it and they are irrevocable and irreversible. You might as well say that birth doesn't matter."

But let's get back to the Lectionary. What are these two readings saying to us? First, St Paul, writing to the Romans, seems to speak right into the economic crisis that we all find ourselves faced with at present. He reminds us of what philosophers have called 'the Golden Rule' – 'Love your neighbour as you love yourself'. But he does so in a very interesting context. In the previous few lines, Paul has been talking about faithfulness in financial matters. "Pay your taxes", he says, "because the authorities are God's servants". Then, "Give everyone what you owe him". Then finally, "Let no debt remain outstanding".

If only this was the basis on which our financial system was built! If only we had not built our entire system on debt, then perhaps it would not have come crashing round our ears as it has done in the last few years. Paul says "Let no debt remain outstanding except the continuing debt to love one another, for he who loves his fellow-man has fulfilled the law".

Just imagine what a different world this would be if the law of loving compassion was the basis of our system of finances and banking! Just imagine how different life would be for billions, if 20% of the world's population did not control 80% of the world's resources. Just think how 'loving your neighbour' would truly transform the world!

It is possible to state the so-called Golden Rule in an opposite way. There is a story about a Jewish Rabbi, a contemporary of Jesus, called Rabbi Hillel. He was once challenged to stand on one leg, to recite the law of Moses. The old fellow was clearly up for a challenge, because he immediately stood on one leg and said (and I paraphrase)

59

"Don't do to others what you would not like them to do to you. That is the entire Law of God...the rest [of the Scriptures] are just commentary".

Do you see the difference? 'Love your neighbour' is a positive action, and potentially a rather passive one. It's relatively simple to go around just loving everybody. But "don't treat your neighbour badly" is a way of inviting us to really challenge our behaviour. "Don't grab selfishly at stuff if you wouldn't like people grabbing at your stuff. Don't wage war if you would not like war waged on you. Don't judge other people's opinions, lifestyles, choices, if you would not like other people judging yours".

So here is Paul saying "wake up, people!". In fact, if we read on a few verses from the small selection of the lectionary, we find Paul saying this:

"The hour has come for you to wake up from your present slumber, because our salvation is nearer than when we first believed."

In other words, death is coming. Our salvation, through death into the Kingdom of God, is coming. Are we content to sleep our way through this 'present slumber' or are we perhaps interested in living Kingdom lives now? Because, let us not forget, the Departed whom we commemorate today, are living in the Kingdom of heaven (or so we pray). Our lives are but dull slumber compared to the true life that awaits all those who are transformed by the love of God.

D.L.Moody, a famous preacher, once said this:

"Some day you will read in the papers that D.L.Moody of Northfield is dead. Don't you believe a word of it! At that moment I shall be more alive than I am now: I shall have gone up higher, that is all, out of this clay tenement into a house that is immortal - a body that death cannot touch, that sin cannot taint; a body fashioned like unto his glorious body".

And that is of course the thrust of the Gospel reading we just heard. Jesus uses a clearly exaggerated phrase to emphasise how unimportant our present priorities are, compared to the priorities of the Kingdom. He says, effectively,

"There is a cost to being a disciple".

"Any of you who does not give up everything for my sake cannot be my disciple. If anyone comes to me and does not hate his father and mother, his wife and children, his brothers and sisters - yes even his own life - he cannot be my disciple".

Jesus, and the Kingdom of loving compassion that he preaches, has a claim on our lives. Eternal life is not something which is only given to the departed. Jesus preached that the Kingdom of Heaven is 'among you' or 'within you' - depending on the translation. In other words, eternal life in the Kingdom of Heaven is something which is offered to us now. Eternal life is life which doesn't stop, even through death, and which can begin today. It is literally 'life which goes on for ever'.

There is an irony that as we pray for the souls of the departed today, Christian tradition has always taught us that those who are in the very presence of God, now, are also praying for us. Our loved ones, who are themselves caught up in the love of God, are praying for us, as we pray for them. By their prayers and ours, a great unending circle of prayer is initiated. It's a circle of compassionate love, in which we, like them, can be caught up. A great powerhouse of prayer which can give us the strength, the commitment, the drive, to live as Jesus and Paul his Apostle call us to live.

In most Orthodox churches around the world, over the Altar, there is an image of Christ celebrating the Eucharist with the 'faithful departed' - those who are in his presence now. Within Orthodoxy, there is a lovely idea that as we celebrate the Eucharist on earth, with the Priest standing 'vicariously' (i.e. as a vicar) in the place of Christ, Christ himself celebrates the very same feast, eternally in heaven with all those he has welcomed into his kingdom. It's a lovely image. It's one that I encourage you to hold in your mind as we pray later 'with angels and archangels and all the company of heaven'.

So today, we pray for our loved ones, who we re-member in this act of worship...but we also pray for the strength to live our own eternal lives by the Golden Rule, and for the strength to make the compassionate priorities of the Kingdom our priorities...for ever and ever.

All Saints

Readings: Rev. 21.1-6a and John 11.32-44. First preached 2012

The Rev'd Richard Coles is a parish priest and public broadcaster whom you may have heard on my favourite Radio Station - good old BBC Radio 4 (or what some people still call 'The Home Service'!). He has published a book called 'The Loves of the Improbable Saints', in which he has written up stories about some of the strange people who have been made Saints by the Catholic Church.

For example, have you ever heard of St Ronald of Buckingham? Apparently, he was born into the world like any normal baby, and immediately preached an amazing sermon....before promptly dying. Then there's a favourite of mine - St Theophilus the Myrrh-Gusher. It's a great name isn't it? It refers to the belief that the bodies of certain martyred saints have the ability to ooze a sweet smelling liquid from their wounds.

I've got a few other favourites. How about St Drogo, the patron saint of unattractive people? There's St Isodore, who in the 1980s was designated the patron saint of the Internet, because he was well known as a scholar and compiler of information. Can you imagine the scene in Heaven when God tells a particular saint that the Catholic Church has just designated him as the patron of something or other? "I'm the Patron Saint of WHAT?!"

Personally, I'm particularly drawn to St Anthony of Padua, who is the patron saint of lost causes! And then there's the number one weird saint of all time, the patron saint of finding a parking place. Apparently, in New York, car drivers circling a block can be heard muttering this prayer: "Mother Cabrini, Mother Cabrini - find me a space for my driving machiny."

Richard Coles says that whilst all these Saints might be jolly good fun for us, there is a grain of truth in many of them. Sometimes, saints become patron saints because of the terrible things they were made to suffer for their faith in Christ. So, for example, St Apollonia is the patron saint of dentists, because she had all her teeth extracted as a punishment for believing in Jesus. I could tell you a lot more horror stories...but it's a bit early in the morning for that!

So, why do we celebrate All Saints? Is it perhaps a feast in honour Southampton Football Club...which, as some of you may know started life as the All Saints Church Soccer Team? No of course not. Besides, I don't get football at all. I've never really understood the attraction of watching 22 people run up and down a field with the sole object of getting a ball between two sticks. And what's all that business with protesting against the decision of referees? Have you ever seen a referee, with a frustrated player up in his face about a red card suddenly change his mind at put the card away again? Why do they bother?

No, the festival of All Saints is nothing about football, and very little about silly or funny patron saints. Rather it is a reminder to us that we are members of a church which is both here on earth, and also in heaven. The Bible refers to all Christian believers as Saints. It's a term which we can all own, if we are followers of Christ. Hmm...St Tom of Portsmouth....has a bit of ring to it?

The Church has always taught that we are members of not just a world-wide church, but a Universal one. We, here on earth are known as the Church Militant, and those Saints who have died and now live with God are called the Church Triumphant. In the same way that we pray for each other here on earth, the Church teaches that we should also pray for those who have died, and that they pray for us. That is why many churches have icons of saints that we can ask to pray for us, as we continue to pray for them.

Our two readings today remind us that, as the Bible says, 'God is the God of the living, and of the dead'. The dead are held by him, in his love, until the great end of days that many of us hope for. Our first reading, from the book of Revelation, paints a picture of the end of the world, when the whole of humanity, living and dead will be united before God. On that day, God will fashion a new heaven and new earth, where death is no more, and where there will be no more crying or pain. It's a wonderful vision, isn't it? Some people take the underlying theme of Revelation quite literally - they believe it to be a sure and certain prophesy that the world will end, and that God will intervene to stop all the slaughter and the hatred. And why not?

Personally, I'm not quite so sure. I tend to see the visions of Revelation as more like poetry that points us towards a spiritual reality that we can claim today. God is already with us. In Jesus, God has already made his home with mortals. For those who truly trust in him, whether they be alive or dead, there need be no more mourning, or crying or pain. But I am not here to tell you how to interpret Revelation. That's a task that you must take on for yourself, as part of your own discipleship.

Our Gospel reading reminds us of the story of Lazarus, rising from his tomb at the command of Jesus. This is given to us, on All Saints Sunday, to remind us that God, in Jesus, has power over death itself. Strictly speaking, Lazarus was not 'resurrected'. Rather, he was 're-vivified'. He came back to life, but he would one day die again. Resurrection, rather, is what happened first to Jesus.

The Bible talks of Jesus as 'the first-born from the Dead'...and describes resurrection as a sort of new birth. Jesus' body was transformed by his resurrection. It was different, unrecognisable by those who knew him on earth, until they heard his voice, or recognised him in the Breaking of Bread. It was a new, eternal body...a body which will last forever....and a body which the bible promises that we will also be given one day. We Saints. We who trust in Jesus.

And that's the crucial point. It is our trust in, and love for Jesus which makes us, and those who have died, saints. It's very little to do with what we have achieved in life; how much we've given or sacrificed. You don't have to be a martyr to be considered a saint. All that is asked, by God, is that we trust in God...in his grace, and his mercy, and his love.

You see, to return to my rant about football in a more creative way, Jesus is the kind of referee to whom you can go and appeal. He might metaphorically hold up a red card, and there might be a real danger of being 'sent off'. But if we appeal to Jesus, telling him we are sorry, he is the one referee who would gladly put his card away, and say 'Play On'. He does that because of his Grace. He does it because of his mercy.

And because of Jesus, we are All Saints.

The Hero's Call - A Meditation for Remembrance Day

Reading: Mark 1.14-18. First preached in 2009

So, there you are at home. Maybe you are digging the garden, or preparing the dinner. Or perhaps you're mending your fishing rod for a day on the river...and there comes a knock at the door. On the doorstep is a wandering preacher, who looks straight into your soul and says "Come. Follow me".

What do you do? You've got a family who are relying on you. You've got responsibilities to them, and to your neighbours. You've got an employer who is expecting you to be at work...or a teacher who expects you in class. But there's something about this preacher. There's something inspiring about him.

Of course, you know something about him already. You've heard some of his teachings, and you've heard the rumour that he's out and about looking for followers. But you never expected that he would knock on your door.

So what do you do? Should you simply follow him out of the door? Should you step out on a new adventure...and let all your other responsibilities take care of themselves? Or should you shut the door in the preacher's face?

What do you do?

But you've been intrigued by this preacher's message. You've already heard him, talking about how the 'Kingdom of God'...the new government of God...is coming. You've heard him calling people to turn away from society's normal ways of doing things. You've heard him saying that people need to 'repent'...to turn away...and to believe that there is good news.

But that's hard, isn't it? Good news. Hmm. Good news for whom? The last time you heard the phrase 'Good News' was when a bunch of soldiers rode through the town. They were proclaiming that there was 'good news' about the Emperor, Caesar. Apparently - according to the soldiers - Caesar had declared himself to be the Lord of Lords and the King of Kings. And this was supposedly 'good news'. Apparently. According to the soldiers, 'there is no other name by which people can be saved than the name of Caesar'. Considering the amount of taxes you are having to pay to Caesar, and considering the number of soldiers all over the countryside, it doesn't feel much like good news to you.

But this wandering preacher - this Jesus-bloke - he's talking about another kind of good news altogether. Or at least that's what you've been hearing. Apparently, his good news is good news for the poor. And for those who are mourning. And for those who are pure in heart. And for those who are peacemakers. That's a bit different than good news for Caesar, and for money-lenders and weapon-makers...

Perhaps Jesus' good news for the poor, and the oppressed, and the meek - perhaps that is worth following. Perhaps that is worth laying aside your family responsibilities for a while.

What do you do? Are you prepared to follow this call to 'Follow me'. Because that's what heroes do. Heroes throughout history are always given a call to follow. Sometimes they resist that call. Like Moses who resisted the call to lead the people out of slavery. Like Jonah who resisted the call to go and tell the people of Nineveh to repent.

Because calls are dangerous. Calls lead us out of our safe, secure lives into lives of adventure, possible danger, and even death. But isn't the case that the best journeys are the ones where there is adventure and challenge along the way?

That's a challenge that many soldiers have followed over the centuries. It's a challenge to stand up and fight for what you believe in. It's a challenge to leave family and home - and to become a peace-maker, often in a foreign land. It's a challenge that will certainly include adventure. It might well end in death.

But's it's a hero's call. It's a call to transform a society - perhaps through fighting, perhaps through diplomacy, perhaps through the transforming power of rendering aid and giving food to starving people. It's a call to stand up against powers of oppression that would seek to dominate an entire population...just like the Egyptians dominated the Israelites.

So what do you do?

Do you follow this preacher - this Jesus? You don't know where he might lead you. Perhaps he'll lead you on a path to destruction. Perhaps he's trying to put together a rebel army to over-throw the oppressive dictator's army. Or perhaps he's talking about another kind of kingdom altogether...a kingdom of God's rule, which God, and only God can ultimately establish.

And if you follow him on this path, and if you die, will anyone remember you? Will anyone sing laments for your passing? Or will you lie in an unmarked grave on some foreign field?

Wouldn't it just be easier to stay at home. And go fishing tomorrow.

Wouldn't it be easier to just settle back in your comfortable chair, tend your garden, dandle your children on your knee, and pretend that everything's alright with the world. Wouldn't it be easier to never give your time, your energy, your skills, or your money to any other living soul?

Yes. It would be easier. But where's the adventure in that? Where's the challenge? Where's the growth? Where's the chance to be changed from glory into glory ever more like the image of God your Creator?

"Come. Follow me. And I will make you fish for people".

You hear the call. You know something of what it means. It's something about doing things differently. It's something about living differently...living for others, not for you. It's something about acquiring scars and wounds, instead of the latest stuff from the market. It's something about giving up home and family, and having nowhere to lay your head for the sake of a bigger vision, a better vision. A vision of a new kind of Kingdom.

You've heard the call.

What do you do?

What do you do?

——

Note: this sermon/meditation was immediately followed by an Act of Remembrance, including the customary two minutes' silence in memory of those who have given their lives for our freedom.

A Christmas Message

First preached in 2011

2011 has been quite a year, hasn't it? In the Middle East, the so-called Arab Spring has brought about an earthquake in politics. In New Zealand there were real earthquakes, while in the UK our summer streets exploded into riots. In Europe, the Euro-zone countries are in crisis. Floods in the Philippines, civil war in the Ivory Coast. In Russia, Vladimir Putin is accused of rigging elections. In the Western World, bankers are getting ludicrously rich while homelessness and poverty is on the rise at least partly because of their greed. America withdraws from Iraq...which quickly plunges into political chaos. Refugees are flooding across borders all over the world...desperately seeking a better life.

And that's just for starters....

But you know all this. You watch the news, like me. I wouldn't be surprised if, by now, you are wondering what the Vicar going on about?! We didn't come to church to hear about politicians and war-mongers, bankers and natural disasters did we? We've come to church to hear lovely things which make us feel good inside.

But perhaps that's the problem...especially the problem with how we have told ourselves the Christmas story. At the centre of the story is a baby...yes. And some sheep and camels, and a manger full of sweet-smelling hay. How quickly we forget the rest of the story, though!

We forget that Jesus was born in an occupied country, governed by the most powerful and war-like Empire the world had yet known. We forget that the story of a baby born in Bethlehem is the story of a baby born homeless, in an animal's food trough. We forget that within months of his birth, the local warlord, King Herod, had ordered the slaughter of all male babies in Bethlehem - because he was afraid of losing political power. We forget that just after his birth, Jesus and his parents had to flee for their lives - becoming political refugees themselves.

There are other aspects of the story we forget too. We forget that Mary was an unmarried, probably teenage mother. We forget that Shepherds - the first visitors on the scene - were thought of as 'the

68

scum of the earth' to much of their society. And we forget that this story which begins with the birth of a baby will end up with the cruel death of a God-filled man, nailed to a cross by the political and religious powers of his day.

No, my friends, we dare not take this Christmas story lightly. And we must not assume that our world is any different to the world into which Jesus was born. Because that is precisely the point. In the babe of Bethlehem, God enters our world. The underlying story of the Christ Mass is that God comes to us in the middle of all the chaos. Surprisingly, God is at work in the middle of all the muddle.

How can this be? How can God be at work when there is obviously so much horror out there?

An animal's food-trough is a surprising place to find God. But there are many other places where we find that God has been startlingly at work; in hospices and prisons, for example. He's been at work in school classrooms, and loving families. In our community cafe here at St Mark's, and in day-care centres and play groups. God has been at work in campaigns for global justice, and in the work of Christian Aid and a thousand other relief organisations. God is at work in lives which are poured out in the service of others, all around the globe - in the lives of men and women who are committed to being peace-keepers of all kinds. God is at work among the Churches Homeless Action Group in Portsmouth, and in the dedication of social workers, nurses, and doctors, serving the needs of drug addicts and prostitutes. God is at work in the Portsmouth Women's Refuge, and the Haslar Centre for Refugees.

Everywhere that there is love, 'Christ is born today'. Every time that a weapon is laid down, and reconciliation is sought, 'Christ is born today'. Every time that the mighty are brought down from their seat, the words of the Angels come true.

And that's why we are here. In the middle of night, in the middle of the darkness, we proclaim that there is light, after all. In the middle of the darkness of the World, in the middle of political and economic chaos, we proclaim that Christ is present; that God remains at work among us.

So, sing choirs of Angels...sing in exultation. Christ is born today!

Mothering Sunday

First preached in 2011.

Right then. Let's start with some basic dictionary definitions. What is a mother? According to the Concise Oxford English Dictionary, a mother is:

"A mucilaginous substance produced in vinegar during fermentation by mould-fungus"

Oh. Hang on. That can't be right. Let's try another:

"A term of address for an elderly woman of the lower class"

Better.

How about "the Head of a Religious Community"

or

"A quality or condition which gives rise to another, as in 'necessity is the mother of invention'"

or

"Artificial Mother: An apparatus for rearing chickens"

Of course we've all heard the word Mother used in many and various contexts haven't we. The House of Commons is sometimes referred to as 'the Mother of Parliaments'. For our friends in Roman Catholicism, St Peter's in Rome is sometimes referred to as 'the Mother Church'. And Saddam Hussein had an annoying habit of referring to his warlike excursions into neighbouring countries as 'the Mother of all battles'.

But of course, the most usual use of the word is the one we give to our Mums...to those who gave birth to us, and who brought us up in the world.

True motherhood though, is much more than the biological function of bringing new life into the world. That part of motherhood is hard, no doubt. It takes commitment, devotion, and (I'm told) a huge amount of pain to fulfil the purely biological process of motherhood. But, as any mother will tell you - it's after the birth that the real work of mothering begins.

Real mothering takes time, devotion, and skill. And many mothers have to learn those skills along the way - often by trial and error. In fact, it is very easy to tell new mothers from more experienced ones - especially by the way they relate to their children.

Apparently, when you have your first baby, you spend a great deal of time just gazing at your baby.

When you have your second child, you spend a good deal of every day just making sure that your first child isn't hitting, poking or squeezing the new baby.

When you have your third child, you spend a little bit of every day hiding from all the children!

But let's face it, not every mother is successful. In fact, in these days of fractured or highly mobile families, it is not at all unusual for a young mum to find herself bringing up a child all alone, with no other family members around. In this City I know of many young mums who are isolated beyond belief. They are stuck at the top of high rise buildings, perhaps with the lift broken down, or perhaps with too many children to be able to go out into the world, even to seek help. For many, motherhood becomes an oppressive almost prison-like experience.

The other uncomfortable fact is that some mothers just shouldn't be mothers. Too many children grow up in homes that are unloving, or where one parent or the other suffers from addictions to drugs or alcohol. Some parents routinely use violence to bring up their children, others are too poorly educated to realise that sticking a child in front of a PlayStation all day does not constitute good parenting!

And that is why Mothering Sunday should inspire us to enlarge our vision of what 'mothering' is. Mothering is something that the whole of society should be involved with. Put it another way: mothering is just too important to be left to mothers alone! Not so long ago, in fact within the memories of most of us here, whole villages or towns were involved in bringing up children. It was perfectly natural for any adult who saw a child mis-behaving to chastise them. Adults from across the community ran scouts and guides and youth clubs and choirs.

When I was growing up, the parenting that my parents did was supported by my school teachers, my brass band, my drama group, and my cub pack and my church choir. But now thanks to some mercifully rare, but very high-profile cases of appalling child abuse, less and less adults are willing to volunteer; afraid that they will be labelled as paedophiles, just for caring about children. Many activities which are run for children now can only happen if parents stay in the room, or at the side of the football pitch.

The danger of this over-protection of youngsters is that children don't get the chance to flap their wings, and find out who they are. Their vision of what life can be is being reduced. For children who are taken to school in the safety of Mum's car, then observed in every dance class or drama group, and taught martial arts only 'so they can stand up for themselves', the world becomes a place to be protected from...rather than to be experienced, relished, and enjoyed for all its beauty, challenge, and yes, even danger.

Mothering though, is something which the Church teaches should be done by the whole community.

In fact, Jesus used some pretty strange language about mothers. Do you remember the time when someone tugged at his sleeve and said "Your mother and brothers are outside"? Here's the whole short story, from Matthew 12. 46-50:

While He was still speaking to the crowds, behold, His mother and brothers were standing outside, seeking to speak to Him. Someone said to Him, "Behold, your mother and your brothers are standing outside seeking to speak to you." But Jesus answered the one who was telling him and said, "Who is my mother and who are my brothers?" And stretching out his hand toward his disciples, he said, "Behold my mother and my brothers! For whoever does the will of my Father who is in heaven, he is my brother and sister and mother."

This was pretty tough stuff, wasn't it? Jesus appears to reject his own Mother, in favour of the larger community of disciples who were following him. What's going on?

For Jesus, the bonds of family were clearly important. They were so important that when he hung on the cross, one of the things most clearly on his mind was the long-term care of his Mother (which is why he asked John to take care of her). But before that, by his actions and by his words, Jesus makes it very clear that the family unit (and even the bonds of love between a mother and a child) must take second place to the wider Christian community.

And that's because the Christian wider community is the whole Body of Christ - and the Body of Christ is called, by Christ, to serve and 'mother' the rest of the world. To those who are sick, or in prison, or hungry, or homeless, Christ says, effectively, "Mother them".

Christ uses a mothering metaphor of himself, when weeping over the lost city of Jerusalem; he says "How long have I desired to gather your children together, as a hen gathers her brood under her wings".

So for the Church, Mothering Sunday has never been just 'Mother's Day'. You could even wonder whether Mother's Day is just a secular scam, designed to sell cards and flowers, and rack-up the profits of restaurants, by feeding on our guilt about not having phoned our mothers! Going further still, someone responded to a few thoughts I put on Facebook recently, on the topic of Mother's Day. They described Mother's Day as 'A patriarchal construct to reinforce women's subjugation and oppression'! That might be a little bit strong...but I know where they are coming from.

To be a mother is to be much more than the one human being whose sole duty is to bring up one or more biological children. Motherhood needs to be understood as a calling that every Christian - man or woman - shares...a calling to 'mother' a world which is need of the kind of wisdom, challenge and upbringing that the very best Mothers are capable of.

And that ultimately is surely what we are called to do. Our churches are called to act like mothers to those around us. A good mother imparts knowledge, and wisdom. A good mother reaches down and picks up fallen children. A good mother inspires their child to be more - to learn more, to grow more...to become the best human being they can become. A good mother introduces her child to other children, so that all the children learn together what it means to grow up together. A good mother picks up a child who is crying, and comforts them. A good mother sits beside the bed of a child who is suffering, and prays for them. A good mother feeds her children.

Our churches, all of us, are called to be that kind of mother to the people of our parish. By our teaching of the Gospel, by our prayers for the sick and the suffering, by our feeding of the hungry poor (in our café, for example), by the visiting of the lonely, by our care for the oppressed, by the provision of opportunities for people - and children - to grow in talent and humanity...we are called to act as a mother to the wider family of the people of this parish.

So here's my prayer for this church, and for us: may we discover the fullness of mother-hood revealed to us through the example of Christ. May we discover the joy of giving loving, motherly service to the lost, the lonely and the poor of our parish. May we know that fulfilment which comes from sharing God's motherly love to more than just our own families: indeed, to the whole world to which Christ calls us.

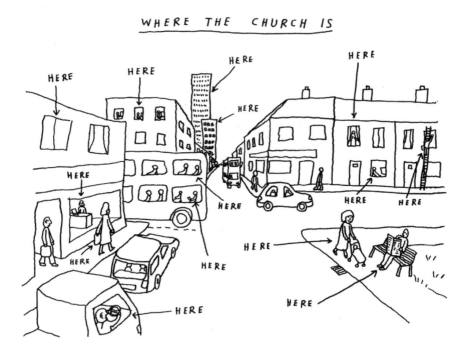

WHERE THE CHURCH IS

Palm Sunday

First preached in 2012

Jesus enters Jerusalem on a donkey...

Palm Sunday. "Blessed is he who comes in the name of the Lord!" We hear these words, we sing these songs but I wonder if we understand the impact of Jesus' entry into Jerusalem on the people of his time? This day marked the end of the beginning of Jesus' ministry and the beginning of his end. He was moving into the final week of his earthly ministry - a climactic moment.

It did not just happen - Jesus planned everything very carefully. He had even arranged for a donkey to ride on, and had agreed a coded message with the owner - so that when the Disciples turned up and took the donkey, the owner wouldn't complain.

It was very important for Jesus that he should arrive in the city on a donkey. He knew the prophecy from the ancient book of Zechariah,

'Rejoice greatly, O daughter Zion!
Shout aloud, O daughter Jerusalem!
Lo, your King comes to you;
Triumphant and victorious is he,
Humble and riding on a donkey
On a colt, the foal of a donkey'

Jesus' actions were an unmistakable claim to be the Messiah, God's messenger to the world. You see, Jesus normally walked everywhere. This is the only time we see Jesus travelling other than on foot. That is why the people pulled branches from the trees and shouted 'hosanna' – which means 'save us'. That's why they threw their garments on the ground to welcome the King of Kings into the holy city...it was a very ancient custom to spread out cloaks for a King...going right back to the story of King Jehu, in 2 Kings 9.

Yes, the crowd certainly understood Jesus' claim to be the Messiah. That is why they began to sing the psalm of praise, Psalm 118 that pilgrims always sang on the way to Jerusalem: a song of victory, a hymn of praise to the God who defeats all his foes and establishes his kingdom:

"Blessed is he who comes in the name of the Lord.

...With boughs in hand, join in the festal procession

up to the horns of the altar!"

But what did his disciples understand by all of this? Throughout the Gospel records we see Jesus struggling to help his disciples understand the sort of kingdom that he had come to usher in. But some of his disciples, even on Palm Sunday, still harboured ideas of Jesus coming to overthrow the Romans and to restore the power of the Jewish State. Whatever Jesus said, whatever Jesus did – it seemed that his disciples couldn't free themselves from some very human notions of power and victory.

You see, Palm Sunday is unmistakably all about power – the power of God. But the power of God is of a different order to the powers of this world. God's power is not a sort of multiplication of the power of Caesar or of Napoleon or of the USA. Somehow just bigger, better, more powerful power. God's power is not like that.

That is the point made in one of the crucial moments of Jesus Christ Superstar - the Rock Opera. Jesus and his followers are seen arriving in Jerusalem. Simon the Zealot is urging Jesus to go ahead and get the crowd to follow him to get rid of the Romans. Simon declares.

"You'll get the power and the glory for ever and ever and ever."

And do you know what Jesus replies? Very gently, against all the noise of Simon the Zealot, he sings,

"Neither you, Simon, nor the fifty thousand, nor the Romans, nor the Jews; nor Judas; nor the twelve, nor the priests, nor the scribes nor doomed Jerusalem itself, understand what power is; understand what glory is; understand at all."

You see - God's power is shown through Jesus and through his self-giving and sacrifice, and suffering. Jesus Christ and him crucified; that is the power and wisdom of God. As St Paul said,

"The message of the cross is foolishness to those who are perishing, but to us who are being saved it is the power of God". (1 Cor 1:18).

It's a different order of power that works not through violence and victory but through love, service and sacrifice.

It is easy for us to see both those kinds of power at work today. On the one hand, we can see the power of violence and victory - as we see armies marching against each other around the planet, as we see selfish companies and individuals grabbing all the riches and wealth that they can, as we see man's inhumanity to man continuing to spread around the world.

But we can see the other kind of power as well. Every time that someone stands up against the violence and greed. Every time someone reaches out a hand to help another human being. Every time a hospital is opened, or a school is started, or a refugee is fed or given a tent - that's the power of God at work. Every time someone decides to give up the latest gadget they desire and chooses to give that money for the benefit of others, there is another power at work...the power of love, service and sacrifice.

Let's imagine counting up all the people in the world who are involved with education, healing, loving their families, relieving poverty, serving their church or their local community, or working for reconciliation. Now let's imagine counting up all the people who are money grabbing war-mongers. You know, I think we'd see, pretty quickly, that God's power is very much in evidence. I think we'd really see who is reigning on Earth.

We hear about the atrocities - the terrorist bombs, the famine and poverty - because they are real, and they are horrible. But what we don't hear about is the day to day normality that most people actually live with. God is the God of normality. God delights in the simple loving acts of families, and communities and churches all over the world. God delights in those communities around the world (like those I met in Ghana recently) who are not obsessed with grabbing power, and working every hour of the day to acquire the latest gadget, or the bigger house. God delights in those communities who take just what they need from the land, and spend the rest of their time pursuing friendship, art and community. His power is found there. He is there.

That's why we can sing, with such joy, that Jesus reigns over all the Earth! Because although we hear more about the bad stuff in the world, the reality is that God is alive. In the confident, hopeful words of that hymn we sing: 'God is working his purpose out as year succeeds to year.'

When Jesus rode into Jerusalem, on that first Palm Sunday, he was profoundly misunderstood. But the power of God that he was embracing and sustaining and sending forth throughout that first Holy Week has continued to shape and affect lives all around the world ever since.

The power of God is not about war and conquest, it's about love and sacrifice.

The power of God is not about gaining wealth, it's about gaining simplicity.

One final thought. By his actions on that first Palm Sunday, Jesus laid claim to the title 'King of Kings'. In this Jubilee year, when we will mark 60 years of our own constitutional monarch's reign, we sometimes forget what it means to live under an absolute Monarch (like kings were in the time of Jesus). A constitutional monarch, like ours, is very limited in their power. Their power is largely ceremonial. They can influence events, but they don't have the power to dictate how the country is run. An absolute Monarch had tremendous power. Their word was law, quite literally. If a King of those days said 'jump', the only reasonable response was to ask 'how high?'

By riding into Jerusalem in triumph that day, Jesus claimed to be the absolute Monarch of all absolute Monarchs. He claimed that his way of living, his way of dealing with other people, his way of loving all whom he encountered – that was the new Law.

What does that mean for us, who call ourselves Jesus' subjects, Jesus' disciples? It means that we are called and summoned to obey the new law of our King of Kings. It means living lives that are poured out in service to others, as his was. It means living lives which seek nothing for us. It means devoting ourselves to the process of 'unselfing'…of giving up all that our fragile egos demand, giving up what we want in favour of what is needed by the whole society around us.

And so as we share today in the last supper of bread and wine, let us recall the new age that Jesus came to usher in, an age not based on military power or might but on suffering and service, love and obedience. And let us commit ourselves anew to being people of his Kingdom. We are people who embrace his way of living; the way of self-sacrifice and love.

As a sign of that commitment, I'm going to ask you to make a gesture this morning. When you come to the rail, to receive the sustaining power of the body and blood of Jesus, we are going to offer you a Palm Cross. After you have received the bread and the wine, or received a blessing, let me invite you to reach out and deliberately take that cross, as a sign that you are taking up the challenge that Jesus offers us. Take that cross home with you and put it in a prominent place.

Let it be a reminder, throughout the rest of this year, of the fundamentally different way of life that Jesus calls each one of us to embrace.

Not the way of power, and wealth, and consumerism.

The way of love, of self-sacrifice, of simplicity, and of peace.

Meanings of the Cross (Good Friday)

Reading: John 3.13-17. First preached in 2012

The Cross is a powerful symbol indeed. It stands, for many, at the centre of their faith, and even at the centre of time itself. A traditional belief, especially in the Orthodox church, is that after his Crucifixion, Jesus descended into the world of the dead, and released those who had died before him, but who were held captive because of their sin. The Cross then, stands at the Crossroads of time. Jesus' atoning death is believed to have effect both forward and backwards in time.

It should not surprise us then, perhaps, to discover the cross, or cross-like symbols, popping up throughout history. Many crosses have been found throughout pre-history...way before it became important as a Christian symbol. In most cases, the cross was a symbol of life. It may be that the cross symbolised the making of fire by rubbing two sticks together...fire being a symbol of warmth, the Sun, and life. In other mythologies, crosses symbolised a connection between heaven (as a vertical line) and earth (as the horizontal line). Worship, therefore, took place at the point of connection between heaven and earth...at the centre of the Cross. There are two pre-Christian crosses that you will probably be most familiar with. The first is the Swastika – which has a wide variety of meanings to many different people of the world (see here for more details). The second is the Ankh – an Egyptian version of the cross, with a looped head at the top...believed to be principally a symbol of life.

Initially, after Jesus' death, the cross didn't feature in Christian worship at all. For many, it was a disgusting and degrading symbol, not worthy to be used in connection with the Christ. For us, a modern parallel might be the use of an electric chair as a religious symbol. Early Christians, as you probably know, preferred the use of the secret sign of the fish - the Icthus, the letters of which could form an acrostic phrase: Jesus Christ, Son of God, Saviour.

However, as crucifixion faded from habitual use by the Romans, we begin to see the sign of the cross emerging in Christian worship...until, by our time, it has become a ubiquitous sign of the Christian religion...like it, or not!

The cross, then, comes to us with redolent history. It is an ancient sign of life and healing - a divine union between heaven and earth. Tradition has it that the 'pole' which Moses lifted up in the desert, for sick people to gaze upon and find healing, was in fact a cross...though in this case it was a 'T' shaped cross. The same symbol – a T-shaped cross with a bronze serpent – is now a universal sign of the healing arts - seen on pharmacies and medical centres all around the world.

The sign of the cross speaks to us of life...and of a mystical union between heaven and earth. But to Christians it speaks still deeper. For it was on a cross that God showed how much he loved the world. In the words of our Gospel reading, 'God so loved the world that he gave his only son, to the end that everyone who believes in him should not perish, but should have everlasting life' (John 3.16). The whole narrative push of the Gospels was that is was necessary for Jesus to die on such a cross.

But why? Why was it necessary for Jesus to die on a Cross? It's frankly what the church calls (for good reason!) a 'Mystery'. My advice is that you should be deeply suspicious of anyone who tells you that they have understood exactly what Jesus was accomplishing on the cross. The writers of the Bible itself wrestle with meaning – at various points they conjure with metaphors like 'paying a ransom to the devil' or 'taking our sins upon him' or 'being punished for our sake'.

Later theologians have sometimes preferred to speak of the Cross as a grand moral example...a graphic, lived-out picture of how far it is necessary to commit oneself to the Gospel. Others have pointed out how the Cross stands as a vindication of peaceful resistance over inhuman violence...because the subsequent Resurrection demonstrates that peace will eventually overcome all war.

Rowan Williams suggests through the Cross, the human power-mongers who promise that violence can rule the world are shown to be false prophets. How can violence rule the world if it ends up pushing God to the margins of society?

So, as I hope you can see, there are many different ways of understanding, or meditating upon the meaning of the Cross. But through them all, one underlying reality holds sway. It was to the

Cross that Jesus turned his face. He was reluctant...praying that this particular cup of suffering may pass him by...but it was clearly vital to Him, and to the completion of his mission.

For that reason, if no other, we look to the Cross. The Cross was important to Jesus...it symbolised the very apex of his mission. And so to us, the Cross symbolises the very heart of our religion. It symbolises the sure and certain hope that we have that, as our Gospel reading made clear, 'whosoever believes in Him, will have eternal life'.

It is perhaps worth pointing out, however, that Jesus did not dictate, in that passage, precisely what we were to believe about him. We are not asked to sign up to any particular theological understanding of his atoning death, for example. We are invited not to believe things about Jesus...but to believe in Jesus. We are invited into something similar to a relationship with a person, not mental assent to a series of theoretical propositions.

Those who 'believe in Him' are those who have studied his life, as well as we can understand it from our distance in time. Those who believe in Him are those who trust that His way of living, his way of giving, sacrificially, of all that he had and was...this is the way to eternal life.

The Cross symbolises the giving up of the last thing a man can give...his very life. For us, may it symbolise the giving of our lives too...offered as living sacrifices for the God who is our sure and certain hope.

Easter
First preached in 2012.

Easter means many different things to many different people. A sign of new life. The defeat of darkness. The Spring Equinox, with all the promise of new life - chicks and eggs. Or, perhaps, the single most important event of all history!

What do you believe?

Let's first review the claims made about Jesus, which we demonstrated just now in the signing of the new Pascal Candle. He is the Alpha and Omega. The Beginning and the End. He is the one who has the power to make all things new...and who promises a new heaven and a new earth. C.S. Lewis spent some time in his book, Mere Christianity, thinking about what it meant for Jesus to come and live as a human being. He wrote: "The Eternal being who knows everything and who created the whole universe, became not only a man, but (before that) a baby, and before that a foetus inside a woman's body. If you want to get the hang of it, think how you would like to become a slug."

Jesus, having emptied himself of his divinity, came to live among us as a human being. It's worth remembering that. Sometimes, when we struggle to live like Jesus, it's tempting for us to think "Well, it was easy for Jesus – he was God!". But that is not the message of the Gospels. Jesus emptied himself of all Godly power. He became fully human, to show us what a truly full, human, life looks like. As a human being, he lived and he loved, and he gave up all that he had for others. He taught us what God was like, and offered us the chance to choose God's way of living.

But if it wasn't for Easter...these remarkable actions on the part of God would quite probably have gone unknown, and un-remarked by the rest of humanity. Jesus wasn't the first man to die in a horribly painful way...and he wasn't the last. His disciples knew that, and the historical records of the time - the Gospels - tell us that after his death they thought that the whole thing was over. They hid in an upper room - terrified.

But the fact is that Jesus shrugged off death! Taking back the divinity he had laid aside as a human, he rose from the tomb! And what a dramatic impact that had! It transformed the lives of Jesus' friends, and from there it transformed lives throughout the whole world.

It is sometimes said that it doesn't really matter whether or not we believe in the Resurrection. Some people have suggested that Jesus didn't actually rise from the dead...it was just that his presence with the disciples seemed to live on with them, after his death. Some people suggest that Jesus was only alive in the sense that any dead person is alive to us...in our memories. But I don't think that interpretation matches the facts.

First of all, people don't give up their own lives for a memory. We know that many - if not all - of the disciples were persecuted, hated, tried and martyred for their assertion...their absolute certainty...that Jesus had got up from the grave. They could not deny what they had seen with their own eyes...no matter how much they were threatened and beaten. Now in these days we know that people will give their lives for religious dogma - for what they've been brainwashed with by the mad mullahs of Al Quaida. But the sacrifice of the Disciples was something quite different. For them to have denied that they had seen Jesus rise from the dead, would have been like us having to deny that grass is green.

Secondly, if Jesus had not risen from the dead, why didn't the Roman or Jewish authorities simply produce his body to disprove it? That would have quickly stopped the resurrection rumour in its tracks. But there was no body to produce.

As you know, probably, I'm a pretty liberal Christian. I'm happy to indulge a great deal of latitude in the interpretation of all sorts of dogma! But on this one issue, I am steadfast to the faith we have inherited, in the precise formula that we have inherited it. Jesus calls us to follow him, not only because he died for us...not because we feel grateful to him (although of course we should). The message of Easter is that Jesus calls us to follow him because he lives!

As one of us, Jesus not only died, but was raised from the dead and now lives with the Father. And he says that he wants to share his joy and his life with us. Jesus isn't looking for our sympathy; he's inviting us to get involved. He's looking for us to join his followers in proclaiming that there is another way than the way of war and violence and hate, of greed and consumerism and poverty. And he's inviting us, ultimately, to come home to the love of our heavenly Father.

That's why he died...to give us life, and to call us home. Not to illicit our pity.

So it does matter what we believe. If we believe that Jesus only lived in his disciples' memories...then he died there too - when they died. And our faith is based on nothing more than a vague wishfulness - a unprovable hypothesis that maybe God exists, and maybe we have somewhere to go after we die.

If, on the other hand - as all the evidence suggests - he really rose from the dead, still lives today, and calls us to life and to heaven...then that is worth something. That is a truth worth hanging on to. That is a fact worth telling our neighbours about. That is something worth celebrating.

Alleluia...Christ is Risen!

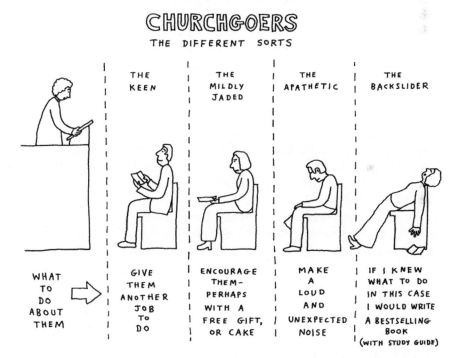

CHURCHGOERS
THE DIFFERENT SORTS

	THE KEEN	THE MILDLY JADED	THE APATHETIC	THE BACKSLIDER
WHAT TO DO ABOUT THEM	GIVE THEM ANOTHER JOB TO DO	ENCOURAGE THEM - PERHAPS WITH A FREE GIFT, OR CAKE	MAKE A LOUD AND UNEXPECTED NOISE	IF I KNEW WHAT TO DO IN THIS CASE I WOULD WRITE A BESTSELLING BOOK (WITH STUDY GUIDE)

Pentecost: Heaven on Earth?

Reading: Acts 2.1-21. First Preached in 2009

What fantastic weather we've been having...at last! It's been lovely, hasn't it? A chance to sit in the garden without your raincoat on. The flowers are blooming, and it's too early in the season yet for wasps! For many of us, these last couple of days have been like a little piece of heaven.

We human beings like to try and find little bits of heaven, don't we? Some of us go in search of sun to some foreign shore...a few days on a beach, with a book, some sunglasses, and a cool beer is just what heaven would be like, we think. The trouble is, reality is so often disappointing isn't it?

The problem for me and my family has always been that once we get to the beach, the first thing we discover is that it is full of other people...who got there before us! So we stare across the sea of slowly roasting people, and we think we might be able to see a spare yard of sand that has not already been occupied. It is then that we find ourselves wishing that we had not worn flip-flops! Flip flops are designed for walking a few yards down to the shore...not for 3-mile route-marches across scorching sand.   And then there's the luggage...because of course we've taken our sun-lounger, a parasol, an enormous picnic basket, a ball for the kids, a tyre, towels, swimming costumes...and the dog...who is much more interested in stealing other people's ice-creams than following us to our destination. That's when the shouting starts...

"Look, you wanted to bring the darned swing-ball, so you can carry it! Darling, what is in this picnic? Are you intending to feed the whole beach? Dog! Stop it! Come here!"

When we finally arrive at our target square yard of sand, we prepare to put up the defences. Out comes the wind break...which we proceed to erect around the whole square. It's about marking out your territory...staking a claim. This is my bit of beach! Don't you dare step on it! All the people round about start looking excessively grumpy. You can almost hear their thoughts: "We got here early and picked a nice spot, with that nice bit of sand in front of us...and now the family from hell have turned up. Oh no! They've brought a dog too!"

Then, after an hour of banging in stakes, putting up the parasol, laying out the towels, getting out the picnic - a stunning realisation suddenly hits us. The tide's coming in! Action stations! We, and everyone around us, start to inch our way back up the beach, above the tide-line...until we are all jammed like sardines up against the sea-wall.

And that's the problem with trying to find a little taste of heaven! Heaven so often proves elusive for us, doesn't it? We plan a nice quiet evening at home, pizza in one hand, a bar of chocolate in the other...and a good movie on the box. That'll be a taste of heaven, won't it! And then the phone rings and its Aunty Mabel; you know, the aunt who can't stop talking, and wants to give you the latest instalment in her long-running bunion saga.

The problem is that we think that heaven is a place. We imagine that if only we can get all the circumstances right, we will find peace and harmony. Heaven, we imagine, is a place where the sun always shines, and where there are no screaming toddlers. But heaven is not about a place. We don't find heaven by getting in a car. Yuri Gregarin, the first man in space, discovered that we don't find heaven by getting in a rocket either. Heaven is not up there. Heaven is in here. Heaven is not a place on earth. Heaven is a place of mind and spirit.

Jesus spoke about heaven quite a bit. When he first started out on his ministry, he declared that the Kingdom of heaven is 'at hand'. Another time he said 'the kingdom of heaven is among you'. Jesus declared that heaven is there, at hand, among us, ready for us to touch and experience.

I once heard Tom Wright, the Bishop of Durham, suggest that heaven can be thought of as being with us in a very immediate sense. If I understood him correctly, he suggested that heaven is a spiritual state of being that is around us all the time, separated from us by a kind of invisible curtain. He suggested that there are times when we are capable of lifting the veil of that curtain, and of stepping through into a different reality. And that sometimes, heaven itself sort of 'bleeds through' the curtain, and shines its light into our reality.

That, I suggest, is what happened on the day of Pentecost. When God poured out his Spirit on the disciples, gathered in that upper room in fear and trembling, heaven broke through for a while. Afterwards, the disciples told people that they had heard a sound; something like a rushing wind. They had seen what looked like tongues of fire, which spread out and touched each person. And then something truly remarkable happened: they all began to speak in different languages. Filled with this wind from heaven that had blown through the curtain, they spilled out into the street in excitement. Some people in the street thought they were all drunk (Acts 2.13). But others found that they could understand what was being said by these excited, spirit-filled, heaven-touched people.

So let's see what the result of that taste of heaven was. What were the tangible signs that God was at work? And how can we recognise heaven for ourselves from this story? Any significant event in human history can only really be judged by its effects. The effects of the day of Pentecost were these:

First, there was a breaking down of national barriers. Luke uses the story-teller's technique of strange tongues being miraculously spoken. But what he is pointing to is that on that day, more than any other in biblical history, God's good news became good news for all the world. No longer was God to be seen as the small God of one small nation. Through whatever actually happened that day, God showed himself to be the God of the whole world...the God of Parthians, Medes and Elamites. The God of Mesopotamia, Judea, Cappadocia, Pontus, and Asia. The God of Phyrgia and Pamphylia, Egypt and Libya. He was shown to be the God of Rome, Crete and Arabia - in other words, the God of the whole world.

This was, of course, a reversal of the much older story of the Tower of Babel. This was a God who was no longer to be understood as a partisan God of one tribe; but the Father (and Mother) of all humanity. That means that heaven can be found when all nations lay aside their petty squabbles over resources, and unite in the pursuit of justice. Heaven is found when all nations and peoples begin to work together for God's purposes. Heaven is found when neighbour begins to truly love neighbour. Heaven is found when our love for God becomes greater than our love of profit.

The Bible's word for these kinds of actions is 'repentance'. On that first Pentecost, the crowd asked Peter and the other apostles "what, then, shall we do Brothers?" (Acts 2.37). Let's take note of Peter's response.

(Acts 2.38) "Peter replied, 'Repent and be baptised, every one of you in the name of Jesus Christ, for the forgiveness of your sins. And you will receive the gift of the Holy Spirit."

That word 'repent' is crucial. It can conjure up unfortunate images of hell-fire and damnation preachers (i.e. "Repent, ye sinners, or burn in hell!")! But what does it actually mean to 'repent'? To repent, according to the Greek word attributed to Peter and Jesus, is to literally 'turn away' or 'turn around'. Those who repent are those who turn away from destructive, hellish ways of living, and who turn towards Godly, life-giving ways of living. Those who repent are those who give up hating and resenting, and begin loving and forgiving. Those who repent are those who stop embracing selfishness and greed, and who embrace self-sacrifice and generosity.

Those who repented on that first Pentecost very soon found themselves living in very different ways. According to the final verses of chapter two, they began living communally; sharing their goods and resources and giving to everyone as he had need. Luke paints a picture of a community who had put aside all notions of gain, of racism, of selfishness - and who had instead begun to live generous, sharing, joyful lives.

For a while, these people really began to get a little taste of heaven. As God's spirit flowed out through them, their response was a joyful self-giving; to one another, and to God.

It didn't matter to these people what the weather was like. They could have been just as joyful in the rain or the sun, on the beach or in the country. Heaven, for them, was not a place, but a state of mind. It was a Spirit-filled, transformed state of mind in which generosity, love, forgiveness, and self-sacrifice were found to be the way that heaven comes to earth.

How I pray that our world, our country, our city, and our church could truly learn what it means to live that kind of spirit-filled, Pentecostal, heaven-touching life!

Then we could really know what it means to pray 'thy kingdom come on earth as it is in heaven'.

What Price Unity?

A Sermon for the Week of Prayer for Christian Unity 2012

Reading: Titus 2.1-11

The Week of Prayer for Christian Unity is a good week for us to be meeting together. Although we are all Anglicans here - as far as I know - we are Anglicans from various and different traditions. A little later we will participate in Benediction, during which some of us will believe with all our hearts that we are somehow even more in the presence of Christ than we are at other times. Others of us will be slightly bemused, and see the ceremony of Benediction only as a metaphorical guide to prayer. Under this one roof, to my certain knowledge, are gathered tonight people whose Christian faith is best described as Catholic. Others, have evangelical backgrounds, but might now describe themselves as 'central'. Others have an interest in Orthodoxy. Some like their music to be really ancient...I know one choir member at least who considers anything newer than Mozart to be dangerously modern. Others take real joy in singing the latest anthems of living composers, or even the odd upbeat, rock 'n' roll chorus!

This, for me, is the heart of what it means to be Anglican. We belong to a church which systematically and deliberately attempts to be a communion in which people of different opinion, styles and preferences can nevertheless gather under one roof; all declaring a common belief in Jesus Christ. We don't always get that right. Clearly there are big tensions between us over issues like sexuality and the consecration of women bishops. (Isn't it interesting that the primary issues which divide us are usually about sex?)

For many years, the Churches Together movement has been a beacon of hope to those who lament the divisions in the church around the world. But, unfortunately, after 30 or more years, the flame of the Churches Together movement is beginning to wane. Those who have spent half a lifetime or more desperately praying for the visible Unity of Christ's Church have, in many places, begun to wonder whether God is deaf to their prayers. Or perhaps they are wondering whether God has a different plan altogether in mind.

There remains, of course, a hard core of folks who work hard to bring churches together in common worship and action. I take my hat off to them for their diligence and commitment. There are some great examples of projects out there in which churches of all hues combine their resources, time, and people for the common task of building the Kingdom. Perhaps the best local example is the Churches Homeless Action Group, which this year raised nearly £14,000 from the churches of the city at Christmas. The college at which most of our priests are trained by this Diocese (STETS in Salisbury) is a course which brings Anglicans together with Methodists and URC trainees, to learn from each other's experiences.

But, frankly, these wonderful pieces of work remain the exception rather than the rule. The church remains divided, across the world, because we seem unable to give each other the benefit of the doubt over a wide range of doctrinal and ecclesiological issues. Should the church be ruled from Rome? Should we have women bishops? Gay Bishops or Priests? Even Gay people? Where does our authority spring from - the Bible, or Tradition, or Reason, or Experience, or a combination of any two or more of those four. Styles of liturgy, the place of Mary, praying to the Saints, whether or not to follow a lectionary, or simply preach on what the Spirit suggests. Hymns or choruses? Organs or guitars? Robes or everyday clothes? The real meaning of the Eucharist (a simple memorial, or a transubstantiated real presence of Jesus, whose flesh we really eat as spiritual food).

That's just for starters. I could go on for a very long time. And I imagine that for world outside these doors must be tempted to proclaim, with Shakespeare, 'a plague on all your houses!'

Into this maelstrom of confusion comes tonight's reading from Paul's Letter to Titus. It's a very short letter - only three chapters long, covering just a couple of pages; and it often gets overlooked. But on this Sunday during the Week of Prayer for Christian Unity, it has the capacity to speak volumes.

In the letter, Paul writes to Titus, whom he has appointed as the Bishop of the Island of Crete. It is clear from Paul's text that he is very concerned about divisions which have already begun to erupt in the early Cretan church. Paul describes the 'many rebellious people, idle talkers and deceivers' who, Paul says, 'must be silenced since they are upsetting whole families'. He goes on to describe them as those who 'profess God, but then deny him by their actions. They are detestable, disobedient and unfit for any good work'

What is Paul's remedy for this problem...this problem of rebellious factions? His advice to Titus is essentially two-fold:

First, Paul encourages the Cretans to live Godly lives. Men are to be 'temperate, serious, prudent, and sound in faith, in love and in endurance'. Paul then goes on, in the context of his time, to give other lists of good behaviour for women, (young and old), young men and even slaves. Much of those lists might make us wince a little today, including the idea of young women having to be submissive to their husbands! But the underlying point which Paul makes is clear: being a Christian means living in a way which becomes 'an ornament to the doctrine of God our Saviour'. Our lives should be those which look like polished jewels - ornaments - on the crown of faith. Put another way, as the Apostle James wrote in his letter, "Faith without works is dead" (James 2.26)

A Christian will be judged - by God and other people - not by what they say or profess, but by the kind of lives they lead. Remember Paul's words to Titus: there are those who 'profess to know God, but they deny him by their actions'. (Titus 1.16)

Paul's second point to Titus is the most important of all, in the context of a discussion about Christian Unity. He says this, in chapter 3 of the letter: "Avoid stupid controversies, genealogies, dissensions and quarrels about the law, for they are unprofitable and worthless." Paul goes on, even more forcefully..."have nothing more to do with anyone who causes divisions, since you know that such a person is perverted and sinful, being self-condemned".

Wow. Those are strong words. "Have nothing more to do with anyone who causes divisions. They are perverted and sinful."

These then should be our watchwords when dealing with any other Christian. True Christians are judged by the kinds of lives they lead. Paul encourages his readers to be those who are 'obedient, ready for every good work, speaking evil of no-one, avoiding quarrelling, being gentle and showing courtesy to everyone." (Titus 3.2).

That's why we are here tonight. Even though some of us might have personal theological qualms about, for example, the ceremony of Benediction, out of gentleness and courtesy, we will kneel in contemplation before the Host when it is displayed, open to what God may show us through the practices of others.

That is why we are Anglicans: because out of a desire not to speak evil of anyone, and to avoid quarrelling, we will continue to worship side by side with people with whom we might profoundly disagree, for example, over whether or not a Priest or a Bishop can be a woman.

That is, ultimately, according to Paul, a clear sign of our Christianity. We are willing to lay aside quarrel and dissent, finding ways to respect and accommodate each other. We are those who chose to focus on the heart of our calling - to be 'ornaments to the doctrine of God our Saviour'..

May we discover what it means to put our love for God, and our love for neighbour, above and before any doctrinal dissent. If we could all do that, I believe that the issue of Christian Unity would quite simply take care of itself.

ECUMENICAL RELATIONS

HOW TO GET ON WITH THE CHURCH DOWN THE ROAD

INVITE THEM TO A 'BRING AND SHARE' LUNCH

INVITE THEM TO A PRAYER MEETING

TELEPHONE THE MINISTER, TELLING HIM THAT IF HIS CHURCH EVEN THINKS ABOUT STEALING ANY OF THE YOUNG PEOPLE FROM OUR YOUTH GROUP YOU WILL BE ROUND THERE SO FAST THAT HE WILL NOT EVEN KNOW WHAT HAS HIT HIM

A sermon for Joseph

Preached on the first Sunday of Christmas 2020

Last Sunday was a long time ago, wasn't it? Since then we've all we've attended overflowing carol services, celebrated the midnight Mass, feasted on TV programmes galore, and, if you're anything like me – promised faithfully, again and again, that the diet will start after Christmas!

But if you can cast your mind back as far as last Sunday, you might remember that I sat on a chair, and read a story of Mary being visited by the Angel. In my words of introduction, I explained that even though Matthew's gospel reading focused very heavily on Joseph's role in the annunciation, I felt that, being the fourth Sunday of Advent, we should properly give attention to Mary. Which I then did.

I also said that it was a curious fact of Matthew's Gospel that his focus is pretty-much entirely on Joseph. I suggested that this was because Matthew himself was a Jewish man, who tended to view life from a patriarchal perspective. Luke, on the other hand, appears to us as more of a gentile, and certainly his Gospel seems aimed at gentile Christians – and that women feature much more strongly in his narrative.

But after our service, I was gently chastised by one of my very good friends in this congregation, who rightly implored me not to overlook Joseph's pivotal role. (He also told me that he had enjoyed the re-telling of Mary's story – so he wasn't actually cross with me!).

And of course, he was right. As today's Gospel demonstrates very well indeed, Joseph's role in the birth of Jesus was absolutely front and centre. It was Joseph who could have (in the words of the King James Bible) 'put Mary away' in disgrace when her pregnancy became obvious. But Joseph trusted what he had been told in a dream, and stood by his wife-to-be. It was undoubtedly Joseph who negotiated a safe place for the birth of Jesus from a reluctant innkeeper. It was Joseph who responded to another dream, and led his new family to safety, as refugees from Herod's power-crazed murder of Bethlehem's children. It was Joseph who carefully shielded

Jesus in Egypt, and then, when the time was right, settled his family in Nazareth.

Incidentally, it's a little-noticed fact that Matthew's account of the Nativity, unlike Luke, doesn't describe Joseph travelling to Bethlehem from Nazareth. In fact, if we only had Matthew to rely on, we could quite easily believe that Joseph was already a resident of Bethlehem (just as the prophets had foretold). According to Matthew, Jesus only became a Nazarean because of the threat to his life as a child of Bethlehem. According to Matthew, the Wise Men visited the baby in the 'house' where Mary and Joseph were living, not in a stable at all.

But those are just fun facts for bible nerds!

The important, underlying emphasis of Matthew's narrative is the vital importance of Joseph doing what God asked him to do. As the head of his brand new family, it is Joseph's faithful obedience to God which saves and preserves Jesus for the ministry that is to come. Joseph does not do what we might expect a man in his position to do. He does not divorce his wife for shame. He does not ignore the messages he receives through his dreams. He doesn't act all macho and try to protect his son from Herod's soldiers with his own strength and cunning. No, he simply trusts and obeys what God tells him to do. He welcomes the new born king, and then safely shields him from harm until the danger of Herod is past.

There are two heroes in the Nativity story, therefore. Mary is a hero for accepting her fate to be the unmarried mother of a heavenly child. And Joseph is a hero for welcoming and then protecting the fragile baby Jesus, even at the cost of a massive journey into Egypt.

In the Bible, consistently, the heroes are always the ones who do what God asks or expects them to do. It's one of the central, over-riding themes of Scripture, that God always has a plan for his people. Only by following the plan – doing what we are told – can we ever hope to establish God's lasting rule on earth. The trick, of course, is to understand what God is, or isn't, telling each of us to do.

As a priest, I quite often find myself being asked the question 'what does God expect of me?', or 'what should I do in this or that situation?'. I honestly think that the questioners think that I must have a unique way of contacting God and asking for his opinion! Should I take the drugs my doctor has given me? Should I apply for a new job?

Should I have another baby? How should I vote in the general election? How should I know?! You see, unfortunately, I don't have a hot-line to God – and frankly I'm rather suspicious of anyone who tells me that they do – although the Bible certainly bears witness to the idea that from time to time, at pivotal moments in history, God will speak directly, or through an angel.

But in the every-day business of living, God actually leaves us alone, most of the time. He has already stated, abundantly clearly, how we are to live our lives. He then gives humanity the free will to decide whether we will choose to live as we've been called.

We are to love God, and love our neighbours. Or, if you prefer a more poetic phrase, we have been instructed through the prophet Micah, to "do justly, love mercy and walk humbly with God." Say it with me – 'Do justly, love mercy, and walk humbly with God'.

These were, in fact, the precise attitudes of Joseph. Doing justice meant that he could not 'put away' a young woman whose unplanned pregnancy was not her fault. Loving mercy meant that he needed to give her the protection she and her baby needed. Walking humbly with God meant trusting that God's plan for the baby were far superior to anything that Joseph himself might have tried.

Jesus too had to follow that plan of doing justly, loving mercy and walking humbly with God. It was that plan which ultimately led to his saving death on the cross, as the writer to the Hebrews reminded us earlier on.

So, as a new decade comes into view, you may be someone who is wondering what God is asking of you. Perhaps you are facing one of those decisions which comes along in every life, from time to time. I cannot make that decision for you. What I can do is invite you to consider whether the choice you have to make will extend God's kingdom of Love, or crush it. All I can do, with the full weight of Scripture and God's story behind me, is invite you to carry on doing justly, loving mercy, and walking humbly with God. Just as Joseph did. Perhaps that's the greatest new year's resolution any of us could make. Amen.

John the Baptiser

Matthew 3.1-12. Preached 2020 – adapted from previous sermons

John the Baptiser is one of the stranger characters of the New Testament. He wore clothing of camel hair – which I imagine was rather itchy – who seems to have lived exclusively on locusts and wild honey. I imagine that getting wild honey out of a wild honey-bee hive is rather a tricky thing to do. So poor old John was probably covered in bee-stings as well.

John was the last of the Old Testament prophets. He followed the tradition of living apart from civilisation, and of calling people to repent of their evil ways. So, let's picture the scene – picture a rather dirty fellow, who has probably never visited a barber, dressed in camel-hair, covered in bee-stings and with honey stuck to his shirt, munching on a locust...and declaring at the top of his voice "Repent! For the kingdom of heaven has come near".

I wonder what our reaction would be if we met someone like that in the streets of Havant – or even here inside the church. I think we'd probably try to get him sectioned – for his own good! There are, actually, some Vicars who have been known to dress up in 'hobo' clothes and sit in the porch of the church, just as worshippers are arriving...to see whether any of them would stop and ask if he needed help. Of course, I know exactly what would happen if I did that here. Jackie Martin would put on her Havant Homeless Trust hat and ask me 'would you like one of the sleeping bags we've got in the office?'!

But, despite his strange appearance, there was something about John that attracted people to him. There was something about his message that had people coming out to him in the wilderness from "Jerusalem, all of Judea, and all of the region along the River Jordan" (Mt 3:5) And let's remember, these weren't Sunday drivers out for a laugh at the strange fellow in the desert. These were people who would have travelled many hours, and in some cases many days – to hear for themselves the amazing – even scandalous - things that this man of the desert was saying.

John was not a man to mince his words either. He called the religious leaders of the day a "viper's brood" (Mt 3.7) He warned them against the complacency of their religion. "Just because you are

97

Abraham's children," he would say, "don't go thinking that gives you an automatic right to heaven" (Matthew 7.8 - paraphrased). He warned them to be afraid of the Messiah who would 'put an axe to the tree' of their systems and laws.

There are a number of strange inconsistencies about John. First there is the fact that he didn't join up with Jesus. Why didn't he set aside his baptising, and become a follower of the Lord? And then there's the fact (as we will hear in next week's Gospel reading) that when he was in prison he sent word to Jesus - to ask him if he really was the Messiah...despite having recognised him as such by the Jordon at Jesus' baptism.

It seems that John had a different vision in his head of what the Messiah would be like – he seemed to expect a Messiah who would be full of swift judgment against the evil people of the day. See what he says in today's gospel, in chapter 3:

"...he [that is the Messiah] will gather his wheat into the granary; but the chaff he will burn with unquenchable fire". (Mt 3: 12) John's mental picture of the Messiah was based in the language and concepts of the Old Testament. He expected the 'great and terrible Day of the Lord'. And when it didn't happen quite as he expected, he perhaps proved more reticent to join up with Jesus. Maybe that's why he sent word from his prison – saying to Jesus, "are you really the Messiah?".

But Jesus has a subtly different agenda. He also speaks of the coming day of judgment, and the separation of sheep from goats – later in Matthew's gospel in fact. But Jesus places that event at some distance in the future. First, he has work to do – to call as many people as possible to repentance, and to give the greatest possible opportunity for people to choose God's way of living over their own.

There's a difference, you see, between John's angry, passionate cry of 'repent', and Jesus' loving invitation to 'repent'. The emphasis that we put on words really matters, doesn't it? John's cry of 'repent' is angry, frustrated, and intolerant of the world he sees around him. He is motivated by anger, and longs for the vipers and the chaff to be burned up in unquenchable fire! But Jesus has God's perspective on the world. He looks on the mess of the world with compassion and love – like a parent looks on a wayward child. He preaches tolerance, forgiveness and peace, and even prays for forgiveness for those who crucify him – "for they know not what they do". Jesus is prepared, with God's longing patience, to give time to the establishment of his Kingdom.

He is so committed to that path – and so reluctant to embark on the eventual task of judgment - that he is prepared to give up his own life so that we might find our way back to God.

And I wonder whether we ourselves can sometimes be a bit like John. Certainly, as a human race, we have often been guilty of making God in our own image. How many wars have been fought in the belief that God approves of them? How many acts of cruelty have been perpetrated in the belief that God is somehow being served through them? Are there ways in which we conduct our lives which are inconsistent with the reality of Jesus – and the way in which he calls us to live?

I wonder if you've seen that bracelet that teenagers sometimes wear. It has the four letters "WWJD". They stand for "what would Jesus do" – of course – and it's a phrase from the 1970s (at least!) which has perhaps become dulled by over-familiarity. But it's still a good question. What would Jesus do in the face of the rampant poverty of the developing world? What would Jesus do in the face of corruption among leaders of so many nations? What would Jesus do when faced with the commercial pressure to 'spend, spend, spend' at this time of the year? What would Jesus do in the face of globalisation and the climate emergency? How would Jesus vote in the coming election? – assuming he doesn't establish his Kingdom in power before next Thursday!

During this time of advent, the story of John invites us to prepare for the coming of Jesus – the true Messiah – who will probably be nothing like we expect him to be. We are invited to prepare for the Lord who says "love one another", and who shows us what real love is like through radical self- sacrifice. The story of John reminds us that our understanding of who Jesus was, and is, needs to be re-interpreted. It needs to be seen in the light of Jesus' advent as the forgiving, accepting, non-retaliatory, suffering-servant-king – whose strength is precisely in his meekness.

May you know the peace of Christ as you prepare to celebrate his coming once again this year. May you know the reality of who Jesus really was and is. By soaking up the stories about him in the

Bible, may you deepen your understanding of who he was and what he stood for. And may that knowledge transform you. Day by day. So that you may truly know who you are...a loved child of God, gently and loving called to repentance. And by depending that knowledge, may you come to know what you stand for too.

THE VIEW FROM THE PULPIT

A sermon for Harvest-time

First preached in 2019

Looking back on it now, I had a very privileged child-hood. I grew up in the countryside of Devon and Somerset. I took long walks with my dog along country –lanes, I cycled and camped all over the southern moor-lands. And in the summer holidays, I worked on a local farm, tossing hay-bales onto trailers, and learning to drive tractors and land rovers well before the age at which I could take a driving test. In my home churches, Harvest was a time of great abundance, with goods from fields and gardens displayed in complete profusion all over the place.

As such, I have a great affinity for the season of harvest. It is perhaps only those of us who have sweated in the fields to bring a harvest in, who can really understand the sense of satisfaction at a job completed. In past times, the celebration of Harvest was as much a sense of relief, as anything else. Relief that drought had not visited the crops. Relief that the hard work of harvest itself had not resulted in injuries to farm workers. Relief that winter was coming, and a quieter rhythm of life could take over.

All is very different today. Harvest now takes place every day of the year. If plants will not grow in the fields, we grow them in green-houses – resulting in hundreds of square miles of plastic-sheeted fields. If we can't grow them in England, we buy them from other parts of the world where they will grow. Labourers are still needed, but mechanical systems of picking food are taking over, more and more, and no-one tosses hay onto trailers anymore. If drought beckons, irrigation systems can compensate.

More to the point, we are no longer a rural society, in the main. Even those who live in the villages and hamlets of England have usually made their living in the city, then used their wealth to buy-up and convert old farming buildings. The word 'Harvest' just doesn't have the resonance that it once had.

And yet, at the same time, the world of nature has perhaps never been more in our minds. We are far more aware than we were in the 1970s of the interconnected nature of all living things. On our TV screens we witness the destruction of the rain-forests, and the rising of toxic chemicals in our atmosphere. We worry about the death of the bees, and the arrogance of genetically modified crops. We watch the melting of the glaciers and ice-fields, and we build our heightened sea-walls against the rising of the seas.

Never has there been a time when we have been less connected to the land, and yet more worried about it.

The same time period, from the 1970s to now, has seen a marked shift in the way we think about God's relationship to creation and harvest, too. In a short while, we will sing that 'we plough the fields and scatter', and celebrate that our crops are 'fed and watered by God's almighty hand'. But actually, I doubt that many of us really believe that anymore. The Book of Common Prayer, from which today's service is taken, includes prayers for rain at times of drought. But, in fact, we have far more faith in the science of weather-forecasting than we do in the idea that God sends the rain.

Now you might think that I'm sorry about that. After all, isn't this loss of faith in a God who sends rain a dangerous thing for the church? Surely, if people stop praying to God for rain – or any other need – the churches will empty?

Well, perhaps they will...or at least they will empty of those people who think of God like some kind of genie, or fairy godmother, who will grant wishes in return for the right words. My hope and observation, however, is that with the advance of our scientific understanding of creation and the harvest, we are in fact growing up. We are moving away from the agricultural God in the sky, who granted the wishes of his farmers, towards the God who is the energy at the centre of all things. Our God is the one who inspires us to use the intellects we have been given to shape and control our own environments.

Instead of a Father Christmas God, to whom we cry for solutions to our problems, we are confronted instead by the actual God of Scripture. This is the God who, according to the great Genesis myth, creates a beautiful garden and then gives it to his children with the command that we should 'take care of it'. The ancients, who wrote our Scriptures, would have had no truck with the idea of God who controls the weather. Which is why, as Joseph did in Egypt, they made provision to store up harvests, so that food could be distributed in times of famine. And it's why, as the Laws of the Hebrew Bible

102

dictated, the poor and the widow and the stranger should be cared for out of the stored and tithed bounty of the community.

We have not learned from those times. The tithe barns that we once possessed to soften the ebbs and flows of the harvest have all been turned into luxury dwellings. Our society has moved so far from the idea of long term storage against times of difficulty that we proudly talk about 'just-in-time' delivery. That's the most efficient way of dealing with our needs. Being 'just-in-time' means that we don't have the costs of long-term storage, and that means more profits for our companies. But it also means that we are extremely vulnerable to the vagaries of weather. Or as the Brexit debate is showing us, the vagaries of politics. If the direst warnings of 'Operation Yellowhammer' should come to pass, and medicines and food cannot be shipped 'just-in-time' from the continent again, perhaps we will have to learn once more the value of prudent stock-piling against disaster and famine.

So, as a church minister, I do not mourn the passing of a belief in the Weather-God, or for that any idea of a God who, in response to the right words, said in the right way, will supply all our needs – like a sort of heavenly drinks-machine. Instead, I pray for a church which will teach the world of a God who inspires us to take care of creation, and to share the bounty we possess for the good of all.

The Lord's Prayer

First preached in 2019

Today, the Lectionary invites us to contemplate St Luke's stripped-down version of 'The Lord's Prayer'. The longer version of the prayer – the one we say or sing in our services - is found in the Gospel according to Matthew, as part of the Sermon on the Mount. Strangely, Luke's account comes somewhat later in the chronology of the texts…so it's possible that Jesus himself sought to edit-down his original teaching into something really simple, and really fundamental to the faith he was sharing.

The Lord's Prayer is essentially the Gospel, wrapped up into a neat package – which is why it has had such longevity, and why, incidentally, that we sing it sometimes. This is more than just a prayer for help. It is a statement of who God is, it is a reminder of the coming kingdom, it is the cry of a spiritual child reaching out for help, it is a promise of forgiveness, and a commitment to live holy lives.

In fact, The Lord's Prayer contains so many complex ideas, that we could easily have a sermon on each one of its lines. But let me try to outline some of the basics for us to ponder:

And, so quote the famous philosopher Julie Andrews, 'let's start at the very beginning'…

Father. Our Father. Our Father in heaven. Our heavenly Father.

We take the idea of God as 'Father' for granted these days. But to Jesus' first listeners, God was the awesome creator of the Universe, the rumbling God of the mountain and of the Holy of Holies. He was so far beyond human understanding, that they would not even utter his name. And whilst all those things remain true, Jesus chooses as different word, entirely. Not just 'father', but 'Abba' – Daddy. An intimate word. A word designed to help us to see God as the one who cares for us like a parent. By using the word Abba, Jesus de-emphasises the stern, masculine stereotype into something much more nurturing, much more loving. The God who made all of us in God's image – male and female – is given a title which points us towards a feminine, nurturing, life-giving identity.

This is a Gospel message. It's good news. We don't worship a distant God on a cloud, or a terrifying Warrior-God on a mountain. We are called into relationship with a nurturing, caring, Daddy in heaven.

And that essential insight gives us a hook by which the rest of the prayer can be understood.

Hallowed – or Holy - is your name.

This loving, nurturing, parent God is nevertheless holy. He is not to be taken lightly, nor gently ignored like some geriatric parent left in an old folks' home. The idea of God is generally still revered today, but few people take the trouble to really spend time with the 'old fella', or to listen to his ancient wisdom. So in just two lines, Jesus shows us the Daddy – the Father/Mother God – but he also warns us not to confuse gentleness with uselessness, or omnipotence with impotence. This gentle loving God still has power. He is still a force to be reckoned with.

Your Kingdom Come

…and to which Matthew's account adds those lovely words about God's Kingdom being about his will being done on earth as it is in heaven.

This is Jesus opening our eyes to God's cosmic vision of the universe, and God's over-riding desire for his children. God's whole being is bent towards the redemption of the world, so that everything in our physical realm might be as holy, just, peaceful and glorious as it is in the spiritual realm. And by putting that hope into our mouths, and onto our tongues, Jesus invites us to co-operate with God in God's mission.

Give us each day our daily bread.

This is a prayer of dependence. Jesus invites us to ask only for daily bread. Not monthly bread. Not to long term security of any kind. Only for enough for each day. In other places, Jesus reminds us that we should let tomorrow take care of itself, or that the Son of Man has no-where to lay his head, or that those who store up wealth for themselves on earth will one day lose it all. For the Kingdom to come, and for God's will to be done, Jesus wants his army of ordinary people to be fleet of foot, ready to answer his call to action at a moment's notice. He wants people who are not shackled to earth by the possessions they carry, but ready to fly for the Gospel.

Forgive us our Sins – as we forgive those who sin against us.

Forgiveness is, of course, the heart of the Gospel. But what good is it for God to forgive us, if we are unwilling to forgive others. In this one line, Jesus opens us to an ever-rotating circle of forgiveness. As we find ourselves forgiven, each week in this Eucharist, we then forgive others. A virtuous circle of forgiveness rolls out from this building and from every church, bringing healing to all.

And let us be in no doubt…such forgiveness needs to be real. When we forgive others, we give up, we for-give, any further possibility of being hurt by the person we forgive. Such forgiveness may do nothing for them. It may not change them, at all – and we would be wise to always treat them with caution. But forgiveness does allow us to move on, unshackled by bitterness, ready to do the work of the Gospel.

And lead us not into temptation…

to which we might add Matthew's insight "but deliver us from evil'. We need to understand this line carefully. This is a much contested phrase. You may have heard of recent debates at the Vatican, where the translation of this line has generated a lot of discussion. The essential premise is this: that it is not God who leads us into temptation. God's whole will is bent towards our redemption. Why would he then tempt us away from his love? As the Pope has said, "I am the one who falls. It is not God pushing me into temptation to then see how far I have fallen'. So various other ways of rendering the line have been tried – including 'abandon me not to temptation'.

For thine is the Kingdom, the power and the glory, for ever and ever. Amen.

This final line, not included at all in Luke's account, is what's called a doxology...essentially a hymn of praise to wrap up a prayer, or a psalm. It actually doesn't appear in the earliest manuscripts of the Gospel, which is why Cranmer excluded it from the version of the Lord's Prayer in the Book of Common Prayer. It was probably added at a later date by well-intentioned editors. Some might even suggest that by focusing on God's Kingdom, power and glory, this was an attempt to balance out some of the more 'touchy-feely' aspects of the rest of the prayer. It was an attempt to draw us back to the utter majesty of God, reminding us that this is not a God with whom we should trifle.

Time is against us – but here's one last thought. In Luke's account, this prayer comes in the context of Jesus' story about the persistent friend, who keeps banging on his mate's door for bread in the middle of the night. That's because, above all, Jesus wants us to get that persistence in prayer is at the heart of our relationship with God. If we pray nothing else each day, let us never cease from at the very least praying this simple Lord's Prayer.

Prayer is unlikely to change God, who already knows what he wants to accomplish. The Lord's Prayer is not so much a petition – an attempt to put the right prayer coins into a heavenly slot machine of answers. But rather, it's a kind of basic catechism of the Gospel. It is not intended to change God's mind, as Abraham sought to do over Sodom and Gomorrah, but rather to remind us, over and over again, of the simple basics of our faith.

We serve a loving, parenting God, who must nevertheless be taken seriously.

This God has a plan for the world, to being about his Kingdom.

Each of us needs to be ready to carry out God's mission, needing only our daily bread.

The engine of that mission is forgiveness.

We need to stay on course, and not be tempted off the narrow path.

Religion and Politics don't mix…?

Preached at a Civic Service of prayers for the new Mayor of Havant, 2019

It is often said that religion and politics don't mix. Well, what a load of complete tosh that is! But before I try to explain my reasoning – let's start with a little bit of etymology.

The word 'religion' comes from the Latin word 'relegio' – which means 're-connect'. It's the same root word from which Lego comes. Think of that, the next time you are building an edifice of plastic bricks with a grandchild or child. So 'religion' is the practice of 're-connecting' ourselves to the divine source from which all life springs. For Christians, that divine source is the originally Jewish concept of God. But for others, its Allah, or Vishnu, or Mother Earth…or any other number of creative sources. All religions have in common the idea that if we could just re-connect ourselves to the Love which brought us forth, our lives would be fuller, more complete, more worthwhile.

Politics is, of course, the business of the polis – another Latin word meaning 'the people'. It is ultimately about the way that we people choose to live together. It's about the framing of laws, and the distribution of the community's wealth. It's about caring for the vulnerable in our midst, and, in short, loving our neighbour as ourselves.

So, if religion is – at the core – about reconnecting ourselves to whatever God we perceive, and if politics is about the way that we connect ourselves to one another, we have a simple concept to hang our entire world-view upon. It was a concept that Jesus expressed most clearly, but which is also common to every great religion. It's a concept which can be summed up in five words: Love God. Love your neighbour.

Around the time of Jesus, there was another great teacher doing the rounds. His name was Rabbi Hillel, and he was once, famously, challenged to stand on one leg and recite the entire law of God. He accepted the challenge, stood on one leg, and said: "Love God, and love your neighbour as yourself. All the rest is just commentary".

108

When you think about it, the command to love our neighbour is a profoundly political statement. Truly understood, it would radically reform the kind of nasty politics which we see around us so often these days. You know the kind of politics I mean – the kind of politics which blames the homeless and the poor for their own misery, or blames the collapse of our financial system on immigrants.

Margaret Thatcher knew that religion and politics belong together. Which is why she famously quoted the words of St Francis of Assisi on the steps of No. 10 in 1979. "Where there is discord, may we bring harmony. Where there is error, may we bring truth. Where there is doubt, may we bring faith. And where there is despair, may we bring hope'. I know, it was rather cringy…but we perhaps all remember her entry to No 10 better than any other Prime Minister, before or since, because she had the courage to quote a religious text.

All of this is essentially my way of saying how delighted I am that one of the first things we do, in this Borough, after electing a new Mayor, is that we bring them to church! For I believe, passionately, that any politics which divorces itself entirely from some form of religion is a poorer politics. It's something I believed when I worked as a Government advisor in the early years of this century. And it's something I continue to believe as a humble parish priest.

Party politics is essentially the battle of ideas. It is the assertion of one group of people that their ideas about how the world should be are better than another group of people's ideas. The great religions of the world have often inspired politicians to rise beyond narrow party politics, and to embrace a fuller, wider, kinder sense of how the world should be. A quick glance into history should remind us that it is religions which first inspired the idea of charity. It remains one of the five pillars of Islam. It is central to the teachings of the Buddha, and of course to the teachings of Jesus Christ.

Religions were most often the founders of systems of healthcare, and education. They were often flawed, sometimes rather narrow in their focus. But the essential idea that all human beings should have the right to see a doctor, and chance to expand the mind is essentially a religious idea.

Arguably, the state does a much better job of these things – not least because it has the resources to do so through taxation. But let us never forget that charity, healthcare and education all arise out of the religious imperative to love our neighbour.

In fact, I would argue that we need more religion in our politics. When we contemplate the various secular political systems under which we live, we find that we need religions to correct and steer. All too easily we accept the mantras of secular gurus, without asking ourselves what religions might have to offer as an alternative view.

Take, for example, the concept of economic growth. The success, or failure, of most modern politics is measured on the basis of GDP. The stated aim of most western governments is to achieve economic growth of around 2% per year. That doesn't sound too bad, does it – until you realise that 2% growth over 10 years would equal 20%. So we live with an economic model which believes that in 10 years' time, we could – indeed should - use 20% more of the world's resources. Which is nuts, of course.

We find the concept of economic growth in the Scriptures too. Many times, prophets promise the people that if they will obey God, their flocks will multiply, and their cattle increase. But set against this are the imperatives of religion too. Such growth, according to the Scriptures, will only be achieved by a people who give a tithe of all their wealth back to God, and who welcome the stranger, and care for the poor, the sick, the widow and the orphan. This is a true blending of religion and politics. Economic growth is achieved not on the backs of the poor, but as a result of generosity to the poor.

So, I'm delighted that in this Borough we continue the debate about religion and politics. By appointing a Chaplain each year, you open yourselves to the possibility that whatever suspicions we might justifiably have about the motives of some religious people, religions themselves do still have the power to shape and mould our politics. I yearn, as do most of us I suspect, for a kinder, more humane, more caring society. And I pray that the interplay between our religion and our politics will continue to march towards such a goal.

Doubting Thomas

John 20. 19-31. First preached in 2019

This week, we've received the exciting news, that there is to be a 25th James Bond film. How exciting, for all of us who enjoy a few hours of complex villains and testosterone-laden conflict!

Back in 1983, Hollywood was stunned when Sean Connery decided to reprise his role as James Bond. By that time, he was decidedly middle aged - and had not played Bond since 1971. Movie-legend has it that after he finished filming for 'Diamonds are Forever' he said to his wife "never again". But she was horrified, and replied "no - never say 'never again'!"

The title of the 1983 movie was a bit of a joke at Connery's own expense. It was a way of him recognising that he had been a bit rash in his original statement.

And that's something I think we've probably all done at one time or another, isn't it? I know I have.

As a young evangelical, I know that I said I would never ever be seen dressed up in clerical robes.... look at me now. I was quite certain that I had understood everything that God had to say on every subject. Now, after 30 or more years of serious study...I'm not so sure.

It's the same in my personal life. I grew up on a diet of good old fashioned English food...and I remember a time when I was being taken out to dinner by friends to an Indian restaurant. "I could never eat that stuff", I said. "I'll only go with you if they also serve egg and chips". But when we were there...someone persuaded me to have just a little taste....and I was hooked!

When Peter and the other disciples told Thomas that they had seen Jesus raised from the dead, his response was pretty unambiguous, wasn't it? "Unless I see the mark of the nails in his hands, and put my finger in the mark of the nails and my hand in his side, I will not believe". In other words -"never - I'll never believe what you tell me...unless I see it with my own eyes". (John 20: 25)

Just imagine the embarrassment that Thomas felt when Jesus appeared to him in that upper room! He must have felt like an absolute idiot! "Why did I say I would never believe?! What a fool I was?! Why didn't I believe my friends?!"

111

You see, the thing about Jesus is that he has a way of over-turning all our expectations. His whole life-story is one of apparent contradictions to the way that others expected he should act. He was born in a stable, not a palace. He ate and drank with sinners, not the religious leaders. He taught about love and forgiveness - even towards the Roman occupiers. He stubbornly refused to stay dead...and rose up from the grave.

Jesus overturns all our expectations. Thomas expected that he could cling to objective proof - that he could depend on his eyes and his own sense of touch to establish what was true. And that is the fundamental mistake that is made by so many non-believing people today...

God is separate from all that God has made. Above it. Beyond it. Outside of it. We should not be surprised that God cannot be found in a test tube or at the end of a microscope or telescope. God doesn't want to be found in a test tube. Instead, God wants us, like Thomas, to discover God with the eyes of faith, and the hands of trust.

Why should that be? Why is it those who believe without seeing who are blessed? Wouldn't it be easier for God to make himself touchable, scientifically prove-able?

Well, I would argue that if we could reduce God down to something we could see in a test tube - it would not be God. God is as far above such reductionism as the sun is above the earth. God is far more than anything which can been seen or touched. God is a mystery that our tiny brains can only begin to glimpse. Belief - or faith - in God is not about believing certain facts about God, and rejecting other theories. It's about setting off on a path, with God as an end-point...being willing to be shaped and changed by the journey.

Evangelicals talk about have a personal relationship with God - which is a phrase I have sometimes lampooned (to be honest). But actually, the idea of a personal relationship is quite powerful.

I have a personal relationship with many people - not least 'the present Mrs Kennar' (to borrow from Terry Wogan). In that relationship, which she has so far heroically endured for 32 years, we have learned many things about each other. But we still can't read each other's minds. (Though I do think Clare has a pretty good idea of what's going on in my mind when I see a table of cakes). But we still have much to learn about each other. New facets of our personalities, thoughts, preferences, ideas are constantly being revealed, and sometimes surprising each other.

So what does this mean for us - in our daily lives, and in our life as a church?

For our life as a church it means that we - like Sean Connery - must 'never say never again'! Rowan Williams has helpfully said that all our language about God must be provisional...it must always be open to being shaped and changed by the God who is outside of all human methods of proof. That means never saying that we could never do things differently. It means never saying that we could never change our view about what God is like. It means accepting that the way we worship, the way we pray, the way we use our time and our money in the service of God must always remain open to the reality of God.

In our daily lives, it means growing in our attentiveness to God in all aspects of our life. God is not tied down by our decisions, or even by our circumstances. God has the capacity to break-through even the hardest of situations that life has thrown at us. He can heal, because he is beyond all human capacity to heal. He can comfort, because he is beyond human systems of support. He can challenge, because he is greater than all human challenges. He can change our minds about priorities, life-style choices, jobs and political allegiances - because he is beyond all such limitations.

God can neither be touched, nor seen...and yet God is present with us in every circumstance of life. God cannot be boxed or sold - and yet he is the ultimate manufacturer. God cannot be seen, and yet he is the light. He cannot be touched, and yet he is the ultimate ground of all being.

At the end of the day, we can, and should, do no more and no less than our brother Thomas the Twin - fall on our knees and cry out, "My Lord and My God".

From the Mountain-top

Luke 9.28-36 - The Mount of Transfiguration. First preached in 2017

Have you ever had a mountaintop experience? You know, one of those experiences that blows your mind - something you'll always remember? I've had a few. I've been at fantastic worship events, where emotion has overwhelmed me. I've been at family celebrations, which I will always remember. And I've had literal mountain-top experiences - breathing in the cool air and amazing views at the top of various hills and peaks.

Weddings are mountain-top experiences. For weeks, months, or even years (sometimes) people look forward to their wedding day. Everything has to be perfect...the music, the dress, the cake, the food...it's all vitally important. And then, at the wedding itself...as I well remember...you find yourself caught up into one of those mountaintop experiences. Your senses are in over-drive - sound, sight, smell, hearing, touch...all are at peak efficiency. You become determined to drink in every moment.

But you have to come down the mountain again. The next day, there are bills to be paid, journeys to be made. New wives discover that their new husbands have smelly feet! And new husbands discover that their beautiful new wife now wants to change them, stop them drinking and introduce them to couscous! Reality comes flooding in, and life has to be faced again.

Our Gospel story today is of just one such mountain-top experience. It's called 'the story of the Transfiguration'. The disciples find themselves caught up in an event which underscores the whole ministry of Jesus. There is a view back through history - as Jesus meets with people who have been part of the story of the past...Moses and Elijah, and is affirmed by them. And then there's a peering into the future, as God's voice from heaven confirms again who Jesus is, and the importance of his mission. "This is my son, the Chosen One...listen to him!"

The disciples who have accompanied Jesus to the mountain-top are having the time of their lives. They don't want to leave...and they even suggest building shelters for Jesus, Elijah and Moses. They seem to want to capture the moment, and stay in it forever. But the thing

114

about mountain-top experiences is - you have to come down from them again. Discipleship involves following, and going on.

Today, we have heard Luke's account of the 'Transfiguration'. Scholars believe that it is based on Mark's account - because they are remarkably similar, and Mark is believed to be the earliest gospel. Mark places this story in a pivotal place...it is dead centre at the middle of his 16 chapters. Before the Transfiguration, Mark deals with Jesus' ministry around Galilee - his teachings and his miracles. Then comes the mount-top experience of the Transfiguration - Elijah, Moses and even the voice of God meeting with Jesus - strengthening him for what is to come. Then, in Mark's narrative, Jesus sets his face towards Jerusalem...towards challenge, torture, death and ultimately, resurrection.

Mountain-top experiences are part of life - and they are often part of the life of faith. Some people spend their whole lives trying to regain such experiences. Mystics and saints have lived lives of ever increasing discipline and piety in the hope of touching, once more, the face of God.

But faithfulness is not achieved by freezing a moment of time...and trying to live in it forever. Faithfulness, and true discipleship, is achieved by following-on in confidence that God is leading...and that what lies ahead is even greater than what we have already experienced. You have to come down the mountain again...and take what has been seen, learned and experienced on with you...on into the journey.

My hope is that our Sunday services are mini-mountain-top experiences. They are a moment in the week when we experience God together, and through each other. They are a couple hours in the week when we climb the mountain, and look beyond ourselves, beyond our day to day lives, and briefly touch the face of God.

But we have to come down the mountain. We have to keep following on...following God into our every-day lives...taking what we have said, done and experienced with us. We allow our worship, the words we say, the actions we do, to permeate our daily lives...colouring them, perfuming them. Because of our mini-mountaintop experience we somehow live lives that are more infused with meaning, more alert to what God is doing in our lives, and through us in the lives of others.

115

One of the things I hear most often as a priest are the immortal words "you don't have to go to church to be a Christian" – usually from someone who is asking for baptism for their child, or to arrange a wedding - or sometimes from church members who haven't been for weeks.

Of course you don't have to go to church to be a Christian...but it helps! It's a bit like learning to play in an orchestra. You might be the most talented musician, who can play every scale and arpeggio at break-neck speed. But, each musician only has one line of music to play. It's only when you play in the orchestra that you see how your one line of music fits with all the others - to create the symphony. Through being together, like the disciples on the mountain-top, we get to drink together from The Source....we get to be inspired for the next week...we receive, together, the same spiritual food for the journey.

But it's never about the mountain-top...it's always about the journey. It should never be about the Sunday Service...it should always be about the day-by-day service...the giving of service to our families, our co-workers, our friends and our neighbours. Inspired at the mountain-top, we go back into the valley to bring the light of Christ to everyone we meet. Just as Jesus left the mountain and then set his face towards Jerusalem, healing and teaching along the way, so we too are called from this mountain top out into the world.

As we shall say at the very end of this service: Go, in the peace of Christ, to love and serve the world...in the name of Christ.

Fishing

Reading Luke 5.1-11, First preached in 2019

There's a technique for contemplation, first described by St Ignatius of Loyola, one of the founders of the Jesuit order. Ignatius taught that our spirituality could be brought alive by active use of our God-given powers of imagination. He advised that we should spend time imagining the great biblical stories – seeing ourselves within them, and allowing ourselves (and our Christian discipleship) to be shaped by them.

So, this morning, I want to invite you to engage in a little Ignatian spirituality with me. I promise you that I won't embarrass you! All I want you to do is close your eyes, and listen to my voice.

First of all – I want you to relax. Focus on your breathing. In, out, in out. Become conscious of your body. Gently wiggle your toes, and feel your nerves sending messages down from your brain and back again. Focus on your legs. Feel how your body is connected to the pew you are sitting on. Feel your breath, going in....and out.

Now, let your imagination run free – sailing through the air to the Sea of Galilee. You are by the shoreline. The sun is hot on your face, and the sound of sea-birds is in the air. All around you are crowds of people. Everyone is here to hear the words of the new prophet, Jesus. There are so many people, all pressing against each other to get close enough to hear what this Jesus has to say. There are so many, that Jesus himself is in danger of being pushed into the water.

Nearby, are a couple of boats. Fishing boats, with rough, tough fishermen on board. You see Jesus hail one of the boats to the shore. He climbs in, and then asks the fishermen to row a few yards from the shore. That's better. Jesus can see the whole crowd now. He can speak to the whole crowd now. He gestures for everyone to sit down on the shore, as he takes a seat in the boat.

There is a moment of silence. And then Jesus begins to speak. What does he say...to you? Perhaps he speaks of what his Kingdom is like. Perhaps he tells one of his fabulous stories – the Good Samaritan, or the story of the wheat and the tares. Or perhaps he says

117

something only to you. Take a moment, in silence, just a few silent seconds together, and listen to what the Master is saying to you.

....

The time of teaching is over. Jesus says farewell to the crowd, promising to teach them again tomorrow. One by one, the crowd drifts away. But you remain on the shore, longing for more. Jesus notices you, and invites you to wade out to the boat, to join him and the fishermen.

Now you are in the boat, and Jesus encourages the men to throw out their nets. One of the fishermen, Simon, is dubious. He says "We've been at it all night, and we haven't caught anything!". But Jesus insists, and so the men throw out their nets on to the water.

Suddenly, the water is alive! Fishing are splashing and slapping the water, wriggling and writhing in the nets. Simon calls you over to give a hand. Together, you, Simon, Jesus and the other fishermen are hauling on the nets, laughing out loud, pulling the nets and all the fish into the boat. The same thing is happening in the other boat, too. There are so many! The boat even looks like it might sink!

When the last of the nets has been hauled into the boat, Simon kneels down in front of Jesus on the deck. You kneel beside Simon too. Together, you both look up at Jesus. Simon has awe in his eyes, and he says, "I think you had better get away from me, Lord; for I am a sinful man."

But Jesus just smiles. He looks down at Simon – and you - and says, "Don't be afraid. Follow me…and from now on, you will be catching people"

How does that make you feel? Jesus has just called you – and Simon – to follow him. He wants you to re-arrange the priorities of your life so that your first task, of every day, will be to lead people to him?

How do you feel? Are you wondering what gifts and talents you can possibly bring to such an awesome task? Are you wondering how you could possibly do such a thing?

Perhaps you've forgotten that when Jesus calls us, he also equips us. After all, if he can fill nets with miraculous amounts of fish, he can surely provide everything you need.

How do you feel?

Perhaps you are excited. Excited at the idea that you might go from this boat today, filled with a new sense of purpose. For Jesus has just given you a mission…a mission to tell everyone you know about him.

How do you feel? Take a moment to let what has just happened sink in. What do you need to change as a result of your encounter with Jesus.

…

And now, it's time to come back home. Become conscious of where you are, physically, once again. Feel the pew underneath you. Sense the people around you. And when you are ready, open your eyes.

I hope you enjoyed that experience. I find Ignatian exercises very useful as ways of bringing the stories of Jesus to life.

There are just a couple of things I would like to say to wrap up.

First – never forget that Jesus called ordinary people to carry out his work for him. He didn't call the lawyers and priests, he called the fishermen, the carpenters, the civil servants. He has never stopped calling them.

Secondly – Let me just leave you with this thought. If everyone here today had the courage to ask just one friend or family member to come to church, this congregation would double overnight. Don't make the mistake of thinking that your excellent church website will do the job for you, nor even your parish priest! The task of calling people to faith – of being fishers of people – is yours.

Epiphany

Reading: Matthew 2.1-11. Preached in this form in 2019, but based on previous sermons

I suppose that many of us will have been on journeys over the last couple of weeks. Some of us have braved wind and rain to visit family and friends in far-flung corners of the British Isles. But I bet none of us had journeys which were as arduous as those of the Wise Men to Bethlehem. They would have crossed blazing deserts, and freezing mountain passes. They would have had to wash in streams, and eat food gathered or trapped along the way. Their journey was remarkable.

We don't know much about the Wise Men. The Bible calls them 'Magi', from which we get our word 'magician' - but that's not the full meaning of the word. The Magi were, as far as we can tell, learned men from another culture. They studied the stars, and no doubt studied the ancient texts of many religions too. They put that knowledge together came to the startling conclusion that a new King of the Jews was being born.

Actually, they were wrong. Jesus never was the King of Jews in any earthly sense...despite the ironic poster that Pontius Pilate had nailed over his Cross. In fact, according to John's Gospel, when Pilate asked him point blank whether he was the King of the Jews, Jesus replied "My Kingdom is not of this world". No, the Magi were wrong. The stars were not predicting the birth of the King of the Jews.

Another accident of the Magi was in their timing. According to Matthew's account, they actually arrived something like two years late. (Matthew notes that Herod enquired of the wise men when they had seen the Star appear, and based on that information he slaughters all the boys in Bethlehem who are under two years old.)

So, the Magi were perhaps not all that wise. They failed to correctly predict the timing of the birth of a new King of the Jews - and they were two years adrift even of Jesus birth. Wise men? Perhaps not.

So, to those who say that our future can be read in the stars, there is a warning here. The stars do not foretell our future, any more than they did for the Magi. We would be wise not to place our future in the hands of star-gazers too.

And yet...and yet... The Magi embarked on a journey of faith. They thought they knew where that journey would lead. They assumed it would lead them to a royal palace in Jerusalem. But God has a way of using the journeys we plan for ourselves, and turning them into something much different, much more profound. Instead of a new prince in a royal cot, the Magi's journey led them, mysteriously, to an unremarkable house in a rural back-water...and to a baby who had been born in a food trough.

And it was when they got there, that the Magi could truly be described as wise men. Recognising Jesus for who he was, much more than an earthly King of the Jews, they knelt in homage to him. When they met him, Jesus was nothing like they expected.

And that's because, in Jesus-of-the-stable, God was declaring a new way of living, and a new way of thinking. Human beings had tended to think of the Universe as a 'top-down' place – with God in heaven, dispensing rules and justice from the sky. But that was a mistake. Through Jesus, especially the Jesus revealed at the Epiphany, God was re-forming our picture of where God is. Not in the sky, looking down...but here among us, one of us, part of us. No longer the 'top-down' God of our ancestors; this is the 'bottom-up' God. The Kingdom of God is an upside-down place – where the poor are the blessed, and the powerful are condemned – as the Magnificat has just reminded us again. It is the Kingdom in which by losing, we win; and by giving, we receive.

But we still fail to recognise this, don't we? Even Christians are duped by the promises of power or celebrity. We find ourselves 'looking upward' in hope towards political dogmas, or individual politicians. We trust that the powerful of our nation know what they are doing – when in reality they are just as confused as the rest of us...stumbling in the darkness. Or we look upward to celebrities, modelling our life-choices, our fashions, our financial decisions on theirs. But we find no peace there either. Or we look to great church leaders, great Bishops, prominent Christian writers - or even our parish priests - to save us. But they turn out to have the same feet of clay as all of us.

The 'bottom-up' Kingdom of Epiphany teaches us to look for God in the simple and earthy things of life. The Sky-God is silent – and looking upwards to such a God, or to other powerful beings – will not help us to find 'him'. As Moses discovered in front of the burning bush, it is the ground which is holy, not the sky.

When we look for God in a stable, we find 'him' in the love of his parents, and the care of a community of Shepherds and Wise Men. God is found in the love between neighbours and friends. God is found in the simple sharing of a meal. 'He' is found in the bread and wine of the Eucharist. 'He' is found in a simple act of charity.

The Wise Men had the wisdom to recognise him, and to worship him, in the dirt and squalor of a back-water town. Their pre-conceptions of palaces and earthly royalty fell away; and the new reality of Jesus took their place.

You see, really wise men and women are open to what the Journey will bring. Wise men and women embrace the possibilities for change and growth which arise whenever we put our journey in the hands of God.

I wonder what our journey this year will be like - our journey with God both as individuals, and yours as a parish. If we are able to listen to God's voice, in the middle of peace and prosperity, as well as chaos and darkness, we will find God speaking into our situation. There is always something to be learned, always some new spiritual growth to take place even...perhaps especially...in the darkest times.

I imagine the Wise Men had some dark times along their road. But through it all, God was with them...guiding them, prompting them in new directions...so that at the end of their journey, they could encounter the God-child himself.

So, my encouragement to you this Epiphany is to be open to the journey. Make a new year's resolution, right here, right now, that you will be more alert, more open to what God is doing in your life as a person, and in your life as a church. Make a pact with God that you will listen to 'him' more, searching the scriptures more, worshipping more, giving more, and receiving more.

If God can lead a bunch of mystics across deserts and mountains to a new Epiphany at the manger, then 'he' can do the same for us.

But we have to be ready to go.

122

Advent. Tired of waiting?

Preached in this form in 2018, based on previous sermons

When, I wonder, did we forget how to wait for something. None of us like waiting, for anything. We want what we want, and we want it now! And, if we are one of the 1% of the world who have enough money to buy pretty much anything we want, we tend to get it...now.

Clare (my wife and partner) came back from visiting a friend's house recently, extolling the joys of the new 'Echo' device. 'It's fantastic', she said. You can just ask it to play the radio, or for a summary of the news headlines, or what the weather will be! I really fancy one for Christmas.'

Three days later, one arrived in our house!

The Season of Advent is the beginning of the Church's New Year, and it is designed specifically to be a time of waiting. For the rest of our society, the New Year starts with a bang and fireworks...with a sense that we've 'arrived' at something important. That's odd, when you think about it. Why should the simple turn of the Calendar be something to be celebrated with dancing in the street and all night parties? But the Church, deliberately, counter-culturally, starts its new year with two important words...'Coming' (which is what 'Advent' means) ...and 'Wait'.

In Advent, we can't help looking forward, because we see the way the world is now. We yearn for God to put things right.

That hope - that God will one day put all things right - is rooted in a long tradition. The Hebrew Bible is full of longing for the day when God will transform society into something fair and just. In today's reading, Jeremiah speaks for God, when he says 'Surely the days are coming when I will fulfil the promise I made'.

When will this happen? Well according to Isaiah – another Hebrew prophet - peace will break out when all the peoples of the world say 'Come, let us go up to the mountain of the Lord...that he may teach us his ways'. In other words, Isaiah says that the reign of God will begin when the peoples of the world finally accept that human ways of doing things don't work. Peace will reign when the peoples of the world turn away from their sin, and ask God to teach them his ways.

And what about Jesus? What will his 'second coming' be like? Well, Jesus himself is rather opaque on the subject, to be honest. The language of Luke's Gospel - based on Mark - is all about the Son of Man coming in clouds...which is a pretty strange metaphor. Could it mean that Jesus' coming will be hidden – obscured in the way that clouds cover a mountain? Then, Jesus says one of the most intriguing lines of the New Testament: "Truly I tell you, this generation will not pass away until all these things have taken place".

Well, that's odd...isn't it? Given that he said these words around 2,000 years ago. Either he was mis-reported (which would mean that the Bible needs to be read with great care). Or perhaps there are still some people alive, walking around in secret, who were alive in Jesus time – as some fanciful theologians have suggested. (Sounds like an episode of Doctor Who doesn't it?).

Or perhaps – and this is what I personally believe – Jesus is, in fact, already come, stealthily, in clouds. That by his Holy Spirit, he is already among us. That he is even now, continually, gathering his elect – his followers – from the ends of the earth. Gathering us into churches, love-factories, for the spreading of his message of Love.

And, while we wait for the completion of the Reign of God, there is a very real sense in which God is already among us, already coming – in fact already here.

Every time a war-monger lays down his weapons, Jesus comes.

Every time a family is raised up out of poverty by the Robert's Centre, or out of fear by the Southern Domestic Abuse Service, Jesus comes.

Every time a lonely person finds a friend in our morning church-opening, Jesus comes.

Every time a family is fed by the Beacon Foodbank, Jesus comes.

Every time one of the homeless people sleeping all around our church is treated like the human being they truly are, Jesus comes.

Every time that an alcoholic, a gambler, a drug user turns up to one of our Pallant Centre support groups, and says 'NO!' to their addiction, Jesus comes.

Every time an exhausted and confused mother finds support and help in our Play Café, Jesus comes.

Every time a young person develops their human potential through Dynamo Youth Theatre, or a person with learning difficulties grows in confidence through Creating Chaos, Jesus comes.

You see - signs of the kingdom are all around us. Our task, like an alert house-owner, is to keep awake. To see the signs of the kingdom with open eyes, and join in with the activity of God, wherever it is found.

CAROL SERVICES

IT IS TRADITIONAL FOR THOSE WHO ATTEND CLERGY GATHERINGS TO DISPLAY THE NUMBER OF CAROL SERVICES THEY EXPECT TO TAKE THIS YEAR

THOSE WITH SINGLE DIGIT FIGURES ARE FROWNED-UPON MERCILESSLY

Who is the greatest?

Reading: Mark 9. 30-37. First preached in 2018

What would you do if you knew that you only had a week to live? Assuming you were fit and healthy, that is. If you had full health, and freedom of movement, what would you do with your last few days on earth?

It's a puzzle isn't it?

If it was me, I'd probably want to spend time with the family that I hardly ever see - because they are scattered around the country. Or I'd want to do something really bonkers - like sky-diving. Perhaps I'd go on that trip to Egypt that I've always promised myself. Who knows?

What about you? What would you do?

Of course, this is all very theoretical. None of us really knows when we are going to die. But that wasn't the case for Jesus. He knew that his journey towards Jerusalem was going to result in his death...and he had to decide what he was going to do with his final days.

He could have gone sight-seeing. Perhaps he could have had a mega-party with all his friends and followers. Being God-on-Earth, he could have held mighty rallies, and shown mighty acts of power to wow the crowd.

But no. Instead, Jesus chooses to spend some of his last days on earth teaching his followers about what it really means to be a disciple. He teaches them about two vital things. Two things that are so important, that he takes his disciples aside to make sure they've got the message. Those two things are:

First, the vital importance of humility, and

Second, a command to reach out to the weakest members of society.

When they arrive at a stop-over in Capernaum, Jesus turns to his followers and asks them "What were you arguing about on the road?" (v. 33). "But they kept quiet because on the way they had argued about who was the greatest" (v.34)

Mark adds a nice little detail now. He says; "Sitting down, Jesus called the twelve and said...". Sitting down was what a Rabbi did when they were teaching their disciples. Sitting down was a sign that serious teaching was about to take place. When a Rabbi sits down, you take notice. Now what it is that Jesus wanted his disciples to take notice of? He says to them...

"If anyone wants to be first, he must be the very last, and the servant of all".

It's the topsy-turvey Kingdom of God again, isn't it? Time and time again, Jesus turns the world upside down - away from people having power over people. Instead, he says that real power is found in service.

The notion of service is absolutely central to the Gospel. Jesus teaches us that it is in serving others that we find the real purpose of life. Rather than being a sacrifice, in fact we find that when we serve one another, there is a kind of freedom, and a kind of joy, that infects us. This is an essential part of what it means to be a follower of Jesus.

Before he died, one of his most significant acts was to wash his disciples' feet. Just imagine that. Smelly, dirty feet. Covered in camel dung. That was a job that usually got done by the lowest member of the household - a slave, or a child. It was certainly not a job that was done by the master of the house.

A member of our Thursday congregation, the theologian Martin Mosse, actually argues that we should take this washing of feet idea much more seriously. His thought is that if, instead of celebrating the Eucharist, we washed each other's feet, we would open up whole new levels of understanding about what it means to be one of Christ's followers. It's a fascinating thought, isn't it?

Ask anyone who works in our charity shop, or who stewards for our visitors during the day in church. Ask them how they feel when one of their regulars, perhaps an elderly widow who lives on her own, comes in for some warmth, a smile, and a chat. Ask one of our pastoral visitors how they feel when they leave the home of a housebound parishioner. Do they feel that they have wasted an hour of their life?

The fact is that the church of God, and the work of God, exists entirely on the voluntary service of its members. Without that sense of service...we could not be here. Without the gifts of time that you give, this church would have closed years ago...and with it would have gone all the good that we are able to do in this community.

127

But Jesus' message in today's gospel was not only about service. After making his great statement that those who would be great must be the servant of all, he "took a little child, and had him stand among them"(v.36). Taking that child in his arms, he said to his disciples, "Whoever welcomes one of these little children in my name welcomes me".

Why did he do this? What's so special about children? Well that's a question you hardly need to ask if you are a parent, or now, (in Clare's case) a grandmother! But, in Jesus day, children were treated rather differently. Children didn't have any of the rights that children have today. There was no 'criminal records bureau' protecting them. There was no state education. There was no right to free medical treatment. There was no protection in law against exploitation and child labour. Did you know that in some circumstances, it was even legal for a father to kill his child!

So children were essentially treated as goods and cheap labour...even slave labour. They were the least powerful members of society. They couldn't change anything. There were no school councils asking for their opinion. There were no youth workers and teachers who tried to help them develop as whole human beings.

Jesus didn't take that child into his arms because he was sentimental about kids. He picked up that child to show that he, Jesus, was on the side of the poorest, the most dis-possessed, the most abused and sometimes despised members of society.

And so that was his message, that day, in the house in Capernaum. Anyone who wants to be considered great in God's kingdom must be the servant of all...and especially a servant to the poorest and most outcast in any society. We are called to bless and serve the poor...not only for the sake of the poor, though that would be a good enough reason. But for our sake too. As we bless others, whether it is with gifts of money or of time, we will ourselves find blessing.

So finally, may you discover the liberation that comes from service. And may you discover the joy of taking the lowest, poorest, most struggling members of our society into your arms - and blessing them.

Mary Magdalene - the wealthy witness

First preached in 2018

There are rather a lot of Marys to be found in the Gospels. Mary was a very popular name in 1st Century Israel and Judea. We know, of course, of Mary the Mother of Jesus. Then there's Mary of Bethany (who is sometimes confused with Mary Magdalene, but who was the 'sinful woman' who anointed Jesus' feet, and wiped them with her hair).

There is another Mary – literally called 'the other Mary' - whom Matthew lists as part of the group of women who were witnesses to Jesus' burial. In fact, I rather imagine that – in those days - if you were to stand in the street and call out 'Mary!' you'd get quite a few responses!

This makes the task of teasing out the story of Mary Magdalene a little bit of a challenge. So let's review what we know – and a little bit of the legends which have accreted around her.

Mary was a Jewish woman, who according to all four Gospels travelled with Jesus as one of his followers. She was a witness to his crucifixion, burial and resurrection. According to Matthew, Luke and John's Gospels, Mary was the one who told Peter and the other male apostles that Jesus had risen from the dead. So, she is often referred to as the 'apostle to the apostles'.

Mary is actually mentioned by name twelve times in the gospels – more than most of the apostles, in fact. Her 'surname', of Magdalene, most likely meant that she came from the fishing town of Magdala, on the shores of the Sea of Galilee.

Luke's Gospel list's Mary as one of the women who travelled with Jesus and who helped support his ministry out of their own resources. That indicates that she was probably a wealthy woman. The same passage also states that seven demons had been driven out of her. Seven is a symbolic number in Scripture – meaning completeness. So to say that someone had seven demons in them was to say that they were completely consumed by whatever illness or malady was afflicting them. Clearly, therefore, Mary had reason to be very grateful to Jesus, for the healing that she had received.

And that, frankly, is all that we really know about Mary in factual terms. During the middle ages, there were many other tales told about her. For a start, as I've already said, she was often mixed up with the sinful 'Mary of Bethany', or even with the woman caught in adultery (whose name we don't know...but it was probably Mary as well!). Even more elaborate medieval legends tell exaggerated tales of Mary's wealth and beauty, as well as her alleged journey to Southern France. There were even speculations, somewhat fuelled by various second and third century Gnostic writings, which suggestively described Mary's as Jesus' wife, or lover. Maybe even the mother, by Jesus, of the line of Merovingians! But there is nothing in Scripture to support such an idea. Not that this stops the likes of Dan Brown from creating some highly entertaining stories about the possibilities.

So if you don't mind, I'd like to focus on what we DO know about Mary – and to ask ourselves what we can learn from her real story.

I think there are two words which we can hang an understanding of Mary on. They are 'wealthy' and 'witness'. Let me see if I can break those down for you.

As I've already said, Mary was clearly independently wealthy. We don't know why. Perhaps she was the widow of a wealthy man? But clearly, she was wealthy enough not to have to work for a living, and to have the leisure to travel around with Jesus. More than that, as I've said, she was one of those who supported Jesus' ministry out of her own resources. We must not miss this detail. It's tempting for us to imagine that Jesus and his first followers didn't need money. Perhaps we imagine that Jesus would just 'miracle-up' some food every time they were hungry, or some new clothes when their old ones wore out. But Jesus's ministry was rooted in the real world, just as ours is. And we know that the Disciples carried a purse – in fact Judas seems to have been the Honorary Treasurer for their little group.

And so, right at the beginning of the story of the church, the way in which we use our wealth becomes an important issue. Mary Magdalene used her wealth to support and enhance Jesus' ministry. She understood that the work of God needs money to be invested in it. It is part of God's way of working with human beings that he chooses to work through us. We are God's hands and feet to a world in need. God uses our hands to touch the world, our feet to spread his

130

good news, and our wealth to build his Kingdom on earth. Mary understood that. I wonder whether we really do?

I wonder what the church of today would look like if all its members really understood what sacrificial giving for the work of God looks like. Perhaps we would spend much less time holding jumble sales to keep the roof on, and much more time devoted to sharing God's love with our neighbours in need.

So Mary Magdalene can be an inspiration to us in terms of the way we use our wealth. And the second word I suggest we hold in our minds about her is the word 'Witness'.

I've already mentioned that according to Matthew, Luke and John, Mary was the one sent to the male apostles with the news of the Resurrection. We must not miss the significance of this. According to Jesus law, women were unreliable witnesses. Anyone from Jewish society of the time who heard that a woman had been sent by Jesus to tell men the news would have struggled to get their head around it. Even at the moment of his greatest triumph, it seems that Jesus was still keen to declare that in his Kingdom there was no room for old fashioned, patriarchal, misogyny. The word 'apostle' means 'someone who is sent'. By being the first witness to the news of the Resurrection, Mary, despite her gender, became the first 'one who was sent' – and so, effectively, the first Apostle.

Now I realise of course that as a church which has recently experienced the ministry of women, this congregation is not likely to be holding on to out-dated notions of male and female roles in ministry. But it is our task to make sure that we use each and every opportunity to tell others that Jesus is never concerned about our gender. Our value to God has nothing to do with whether we are male or female, or perhaps even trans-gender. Each of us is equally loved and regarded by God. And each of us is called, like the Magdalene, to be a witness to the world. Each of us, in some sense, is an apostle – for we are sent out with the good news of God's love for the world on our lips.

By meditating today on Mary of Magdala, may you come to know how much God wants to partner with you in the work of building his Kingdom on earth as it is in heaven. May you learn the joy of releasing your wealth to that task, and the joy of knowing that you too are 'one who is sent' for the work of God.

My house should be a house of prayer!

Reading: John 2.13-22. First preached in 2018

There is a wonderful lady who belongs to this congregation. You'll know whom I'm talking about (if you are a regular member here). Every month, during our First Saturday Coffee Mornings, if the weather is dry, she and her husband stand outside the church selling homemade marmalade and other items to passing customers.... while the rest of us come inside, into the warm.

On the one hand, this act of sacrifice on her part – and her husband's - is a brilliant advert to the community that our monthly coffee morning is on. But what everybody round here knows is that she also has a worry, directly grounded in this morning's Gospel reading, that turning the church into a temporary market-place might not be the right thing to do.

I know – and respect - exactly where she's coming from.

There are two schools of thought, essentially, about church buildings. The first is that they are essentially no more than a dry gathering-place for the people of God and the local community. Many churches meet perfectly happily in school halls, or plain rooms across the country. In Africa, I've experienced churches which meet in barns, school-rooms, or under canopies of palm branches. Their worship has been no less real than ours. No less honouring to God. And it hasn't mattered at all that the same space may be used as a market place the very next day.

But there's another school of thought – in which buildings like ours have something intrinsically Holy about them. To get a sense of what many in this community feel about our building, you only have to check the visitors' book, or the prayer book, or just spend a couple of hours in here during the week, watching the people who come and go to pray.

A couple of weeks ago, I had one of my annual pleasures – that of introducing Year 5 to St Faith's as a building. We talked about the arches – and the way they point us towards heaven. We talked about how the Nave ceiling is like an up-turned ship, reminding us of Noah's Ark, perhaps, and the fact that we are all somewhat at sea on the ship of Faith. We showed the children our beautiful Sanctuary, and some of the silver-ware that we use – telling them how the patten and chalice are made of silver because of the precious blood and body of Jesus that they will contain. We showed them the font, in which some of them had been baptised, and reminded them of its history.

It was wonderful to watch their little faces looking up in awe at the beauty around them – and gaining a sense that there is more to their town than they had thought.

Jesus clearly felt something very similar about the Temple in Jerusalem. As a Jewish boy, growing up outside the big City, the Temple was a special place indeed. It was the place in which God was said to dwell – although Jesus clearly knew that God was present everywhere, because he talked to God all the time. But the Temple was special. It was somewhere where God was especially present, somehow more tangible than in other places.

So when he arrived at the Temple, perhaps 20 years after his first visit as a 12-year old, he was incensed at what he found. There were money changers, everywhere – because the Temple authorities had insisted that the people's tithe could only be paid in Temple coins. So, if you wanted to give a gift to the Temple, in penance for your sin perhaps, you had to exchange your Roman coins – at a loss – with the money changers. It would be like me printing our own St Faith's bank notes, and then telling you that you can only give your collection in our money. And you could only exchange your pounds with us…at the exchange rate I set!

And, Jesus found, the place was full of animals. The ancient system of sacrifice required that a penitent sinner had to provide an animal to be slaughtered on the Altar. So, the Temple Authorities set up animal pens, and allowed worshippers to buy the animal they wanted. A dove, perhaps, for a small sin. Or a cow for one of the really big sins!

So, instead of a place that made God feel more tangible, more real, more present, Jesus was confronted with a load of money changers making profit out of a bureaucratic law about coinage, and a load of farmers encouraging pilgrims to buy their goat! Is it any wonder that Jesus was furious? Is it any wonder that he tried to chase them all out of the place? I'd feel exactly the same if I came in here to find a branch of moneysupermarket.com set up in the Sanctuary, and a local farmer standing in the prayer area shouting 'come and buy my cows!'

This is indeed a special place, and we must be very careful how we use it." There is, however, in our typically Anglican way - a balance to be struck. When all's said and done, this is only – at the most basic level – a pile of stones with a roof on top after all. And because it's an old pile of stones with a roof on top, we have a legal and social responsibility to care for it – as the oldest piece of heritage in Havant. And that's expensive.

English churches have actually always tried to walk the line between being a holy place and a place for the whole community. Communion rails were first established to keep animals out of the Sanctuary – because the oldest churches did indeed double as market places.

Many churches created a separation between the holy spaces and the common places by erecting a screen between the Nave (where the people, or the 'knaves') carried out their business, and the Sanctuary where services were said. The ringing of bells during the Eucharist was first done to invite 'knaves' (in the Nave!) to lift their heads from their commerce, and remember for a moment in whose presence they were.

We used to have such a screen here, in fact. The evidence is up in the wall. A bricked-up doorway would have once led out onto the top of a screen that would have separated you 'knaves' down there in 'the Nave' from the Holy Sanctuary. Such screens were routinely topped off with a big, wooden cross, known in ancient English as a 'rood'. The screens were therefore called 'rood screens' – and were also used as minstrel galleries, before the advent of organs.

This little history lesson reminds us of course that we are custodians of a living breathing, changing building. The rood screen is now gone. The lighting and sound system has been replaced.

My hope, however, is that along with our "Lady of the Marmalades", we will never forget that this is first and foremost a place in which God is tangibly more present, more touchable, more knowable, to the whole of the community we serve.

The Sacrifice of Light

Reading: John Chapter 1. First preached in early 2018

I think I can guess what at least some of you are thinking this morning. "Why on earth are we hearing that Christmas reading again?" Others of you are probably thinking "He's taken down the crib – at last – but he's forgotten to take down the star!"

Well, you'd be wrong. I haven't forgotten, you see. I've left the star up quite deliberately. Because – I think - that poor old star needs a bit more prominence in the Christian story. As for why we are being asked by the Lectionary writers to think about the Word becoming flesh again…. well, let me try to explain.

Everyone loves a story. Stories are powerful ways to communicate – which is precisely why Jesus used parables, and why we all love movies and books. The Christmas Story that we've just worked our way through is one of the best. It's the perfect combination of rustic shepherds, visiting magicians, angels and animals….and there's a baby in it, just to finish off the 'Ah!' factor. At least, that's all according to Luke and Matthew.

But John, writing his Gospel some decades after Luke and Matthew, is not interested in shepherds and wise men. Scholars tell us that John wrote his Gospel in his old age – after a lifetime of spreading the message of Jesus. No doubt the stories about wise men and shepherds were already circulating widely. John didn't need to re-hash them. So he goes deeper…much deeper than a typical Christmas congregation is ready to grasp. Such congregations are usually too high on Christmas Spirit (of one form or another) to want to do any meaningful theology. Which is why, I think, the Lectionary writers give us one more bite at the cherry, at this moment in the year.

After a lifetime of teaching and learning, John wants us to grasp the enormity of the Christmas event, the coming of Jesus, what scholars call the 'Incarnation'. 'Incarnation' describes the in-dwelling of God in human form. The 'Incarnation' is that moment when God, who is Spirit, takes on human flesh.

There are two words which John especially plays with, in his poetic Gospel introduction. The first is 'Word', and the second is 'Light'. Let me see if we can't break them down a little.

135

'Word' is the English translation of 'Logos' – a Greek word from where we get the word 'logic'. John is saying that the incomprehensible being we call God is many things – spirit, love, a creative force that binds the universe together. But God is also mind. God has thoughts. He – or indeed she - has desires and intentions for the world that has been created. God's thoughts, God's logic, God's reason – these are the 'Logos' – the 'Word'. "In the beginning was the Word" – the Logos – "and the Word was with God and the Word was God". It's one of those great big thoughts that we human beings struggle to get our tiny brains around – that God can be thought of as having different aspects, but each of them is also fully God'. So, God's reason, his Word, can be part of God as well being completely God. "The word was with God and "was God".

And, John is saying, that 'Word' is the aspect of God which became human and dwelt among us. Again – incomprehensible, isn't it? How can an aspect of God become human, while not dividing God up into different people? If God is on earth, in the form of Jesus, how can he also be still in heaven? And how come Jesus (God the Son on earth) prays to God the Father in heaven? Is he talking to himself? It's enough to make your brain explode! And that's ok. We are limited, created beings. We cannot ever begin to grasp the reality of God – and anyone who tells you that they have understood God is a fool.

So, confronted with the sheer enormity of what he's trying to say, John chooses a different picture. He uses a metaphor. He has stated the truth as clearly as he can grasp it, by talking about the 'Word' dwelling among us. But now he chooses a different tack, and begins to talk about 'Light'.

Ah! That's better. 'Light' we can understand. We know about Light. We see its effects. We know that even a tiny spark of light cannot be extinguished by the darkness. We know that if this church was completely darkened, save for one candle, all our attention would be focused on that single solitary light.

"In Jesus", says John, "was life, and that life was the light of the world. The light shines in the darkness, and the darkness did not overcome it".

And that, ultimately, is the message of Christmas, and the good news of the Gospel. Darkness is all around us. The darkness of war, and famine, and poverty, and homelessness and selfishness and consumerism and racism and fear of the stranger and all hatred and rebellion against the reason and logic of God. "But the light shines in the darkness".

In Jesus, through his teaching, his life, and yes even by his death, life is offered to the world. Jesus' whole life is offered to us, by John and the other Gospel writers, as The Narrow Way to life. His way of living – generously, lovingly, wisely, sacrificially is offered to us as an example of what God's logic and reason look like. Generosity, Love, Wisdom and Sacrifice. These are signposts for us. Generosity, Love, Wisdom and Sacrifice. Lights in the darkness. Clues to how we too should live, if we truly want to find life. And clues about how we can choose to live if we truly want to shine God's love into the lives of those around us.

At the end of our Candlemas service, we lit candles and held them aloft, promising to be lights to the world. Three times, in response to challenges from the priest at the Font, the whole congregation said "Let us shine with the Light of your Love". So let me ask you…how's it going? Where have you shined God's light of love this week, the first week since you made that commitment?

Generosity. What new generosity have you shown this week? Who has been touched, or had their life transformed by your gift. Did you remember to bring a gift for the foodbank to church this morning? Well done, if you did. Has the suffering of one Syrian refugee been relieved by your generosity this week? Thank you. Or perhaps you gave a gift to help pay for the costs of keeping this church shining as a light in its community, such as the repair to the West Door. Thank you, if you did.

Love. Who has experienced your love this week? Who has woken up this morning feeling lighter, less burdened, more deeply regarded because of the Love you have shown them? Well, I bless you for showing that Love.

Wisdom. How have you grown in wisdom this week? Which passages of the Bible that you have undoubtedly been reading have struck you with new insight? What wise decisions have you made about the lifestyle you lead, or the consumer-choices you've made?

And finally, sacrifice. Sacrifice is more than simple generosity. To sacrifice is to give until it hurts. Sacrifice is what Jesus made on the cross. Sacrifice is the change of mind which knows that nothing I own belongs to me…but everything is God's. Sacrifice is the act of giving up everything, all possessions, all rights, all privileges for the greater, deeper, mind-blowing privilege of shining God's light into God's world. It's about putting everyone else first, holding nothing back…but being poured out completely for the good of the world.

Stars make that kind of sacrifice. In order to continue shining their light into the heavens, a star must continue to sacrifice itself, constantly. To shine, for a star, is to burn up its resources in the service of the Universe. Eventually, after all the hydrogen in a star is burned up, the Star will die. It will give itself completely to its task.

That's why I've left the star hanging there for one more week. We have Christmas in our memories, and the promises of Candlemas in our hearts. May we also be reminded that we too, like Jesus, are called to give ourselves completely to the task of shining God's light into our world.

THE CHOIR

MINOR MISDEMEANOURS TAKING PLACE IN YOUR SUNDAY SERVICES

SYNCHRONISED COUGHING

TEXTING THE ORGANIST FOR A HYMN FORECAST

FLIRTING WITH THE BASSES

PLAITING THE HAIR OF THE CHORISTER IN FRONT

DROPPING SPECTACLES

IMMOBILISING THE ALTOS (TOFFEE)

CREATING SPECTACLES

PREPARING TO PRESS THE BUTTON THAT RELEASES THE TRAPDOOR, SENDING THE CURATE PLUMMETING INTO THE SHARK TANK

UNAUTHORISED PETS

FILING GUM UNDER PEW FOR USE AT A LATER DATE

APPLYING MAKE-UP, CLIPPING NAILS, ETC

INTIMIDATING THE SERVERS

PLOTTING WORLD DOMINATION

Can anything good come out of Havant?

Reading: John 1.43-end. First preached in 2018

A few years ago, someone bought me a copy of Grumpy Old Christmas, which suited me down to the ground. One evening, Clare was sitting alone in one room of our house, when Emily and I heard what we thought was crying coming from Clare's room. We were both rather worried, so we looked around the door, and there was Clare, sitting on her bed, with tears of laughter rolling down her cheeks. She waved my copy of 'Grumpy Old Christmas' in the air, and said "It's you! It's you!"

Let me read you a paragraph from the book, by Stuart Prebble, just to see if you agree with Clare. In fact, I won't even read from the book...here's some of the blurb about the book from the dust-cover:

"So...'tis the season to be jolly is it? Well, not in the household of the Grumpy Old Man it isn't. In his case, 'tis the season to have to put up with even deeper layers of vexation than usual! Everything about Christmas gets up our snitches. Everything. From parents videoing their precocious brats at the atrocious school nativity play, to the 150th opportunity to see 'the Wizard of Oz' on the telly, to the Xmas turkey which tastes like blotting paper soaked in a puddle. And how on earth are we really supposed to look happy when someone buys us a tie with a picture of Santa on it?! Eh?"

Now if I'm honest, I suppose I have to admit it. I know it will surprise all of you, immensely, but yes, I am a bit of a Grumpy. There's something about life which brings out the cynic in me. So I know exactly where Nathaniel was coming from, in today's reading, when he responded to Philip's news about the Messiah having been discovered in the form of Jesus of Nazareth. "Huh", said Nathaniel. "Can anything good come out of Nazareth?".

Nazareth was just a humble little back-water...nowhere important, nowhere posh. It was full of hard working people, many of whom - probably like Joseph the Carpenter - were working to build the near-by Roman city of Sephoris. The residents of Nazareth were employed in Sephoris in much the same way as the residents of Portsmouth were historically employed in the dock-yard.

139

I guess that some of us would have pretty much the same reaction if we were told that the Saviour of the World had been discovered in Portsmouth. "Portsmouth?!" we might exclaim. "Can anything good come out of Portsmouth". Or for that matter, Havant?

But when Jesus met Nathaniel, he recognised a true and upright man...despite his cynicism about Nazareth. Nathaniel was clearly someone who was open to new possibilities, however, cynical he appeared. For a start, he was willing to go with Phillip to meet this Jesus of Nazareth...and Jesus saw something in him. As he approached, Jesus said of him "Here is truly an Israelite in whom there is no deceit". Jesus saw great potential in Nathaniel. Rising into poetic symbolism, Jesus said that Nathaniel "will see heaven opened and the angels of God ascending and descending upon the Son of Man". Jesus uses an Old Testament image - the image of 'Jacob's Ladder' to say that Nathaniel will be part of God's great plan to touch earth with the power of heaven. The picture of 'angels ascending and descending' is meant to help us see that God is active and alive in God's world.

It is Epiphany - the time of revelation. We are those to whom, by the grace of God, has been revealed the news that there is more to life than the simple hum-drum. We are those who chose to say 'no' to the encroaching darkness of so much human life. We are those who declare that we believe God has other plans. Like the Wise Men who went to the Nativity, that's why we are here, isn't it? Week by week, day by day, we pray those words that Jesus taught us "thy kingdom come on earth as it is in heaven", and in doing so we declare our belief that God is reaching out to touch this dying earth with his living love. We are those who have learned to see the world with God's eyes...not just a place of terror, war, greed, famine and plague...but a place full of possibility for life, health, peace and justice.

Quite deliberately, Jesus now has no other hands than your hands, no other feet than your feet. If words of comfort to the sick and dying are to be spoken, then they are spoken through you. If acts of hope to the lost and the lonely, the homeless or the desperate are to be done, then it is through your hands that God wants to do them. That's why we talk about being the 'Body of Christ' - we, you and I, are God's hands, feet and loving hands to a dying world.

You see, in answer to the question 'can anything good come out of Havant, let me tell you…it jolly well does! Every day I see good happening in Havant. Every day I see people like you, deciding to rise above the dull monotony of so much human existence, and refusing to give in to cynicism.

A very good example of that attitude can be found in the Portsmouth Street Pastors. It is very easy to be grumpy and cynical about young people who get themselves into difficulties on a Friday or Saturday night. "Well, they brought it on themselves, didn't they? Going out in ridiculous clothing and drinking too much". That kind of cynicism allows no room for the power of peer pressure – the egging-on that kids do to each other. It allows no room for the young woman who has been dumped by her drunken boyfriend, through no fault of her own, miles from home, with no way of getting there – all because her boyfriend took a shine to a prettier girl on the dance-floor. On our behalf, the street pastors go out and offer God's love to such young people…they introduce them to a God who does care about them, and who longs to see them grow to their full potential.

Can any good come out of Havant? I want to tell you a little story, to finish. There is one member of this congregation who is a nurse. I won't identify them…to save them embarrassment. But you might be able to work out who they are. This nurse and their team recently gave such attentive and extraordinary care to one of their patients, that the patient's family wanted to give them a gift of money. The nurse refused the gift – because NHS staff are not permitted to accept them. Instead, our nurse suggested that the patient's family might like to give a gift to St Faith's, in gratitude. On Friday, therefore, I opened an envelope containing a cheque for £3,000.

That story, and that nurse, is a great example of how we can bring God's love into our everyday life, and of the grateful response that such love and service to humanity can generate. And all this is because, in the language of today's reading from Revelation, we are called to be both a Kingdom and priests who serve our God. This is our sacred calling, and our sacred task – to transform our community so that there can never be any doubt about the answer to this question: "Can anything good come out of Havant?"

The Violence of Christmas

A Meditation for the Rotary-sponsored Community Carol Service (including SDAS - the 'Southern Domestic Abuse Service). 2017

I wish that that the Southern Domestic Abuse Service were not here tonight. And that's not because tonight's collection is going to be split between the church and SDAS!

Actually, I wish – as I'm sure they do - that it was not necessary for them to be here tonight. But unfortunately, the violence that human beings do to each other makes it vitally important that they ARE here.

I wonder if you've ever contemplated how much violence surrounds the Christmas story. I'd like to take a few moments to ponder that with you. But first of all, it might be helpful to define what the word 'violence' means. It is essentially the forcing of one person's will on another, by the threat or actual use of physical coercion. It can also mean the forcing of the will of a group of people on another group of people, by physical means. Terrorism is an obvious type of violence. Blowing people up, to force your view of the world onto them, is about the most violent thing you can do. As is military conquest of one nation over another. But there are other forms of violence too – verbal violence, emotional violence, even intellectual violence – which means the forcing of a particular idea onto others.

Ultimately, violence is about the use of power. Violence is the way that power relationships go wrong. When one person (or one group of people) use violence to impose their power onto another, we can usually judge – pretty clearly – that the power-relationship has gone sour.

So what did I mean, just now, when I said that violence surrounds the Christmas story?

Well, first, there is the violence of the state of occupation into which Jesus was born. The Roman Empire was in control – through violent military conquest. Their powerful control of the land of Israel was so complete, their threat of violence was so great, that Joseph of Nazareth had no choice but to force his heavily pregnant wife onto the back of donkey, to trek for many days across barren lands, and to have her baby in a barn. I'm sure that there were countless times along that road that Mary cried out "Why couldn't we just stay in Nazareth?!" But the political violence of Rome drove them in another direction altogether. Violence surrounds the Christmas story.

Then, there is the awful violence of King Herod. Fearful of losing his power as vassal King over Judea, he plots and schemes to find out where the new 'King of the Jews' will be born. He attempts to manipulate the visiting wise men into being his spies – and when that scheme fails, he slaughters all the male babies in Bethlehem. Joseph and Mary are forced to flee for their lives into Eqypt to escape the rampant violence of Herod's henchmen. Violence surrounds the Christmas story.

Those are the obvious examples – but there is other, more subtle, violence too. Take the Shepherds for example. Now when I say the word 'shepherds', I imagine that most of us have a lovely pastoral picture in our heads. We imagine a bunch of hearty old men with tea-towels on their heads. We hear the west-country tones of countless Nativity plays. "Ohh – let's go to Bethlehem to see this thing which 'as come to paaaass!'".

But this is to miss one of the central themes of the Nativity story.

Why Shepherds? Why are Shepherds the group of people specially selected by God to be told the news of the arrival of Jesus. God could have sent his Angels out to knock on the doors of the ordinary people of Bethlehem - "bang bang bang! Wake up – and go down the street to the barn!". The Angels could have sung glory in the highest heaven in the local taverns, or over the palace or temple in Jerusalem. But they didn't.

God chose the Shepherds precisely because they were outcasts of their society. They lived on the edge of towns – they weren't citizens like everyone else. They were rough and ready, and they probably stank from all those sheep, their overnight bonfires, and a lack of running water. Worse still, they didn't obey all the religious laws – not least the law about not working on the Sabbath…because sheep still need looking after, even on a Sabbath. So, in religious terms, they were considered unclean and unholy. Society in general had done violence to them, by essentially excluding them. They were

143

shut out. They were deemed 'unclean' – which is a kind of religious violence done to them.

You see? Violence surrounds the Christmas story.

Power is misused by the Roman conquerors, by the evil King Herod, and by society in general towards the Shepherds. Violence is all around – either threatened or real.

So what is God's response to this violence? How does he seek to intervene in the violence that humanity does to itself – or in 'man's inhumanity to man' as the old Book of Common Prayer has it?

If I was God, I think I would have been very tempted to use my almighty power to just sort them out! If I had sent my son into the world, to establish a new Kingdom, I would have sent him in on a cloud of fire, fully grown, riding a white charger, with all the armies of heaven surrounding him. I would have had him land on Caesar's Palace in Rome, told him to string-up the Emperor from the nearest lamp-post, and jolly well take over. Show them what real power looks like. That's what I might have done.

But I am not God. God knows that the answer to violence is not more violence. No. God's answer to the violence of human beings is to send his Son into the world in the most fragile, dependent, UN-powerful form possible…a new born baby. And not just a baby – completely dependent on his parents for everything – but a baby born in the humblest of circumstances imaginable. Not a palace. Not even a house. A barn. A stable. An animal's food trough.

The answer to violence is not more violence. To quote the great Mahatma Ghandi – "an eye for an eye leaves the whole world blind". SDAS know this. The answer to the violence found in some homes is not more violence in return. It is, first, the gift of shelter and safety – escape, just as Mary and Joseph had to do. And then it is the gifts of love, compassion and care.

The answer to violence in the world today is not more violence – it should be bridge-building, understanding, mutual respect and tolerance. The answer to the violence of terrorism all across the world is not more violence in return – it should be the seeking of understanding, and the addressing of the kinds of basic injustice which drives terrorists to do desperate things. Education, social justice, the fair and equitable sharing of the wealth of our planet – these are the things that will overcome the violence. If only we would give them a chance.

The babe of Bethlehem teaches us by his gentle presence in the midst of the violence of his time that there is another way. And for that simple, profound lesson, we should surely say with all the angels of Heaven, "Glory to God in the Highest, and peace to his people on earth!".

CHRISTMAS CARDS

HAVE KIDS
OR
FAIRLY ORGANISED

A BIT LESS ORGANISED

QUITE
RICH

SPENDTHRIFT, OR
ENVIRONMENTALLY
CONSCIOUS

OVER-
ENTHUSIASTIC
PURCHASER

INCREDIBLY
INTERESTING

RELIGIOUS
(POSSIBLY)

KNOWS HOW TO DO
MAIL MERGE

Adultery, sin and mercy

Reading: Matthew 5.21-37. First preached in 2017

There are times, I confess, when I look at the Lectionary and cry out aloud...What on earth are the Lectionary-compilers doing putting this reading in?! I confess to having had that reaction when I first saw today's Gospel reading. Adultery?! They want me to preach about adultery.... two days before Valentine's Day?!

But that's the thing about reading the Bible isn't it? If we only read the bits we like or the bits we agree with easily, how are we ever going to be challenged and changed?

And the other thing to remember about reading the bible is, as I've said before, that we must always remember the three 'c's. What are they? Context, context context!

So what's the context of this reading? Well, it is a part of the Sermon on the Mount. Jesus has started his sermon with promises of God's favour on the poor, the meek, the pure in heart and the peacemakers. He has called them (as we heard last week) to be lights to the world, and salt. And then, as you may recall, he said that he had come to fulfil the law. "Not one letter, not one stroke of a letter will pass away" he said, "until all the law is accomplished". (Or as the King James version had it, "one jot or one tittle shall in no wise pass from the law, till all be fulfilled!").

Then, as I hope you remember, he went on, "I tell you, unless your righteousness exceeds that of the scribes and Pharisees, you will never enter the Kingdom of Heaven".

That would have been deeply shocking to the crowd who were listening to Jesus, that day. The Pharisees were viewed by many as 'holier than thou'-merchants, who created all sorts of laws and practices which they insisted the faithful must follow in order to be saved. They were a right pain, actually. And here's Jesus saying that his own followers must exceed the righteousness of the Pharisees and Scribes! Whatever could he mean?

That's the background – the context to today's reading. Then Jesus goes on – with a whole list of the ways in which his followers would be even more righteous than the Pharisees. Murder was wrong, of course...but Jesus says that if his followers are even angry with a brother or sister, they will be liable to judgement. If his followers should insult each other, or call them names, they will be liable to judgement. And if a follower knows that someone else has something against him, he should take the initiative to go and sort the problem out.

And then comes the adultery warning...brace yourself...Jesus says "everyone who looks at a woman with lust has already committed adultery in his heart." It would be better to pluck out your eye and throw it away!

And that's not all...Jesus goes on and on and on in a similar vein, through the rest of today's reading and onwards still. Turn the other cheek. God the extra mile. Give to everyone who begs. Love your enemies, pray in secret not on street corners, forgive others their sins, fast with a smile on your face, don't store up wealth for yourself, stop worrying about what you will wear, don't judge others, and so on, and so on.

It's enough to make your head spin, isn't it? Surely, none of us is capable of living up to these standards!

Now of course, I have never looked at another woman with lust in my heart...honestly, Clare! But could I honestly say that I have lived up to all these many calls to righteousness? Have I ever been angry with a brother or sister of the faith? Have I always gone the extra mile, or turned the other cheek? Have I given to everyone who begs of me?

No, of course not. I can't do it. I'm just not that righteous. And that's where the grace and mercy of God come in.

Do you remember what the difference between grace and mercy are?

Grace is when God gives us what we do not deserve.

Mercy is when God holds back the punishment that we do deserve.

If it was entirely up to us to be righteous enough to enter the Kingdom of Heaven, I suspect that none of us will ever get there. I mean...you're all wonderful people. But is any of us that righteous? I doubt it. Perhaps I'm judging you by my own standards – and in judging you, I'm already breaking a commandment of Jesus. But I know how hard I find it to be truly righteous...so I'm guessing you do to.

147

But let's remember the words we sang in our first hymn of this morning:

There's a wideness in God's mercy,
like the wideness of the sea;
there's a kindness in his justice,
which is more than liberty.
There is no place where earth's sorrows
are more felt than up in heaven;
there is no place where earth's failings
have such kindly judgement given.

In these words, directly based on the wisdom of Scripture, we can find hope. We can have reasonable and assured hope that our Father in heaven looks down on his failing and weak children with nothing but love and compassion, mercy and grace. However many times we let him down, however many times we fail to live the righteous lives to which he calls us, 'there is wideness in God's mercy'.

And how shall we respond to this news. Shall we, as St Paul once suggested ironically, keep on sinning and sinning, so that God's grace may be greater and greater? No, of course not. The response to love, is more love. Valentine's Day teaches us that, if nothing else. The response to love, is more love. As God loves us, we love God more and more. Each day, aware of our failings, we are also aware of God's love towards us. However many times we let God down, he keeps on showering us with blessings – life, health, food and shelter, purpose and direction for our lives.

Lent is nearly upon us – and during Lent we will have extra opportunities to weigh up the sum of our lives, to make amends, and commit ourselves to do better, to live better, to live more righteously. But at the end of Lent comes the great feast of Easter, with the death and resurrection of Jesus once more laid before us. In that great story, we will see again the grace and mercy of God – writ large on the Cosmic stage. We will be reminded that however often we fail, however often we fail to obey his commandments, or confuse Apollos with Paul, or behave according to human inclinations…'there is wideness in God's mercy, like the wideness of the sea.'

Slaves for Jesus

Reading: Luke 17.5-10. First preached in 2016

From time to time, people wonder where I got the title of Canon…well let me tell you.

A few years ago Clare and I gave hospitality for a couple of years to a priest from Ghana, who was studying in the UK at the time. When his time with us was over, the Bishop of Cape Coast conferred the title of Honorary Canon on me, as a gesture of thanks. Subsequently, I was made a Canon of Ho as well…after supporting the work of Bishop Matthias there. So you get two Canons for the price of one with me!

One of the privileges of being a Canon is the right to preach at the Cathedral to which one is attached. So, a few years ago, I found myself in the pulpit of Cape Coast Cathedral – looking out over a sea of Ghanaian faces.

Cape Coast Cathedral is a very moving place. The building is, in fact, the former Garrison Church of the British Army, from the days of the slave trade. It is built just a few feet from the walls of Cape Coast Castle, where so many West Africans were sent out in awful slave ships all around the world. I will never forget visiting the Castle, where the guide pointed out the door to the slave dungeons, in the courtyard. Above the doors to the dungeons was a small, white building. The guide asked "Do you know what that building is? It was the very first Christian Church in Ghana!"

I'll leave you to imagine my emotions. There was I, a recently invested Canon of the neighbouring Cathedral, standing with a crowd of tourists in my clerical collar, being told that the very first church in this country had been built over the doors to a slave pit.

Then, the next day, I stood in the pulpit of that same Cathedral. It would once have been filled with white faces and British Army uniforms. But now, I was the only white face in the place. I couldn't help reflect what a remarkable transformation God had achieved in that place. I was grateful, of course, that it was ultimately Christians who brought about the end of the official slave trade. And grateful too that the ancestors of those slaves had been so blessed with God's grace, and filled with loving forgiveness, that they could make me –

and ancestor of their oppressors – a Canon of their Cathedral. It was a humbling moment; I can tell you.

Slavery is, of course, a key metaphor of today's Gospel. At the time of Jesus, slavery was a normal part of human life. Even though later Christian writers, like St Paul, were destined to speak against slavery, Jesus didn't get into that particular inhumanity to man. Jesus was concerned with all inhumanity to man – and prescribed love for one's neighbour as the remedy for all the evil we do to each other. But Jesus also used the world around him, as it then was, to draw out stories to teach his followers. So, in today's Gospel, he uses the analogy of a slave.

Jesus describes how no slave could possibly expect to be able to come in from the fields and expect to flop down at his master's table. Instead, he would fully expect to keep on serving his master – carrying out the functions of a servant. Jesus is saying, effectively, 'don't expect time off for good behaviour when you are my disciple!'. Being a disciple of Jesus is not a part-time occupation. We don't get to decide to be a follower of Jesus one day, and then to ignore him the next. That isn't what the life of faith is all about.

Faith, even as small as a mustard seed, can bring about incredible transformations. But what kind of faith is this?

Our word faith has its root in the Latin words fides and fidelitas – from which we get the word 'fidelity'. We normally use that word today to describe the faithfulness between two people in the bond of marriage. But it has resonance for the bond between us Christians and our Master, too. To follow Christ is to be faithful to the person of Jesus, and especially to his teachings. It means trusting that Jesus's words and teachings have the power to save us from ourselves.

Take the example of Jesus' attitude to wealth. Time and time again Jesus warned us of the dangers of accumulating too much wealth. "Make treasure for yourselves in heaven, where it cannot rust or be stolen". "Don't fill up your barns with wealth – you can't take it with you when you die". "If you have two coats, give one to a brother or sister in need". And yet, we – the slaves of the Master – all have a tendency to only follow his teachings so far – don't we. I know I do. We say to ourselves, that 'a little bit of charity is ok…but let's not go overboard. We might not be able to afford that expensive holiday we fancy, or that new luxury car, or that upgrade to our kitchen'.

There's a story I like, about a rich man who wanted to show his young son what it was like to be poor. So he took his son to live for a few days on the farm of a poor shepherd. At the end of their time, the father asked his son what he had noticed about the differences between his life, and life on the farm. The son replied:

"I noticed that I have one dog in my house, but farmer has a whole flock of sheep and three dogs.

I noticed that I have a swimming pool which takes up half our garden, but that shepherd had a whole lake at the bottom of his.

I noticed that we have lights in our garden at night, but that Shepherd had all the stars of heaven

I noticed that we have high walls around our property to protect us, but the Shepherd had friends coming and going all the time, who would protect him if he was ever in trouble.

I noticed that we are poor, and the Shepherd is very rich"

I've seen just such things in Ghana. My very good friend, Bishop Matthias, is a poor man. He drives a car that is 15 years old, and (as I discovered coming down a mountain last year) has broken brakes. (I'll tell you that terrifying story on another occasion). He lives in a very modest house, and has to scrabble-around every month for enough money to keep the lights on. And yet, his house is always full of children (many of whom he adopts), and the door is constantly being knocked by friends – from all over his Diocese, his town, and the world.

How shall we – each of us – judge ourselves and our faith? How shall we each weigh the level of our commitment to being slaves of the Master?

Well, quite simply, if you want to know what a person's priorities are, find out what they do with their money.

The choice we make about where we spend the wealth God has given to each of us is the clearest indication of the depth of our faithfulness to the Master.

A little matter of Faith

Reading: Hebrews 11. First preached in 2016

Over the last few months we have been grappling with the challenges of this ancient church building, and our buildings in the Pallant. As we've done so, I have been reminded time and time again of the generations of Christians who have worshipped in this place before us. Sometimes we have uncovered evidence of them, in the walls or in secret corners. For example, a few weeks ago we removed a heating flue from the old toilets in the Pallant Centre, and we discovered a pencil drawing of Adolf Hitler on the back of the pipe – with the words 'he is here'. No doubt this was a joke, at the time that rumours were circulating about Hitler not having really died…but quite disturbing for a moment.

Then on Friday, I was poking about in the organ chamber, and I came across a whole load of signatures, scrawled in pencil on one of the old monuments back there. I guess they were previous organ builders who wanted to leave their mark. Again, when installing the refurbished weathervane on top of the tower on Friday, I noticed the number of names that are carved into the cement at the top of the tower steps – quite probably from when the tower was rebuilt in the 1800s.

All these encounters with the past have impressed on me that we are but the latest generation of people who have worshipped here, maintained and improved our buildings, and been witnesses for God in this community. More than that, we are the inheritors of the faith which they have passed on to us down the ages…the faith which we will declare again together in the words of the Creed – in a short while.

But faith is a slippery thing, isn't it? Something I discover more and more as a parish priest is the wide range of things that people believe in. Some believe in aliens, and some in fairies. Some believe that the end of the world is coming any day now, and others believe there is a conspiracy of ancient masonic powers who are really governing the world. Within the Christian church there are also a huge range of beliefs to grapple with. You pays your collection – and you takes your choice. Let me ask you to think for a moment…what do you believe about some of the following questions?

• Is the Bible the inerrant Word of God, a guide-book for every human decision, or is it a collection of writings about how our ancestors sought to understand God?

• What exactly happens at the Eucharist? Is it simply a memorial to the death of Jesus, or does the bread and wine actually (or just spiritually) transform into the body and blood of Christ?

• Is God really three-in-one? Does the Spirit really 'proceed from the Father and the Son' or does he only proceed from the Father? (That, by the way, was an issue which split the Catholic and Orthodox churches around the year 1000).

• How does Jesus save us from our sins? Does he 'redeem' us – by paying a ransom to the Devil? Or does he take our punishment for sin from an angry God?

• Is there such a thing as a Devil? Or is the Devil a metaphor for the sinful things we humans do?

• Is baptism meant for babies, or only for adults who can confess their own faith?

All these questions, and many more, are part of the 'inheritance of faith' that we Christians have received. Before us, generations of Christians have argued, fought and even burned each other at the stake over.

Why is this?

Why has it become so important to believe in certain ideas about God, and reject other ideas? When you think about it, this is actually a rather odd notion. It suggests that what God really cares about is the beliefs in our heads – as if believing the "right things" is what God is most looking for, as if having "correct beliefs" is what will save us.

Following a suggestion of Rob Bell, I prefer to think of faith as being more like a trampoline – a flexible canvass platform that is held up by a lot of different springs. The springs are ideas – ideas which together give the platform its stability. It is quite possible to take off one of the springs from time to time, without the whole thing collapsing. One can examine the spring – see how flexible it is, see if it is still working. Perhaps one might need to grease the spring, or repair it – before putting it back in place.

One of the reasons why we have got into such a pickle about 'faith' is that we use the one word to describe what, in the original

153

languages of the Bible, were rather more complex images. The most common way that we tend to use the word is captured by the Latin word 'assensus' – or assent. We give our 'assent' to a certain idea, whether or not there is any evidence for the idea at all. This is about 'faith in the head' – what we choose to believe about God.

But there are many other ways of understanding 'faith' – ways that I would argue are far more accurate, and far more liberating. If 'assensus' or 'intellectual assent' is 'faith of the head', what about faith that is 'of the heart'. Such faith is 'fiduciary' faith – or faith that is based on trust. That's the kind of faith that Abraham had. He trusted God's plan for his life, and left his home to follow God's Way all across the deserts.

Faith as trust is like floating in a deep ocean. The Christian philosopher Soren Kierkegaard suggested that fiduciary faith – trusting faith – is like swimming in a deep ocean. If you struggle, and tense up and thrash about you will eventually sink. But if you relax and trust, you will float. Just as in Matthew's story of Peter walking on the water with Jesus. When he began to be afraid, when he worried with this brain about what was happening, he began to sink.

Another Latin word often translated as 'faith' is 'fidelitas' – from which we get our word 'fidelity' or faithfulness. Faith as fidelity means loyalty, allegiance, the commitment of the self at its deepest level, the commitment of the 'heart'.

Then, finally, another word for faith is 'visio' – or 'vision'. This is faith as a way of seeing…a lens through which to see the world as God's place, in which God is working his purpose out.

I wish I had time to explore these ideas some more. For now, let me leave you with this thought: true faith is much less about *what* you believe, and much more about *how* you believe. I don't really mind if you believe in angels or not, or exactly by what mechanism Jesus is the Saviour of the world. If you are able to see the world as God's world, if you are able to trust that God is working his purpose out through his people - the Church, if you are able to be faithful to that vision for the world and for Havant, then you are my brother, you are my sister.

Good news at a funeral

Reading: 1 Corinthians 15. Preached at the Funeral of Steve Woods, a parishioner taken early from life by cancer. February 2020

The last time I saw Steve, just days before his passing, he left me with a sacred trust. He said, 'I want you to preach the Gospel at my funeral'.

'But Steve', I said, 'that's not going to be very easy. Who is going to want to hear about a God of Love at the funeral of someone who has been taken from us too early?'.

Steve agreed with me. It wasn't going to be easy. But then Steve himself didn't like to do things easy. Through a life-time of caring for others, in his family, in hospitals, in his community, Steve certainly didn't chose the easy path of life. He chose one which was full of the kind of challenge and adventure, the joy and—sometimes—the pain that comes from serving and loving others.

So I asked Steve to talk about his life and his faith, a little. I wanted to get a clearer picture of what kind of good news he wanted you all to hear.

First he spoke about God—or rather, God's Holy Spirit. 'The Spirit', according to Steve, 'is like wind upon the water. You can't see it, but you can see its effects'. Steve had an unshakable belief about God's activity in the world. Nature shouted to him, of the reality and the beauty of God. Whilst Steve was a committed churchgoer, he never felt closer to God than when he was out in the wind, or on the waves, or in the fields.

But he saw God at work in human lives too. Time and again, through little acts of love, in hospitals and homes, he saw God at work in the hands of others.

'But what about Jesus?' I asked him.

'Jesus', said Steve, 'is my hero'. Which was a fascinating response. Most Christians will describe Jesus as their Lord, or their Saviour, their Master or their King (if they talk in possessive pronouns). But for Steve, the word 'hero' said it all.

It was the Greeks who gave us the first heroes...all those Gods and great men who fought dragons, went on epic journeys, suffered, fought, and finally overcame all the obstacles in their path. For Steve, Jesus was just such a hero.

Jesus, after all, embarked on an epic quest. He came among us to live the tiny fragile life of a human being. He suffered the trials of human poverty, of being a refugee, of being discarded and unwanted by his home town. He suffered the ignominy of being put on trial, tortured and then ritually murdered by the authorities of his time. But through it all, he held on to the core of Love that he brought with him to earth. He never stopped teaching those who would listen to him about the power of Love, and the power of sacrifice. He never stopped offering another way of living...his Way. The Way.

Ultimately, like all great heroes, Jesus conquered the trials of life. He transcended the pain and the brutality of human existence, and rose from the dead, proving to all his enemies that his Way was the Way to life which goes on for ever.

Yes, 'hero' is a pretty good description of who Jesus was, and is. And I thank Steve for teaching it to me.

But what about this stuff about Jesus rising from the dead? Are we really to believe this? Can we? For if he didn't rise, then Jesus' heroics were ultimately doomed to failure, and ultimately meaningless. They came to nothing, and they meant nothing. Just another foolish dreamer, whose dreams came to naught.

Well let's examine the evidence. The fact is that three days after his death, Jesus' tomb was empty. If Jesus didn't rise from it, where was the body?

Perhaps the authorities took it? Perhaps they feared that the tomb of a martyr would become a focus for ongoing civil unrest?

But if they did...why did they not simply produce the body, when the rumours of Jesus' resurrection started circulating. They could have squashed that story in a heart-beat. But the authorities didn't have the body.

Perhaps the disciples took it? Perhaps they wanted to start a lie about Jesus rising from the tomb so that they would look less foolish for having followed him all those years. But...history tells us that each and every one of the Disciples ultimately died for their sure and certain belief that Jesus had risen from the tomb. When offered the choice between life or a grizzly death, surely one of them would have confessed that they hid the body and made the story up? But none of them did. Disciple after Disciple went to their deaths, confident that Jesus' resurrection was real, and that it meant life for them.

That's why they could write, like St Paul, such words as we heard just now in the Bible reading just now. 'Where, O death, is thy sting? Where, O grave, is thy victory?'. For the disciples, the fact of Jesus' rising from his tomb was certain assurance that death is not the end of life...but just the gateway to the next and most glorious stage of our existence. It was nothing to be feared. Love has conquered all.

And that's another word that Steve used in our last conversation: Love. Steve wanted everyone to know that his life had been utterly characterised by Love. Well, actually he said 'Love and Fatherhood' - for it was ultimately as a Father that Steve experienced, and gave, and received Love.

'But Steve,' I asked, 'how can I speak of a Loving God when he has taken you away from us so soon?'

But Steve was having none of that. He told me that his final days had been filled with Love, and he reminded me that the not everyone gets to say goodbye to their families and loved ones before they walk through death's door. There was mercy, in that for Steve. He went on his journey content, enfolded by the Love of his family, of Rachel, and of his friends.

We talked too, about the awfulness of Cancer. And we talked about a theory of suffering that I have been developing over the years of my ministry – often with people who suffer. 'Yes', said Steve, 'tell them that!'. So I will.

It's pretty simple theory reality. Suffering, I suggest, is God's way of reminding the whole world that we are failing to live by the simplest of commands that he gave us. He told us to Love God, and to love each other. But instead, since the days that Jesus walked the earth, we have done exactly the opposite. We've beaten each other, we've conquered and colonised each other. We've raped and destroyed the planet he gave us to care for. We've spent untold fortunes on developing ever more deadly ways to kill each other, from Roman swords to nuclear missiles. I'm given to believe that on average, western governments spend 28 times more on research into weapons design than they do on medical research. 28 times!

Just imagine what a world of 'loving our neighbour' would be like. If, as a human race, we had listened to Jesus' simple call to love one another, we would have found a cure for cancer generations ago.

'Yes', said Steve, 'tell them that'.

So, I've tried to be obedient to Steve's last wish. He wanted you all to know that there is Good News...the good news that life doesn't have to be the way it is. The Good News that we have a loving heavenly Father, who like wind on the water can only be seen by his actions. He wanted you to know that you too have a choice – as to whether to live a life of Love, or follow the human roads of violence, greed, consumerism, and self. It's a simple choice, really. A choice to follow the hero, or to stumble along on your own.

Steve never regretted his choice to follow his hero...and I hope none of us will either.

He who is not against us...

Ecumenical musings – first preached in 2015

One of the joys of St Faith's, is the number of visitors we receive on a daily basis. I have rarely been in the church during the week, when a visitor hasn't shown up from some corner of the world. Interestingly, one of the most frequent questions they ask is 'What kind of church is this?'.

As our weekday welcomers will tell you, it is not always easy to explain what an 'Anglican' church is – especially to someone from outside the UK. It's quite funny to watch people's faces when you say 'Well, basically, we're a catholic church'. When you say that, a light of recognition dawns....most people, anywhere in the world, recognise the word 'Catholic'. They have an image in their head of certain kinds of robes, certain ceremonies. Everyone has heard of the Pope.

But then...you deliver the 'killer fact' and watch their face become all puzzled again..."But we don't follow the Pope...we have an elected church government". Confusion reigns! "How can you be catholic, but not follow the Pope?"

To some people, it really matters what kind of church they are in. In fact some people have been taught from an early age that their kind of church is the only true church. I remember, as a child, having very strange feelings about walking into another kind of church.

In my case, in my little Devon village, it was the URC church down the road. It was weird! It didn't feel like a church. They didn't have stained glass windows. The pulpit was in the centre of the building. The organ was at the back. There weren't any memorials on the walls. Where was the font? It was all very distressing. But worst of all, I found myself asking, 'are these people actually Christians at all?'

Over the years, I have had the blessing and privilege of worshipping in a vast array of churches – all over the world. Some of them have also struggled to see me as a Christian. That won't surprise those of you who know me well...but actually it had nothing to do with my personality! Rather, some churches in foreign lands have simply never heard of us Anglicans.

Take Romania, for example. I first visited Romania soon after the fall of Communism. The Communists had very effectively squashed all the churches of Romania, between 1945 and 1989. By 1990, when I arrived with a delegation from the YMCA, the only churches left standing after Ceausescu were the Orthodox Churches. Orthodoxy has some practices which you and I would find very strange indeed. For a start, there is the screen of icons around the altar. They effectively create a 'holy of holies' where only the priest may enter to celebrate the sacred mysteries. Communion is given on a long silver spoon, so that the body of Christ cannot be defiled by being touched with human hands. Services are routinely three hours long – with some worshippers coming and going throughout for their favourite bits. As you know, Orthodox worshippers put great store in icons – believing them to be windows to the heavenly realm. They may ask Saints in heaven to pray for them to God – because, after all, they are nearer to God.

But for me, a member of the Church of England, the National Church, THE church (as far as I was concerned) the strangest thing of all was to be treated by my new Romanian friends with a huge amount of suspicion. Many of them wondered whether I could be described as a Christian at all. They guessed that an 'Anglican' was another religion all together…perhaps I was like a Muslim, or a Hindu or something. It took some very patient work to listen to each other, and to work out that despite our differences, we were both Christians.

For me, there was a real joy in this encounter. I learned a great deal from my new Orthodox friends. They taught me new ways of seeing faith, and of understanding God.

For example – and it is only one example – I learned a new theological idea, known as 'deification' or Theosis. The Orthodox Church teaches, like the Anglican and Catholic churches, that we are made in the image of God. Like us, they believe that human sinfulness has distorted and spoiled that image. Like us, they believe that through Jesus it is possible for that sinfulness to be removed…and for us to be restored to a right relationship with God. But then, Orthodoxy goes one step further.

Orthodox Christians believe that it is possible for us to attain such a state of Union with God, that we can become 'deified' – or like gods (with a small 'g') ourselves. The Orthodox Saint Athanasius said it most succinctly: "Jesus was made incarnate so that we might become gods" (again with a small 'g').

Now that's a fascinating idea isn't it? It means that the Christian life is much more than a simple transaction - we sin, Jesus dies, we repent, God forgives us. The notion of 'Theosis' invites us on a journey of ever increasing holiness. Theosis offers us the possibility of becoming so much like Jesus, day by day, that we can even obtain the condition of being a kind of god ourselves. Of course, this process doesn't happen overnight. Orthodox saints are those who after a lifetime of prayer, repentance, self-sacrifice, and daily holiness are considered to have become like Jesus in their soul.

I wonder what you think about that idea? Does it encourage you? Does it make you wonder whether, with God's help, you too could embark on a process of becoming so much like Jesus that you might even be described as a kind of god? If you are encouraged, or challenged, then that's the point; that's the point of exchanging ideas across different churches. That's the point of 'ecumenism'. That's the point of movements like 'Churches Together'.

As we saw in today's Gospel reading, the Disciples were rather suspicious of anyone who wasn't in their camp. They came running to Jesus, "Teacher, Teacher…there's this fellow over there who is casting out demons in your name! Help! Panic! We tried to stop him…."

But Jesus is much more relaxed about things. "Don't try to stop him" he said. "For no-one who does a deed of power in my name will soon afterwards be able to speak evil of me. Whoever is not against us is for us".

Jesus, it seems, was an ecumenist. He understood that an infinite God could be revealed in an infinite number of ways. There are many Christians today who get terribly worried about the vast range of churches that there are in the world. To some extent, I share their concern. There are certainly some churches who I think are barely recognisable as Christian – especially any who try to persuade their followers to sign over the deeds of their houses in return for false promises of blessings from above!

But, by and large, the infinite variety of churches on this planet are, themselves, a reflection of the infinite complexity and depth of our God. We can, and should, listen to each other. Each of us has been given something unique and precious. Each of us, if you like, has our own small window into heaven. By sharing our perspectives, and learning from each other, we have the possibility of flooding our churches with the full light of heaven.

Therefore, I welcome the chance to work with other churches in this Town. I welcome the contemporary, modern worship of the Family Church or the Portsdown Community Church at the Beacon. I welcome the radical ecumenism of the URC, a church created out of a vision that it was a church born to die – when all the churches of the world came together as one, United, Re-formed church. I welcome the historic rootedness of the Catholic church, who preserve and hand on the traditions and beliefs of the ages. I welcome the radical social agenda of the Methodists, born among the working classes of England.

And I hope that we Anglicans can add our distinctiveness to the whole too. I hope that with our innate sense of ceremony, our wonderful hymnody and musical traditions, our profoundly rich liturgies, and our inclusive vision of parishes – that we too can offer something to our sisters and brothers of other churches.

He who is not against us is for us.

Wrestling with God

Reading: Genesis 32.22-32. First preached in 2019

Who here remembers Saturday afternoon wrestling? I was hooked, personally. As a young teenager, surging with testosterone, I loved watching the good, the bad and the frankly ugly playing battling with one another. It all came to an ignominious end once the news broke that most English wrestling, like its American counterpart, is fixed. It's therefore not really 'sport', if its fixed. It's really just entertainment.

But most of us of a certain age will never forget the heroes of Saturday afternoon. There was 'Giant Haystacks' – literally a giant of man, with a great bushy beard, who could always be relied on to break the rules and do some dirty deed to his opponent. His arch rival was Big Daddy....whose real name turned out to be 'Shirley Crabtree' – from a time when Shirley was a boy's name too!

Wrestling, of course, is a world-wide phenomenon. And in many cultures, it is still taken very seriously, and never fixed. Japanese Sumo wrestling is perhaps the best-known example, but there are many more, in Russian-speaking lands and further afield. Wrestling seems to appeal to men (especially), as a way of grappling with one another: not to actually hurt one another, but to test each other's strength and resolve. It's about trying new moves, and new positions. It's about balance, and timing.

And that's why, of course, wrestling is such a great metaphor for the act of thinking...and perhaps especially thinking about our faith. As we heard in our Hebrew Bible reading of today, Jacob is said to have wrestled all night with an angel – and angel whom he called 'God'. His name was even changed as a result of this all-night match. He became Israel – which means 'he who wrestles, or contends, with God'. And this is an essentially Jewish characteristic – the idea that human beings wrestle or contend with God.

Remember, for example, the story of Abraham, who negotiated with God about how many righteous people it would take to stop God destroying the city of Sodom. Moses repeatedly argued with God about how to release the captives from Egypt. Remember how the Psalms so often cry out to God in protest, asking him why is this happening to me?! and begging for relief. The oldest story in the Bible, the book of Job, is one long debate, a verbal wrestling match from beginning to end, between Job and his companions, but also with God. God himself is portrayed in the story as engaged in a debate with the Devil.

This line of Jewish thinking was extended into that somewhat over-characterised musical 'Fiddler on the Roof'. As the hero of the story, Tevye, tries to negotiate with God over whether or not he could be a rich man. Biddy biddy bum!

So what does this rich heritage of wrestling with God mean for us?

Well, first I suggest that it prepares us not to accept easy, simple answers to the questions of faith. Like a wrestling match, the journey of faith requires long, sustained, skilful action on our part. It is not enough for us to listen to one preacher, or read one book, and say "Ah! I've got it! That's what I believe!" When I was training for this ministry, one of my tutors said to me that the primary task of the preacher is to help congregations to think for themselves…and that's something I've always tried to do. Spoon-fed Christianity is simple Christianity. Faith which offers easy answers is not real faith, and it rarely stands up to crisis and trouble.

That's why FaithTalk, which we held yesterday, is such an important event in my monthly calendar. It's a chance for us to ask the questions that we all have. Where is God? What is God like? How does God act in the world? How can I get to know God better? What happens after we die? How can we live well in this life? Where is God when things go wrong? Truly wrestling with God means that we shouldn't be afraid of asking the tough questions about God.

Secondly, I suggest that we shouldn't be surprised when God wrestles with us! Jacob didn't seek a wrestling match with the angel of God. The angel sought him out, and then wrestled with the poor fellow all night long.

For us, that means that life will sometimes throw us curve-balls which we really don't expect. A loved-one dies, suddenly. Or we lose a job. Or a hurricane blows our house away. And whilst, with the Psalmist, we might well cry out in frustration 'why is this happening to me?!' – the lesson of Scripture is that God is at work, always at work, wrestling with us, and going with us through every tough circumstance of life.

At the end of Jacob's encounter, he ended up with a broken hip. Even to this day, Orthodox Jews will not eat the tendon which flows from an animal's hip, in remembrance of this event. Wrestling with God, or indeed wrestling with Life, may well leave us scarred. The journey of faith is not an easy one...but it is a worthwhile one.

This was true for Jesus, of course. Remember how he wrestled with God in the Garden of Gethsemane. "Oh, if only this cup of sorrow would pass me by...!". But having wrestled, Jesus accepted God's will, and the forces of evil which pressed on his life. He absorbed them, let them overcome him...and then he rose up above them, beyond them. He took all the pain of his torture and execution, and used it as a seed to plant in the garden of eternity. Instead of his death being shameful and pointless, he transformed it into the very means by which we, through the Eucharist, can gain food for our spiritual journeys!

May you know the ultimate joy and sense of fulfilment which comes from wrestling with God. May God you be always open to what God wants to teach you through everything that happens in your life. Like the persistent widow, how hammers on the door of the reluctant judge, may you never stop wrestling with the Almighty...and may you find the peace which passes all understanding, when the wrestling is over.

Quinquegesima

Reading: Mathew 17.1-13 First preached in 2020

Quinquegesima. It's a lovely word to get your tonsils round, isn't it? Say it with me … Quinquegesima.

That's the ancient Latin name given to this Sunday, the last Sunday before Ash Wednesday. What does it mean?

It ought to mean something really exotic, didn't it? You know, something like "the Feast of St Quinque, holder of the golden orb of Gesima, slayer of dragons, and defender of the poor".

'Friad not.

It just means 'fiftieth'. Today marks the fact that in 50 days from now, we will celebrate the rising of Christ from the tomb at Easter.

But hang on. Some of you are doing the math, and thinking to yourselves 'that can't be right! If Lent starts on Ash Wednesday, and its 40 days long, how can today be 50 days from Easter?

That's because many of us forget that the 40 days of Lent do not include the seven Sundays of Lent. Sundays are days of celebration – each one a mini-Easter, during which the triumph of Christ over the grave is remembered and praised. They are also days of relief from the strictures of Lent. So for those of us who face the prospect of 40 days of abstinence with dread, the church kindly provides us with one day in seven when we are permitted to eat chocolate, or drink that glass of beer!

More importantly than any ecclesiastical numbering system, today's focus is really on the story of the Mount of Transfiguration. Our Gospel reading of this morning reminded us of how Jesus met on the mountain with Moses and Elijah – The Lawgiver and the ultimate Prophet (before Jesus himself). They strengthened him and encouraged him for the journey ahead…the journey to Jerusalem and the cross.

This evening's readings pick up the same theme. The first reading came from one of the apocryphal books of the Protestant Canon…. not part of the Canon of Scripture, but an ancient reading which still has something to teach us.

Ecclesiasticus is another juicy word to get our tongues around. It actually means 'church book' – because it is a text which was readily available to early Christians, and so it was often read in services. Its proper name is 'the Wisdom of Sirach' – or even more fully, 'the Wisdom of Joshua, son of Sirach'. It was written around 200 years before the coming of Christ, and, as such, is one of the latest pre-Christian books that we have.

Sirach's wisdom was a very personal thing. One the one hand, he advocated the use of physicians to heal the sick – demonstrating that 200 years before Jesus, the notion that sickness was a punishment for sin was beginning to lose its force. That, of course, was something that Jesus himself would go on to teach.

On the other hand, Sirach was certainly a man of his time. He advocates the use of harsh punishment to control both slaves and women! Which is one of the reasons why the Protestant church has never recognised his writings as canonical.

Nevertheless, Sirach was well known to the people of Jesus' time, and the passage that we heard just now was one that had particular relevance. In it, Sirach praises Elijah for being the great prophet that he was, and also, intriguingly, promises that Elijah will return to 'calm the wrath of God before it breaks out in fury'.

This one line, from a dubious and idiosyncratic writer, had huge intellectual force in its time…and it still resonates today. It is why the people of Jesus' time kept asking whether he, or John the Baptist, were Elijah. It was somewhat of an obsession of theirs, because the Book of Sirach was so well known to them. Which just goes to show that if you repeat even a stupid idea enough times, people will begin to believe it – as we have seen in the recent politics of our own time.

The idea that Elijah would return to 'calm the wrath of God' is one of the main foundations of the idea that Jesus died to save us from an angry God. Which, again, I want to suggest to you is an idea that needs serious examination.

God might well be angry with humanity. In our second reading, which takes place immediately after Jesus comes down from the mountain, there is certainly a lot of frustration building up in him! "You faithless and perverse generation, how much longer must I be with you? How much longer must I put up with you?"

And then, when the disciples report that they couldn't cast out a troublesome demon, Jesus thoroughly excoriates them for their lack of faith. "If you just had a little faith!" he says, in exasperation, "faith as tiny as a mustard seed, then you could move mountains!"

Yes, God certainly is capable of wrath towards his faithless and perverse generation. But, to then make the leap of saying that Jesus had to die to somehow appease that wrath seems, to me, to load the meaning of the crucifixion with too much weight.

After all, we teach and believe that Jesus is God. There's a certain weakness of logic in suggesting that God had to die in order to appease God's own wrath. Isn't there?

I rather prefer the theology of the 10th century office hymn which we just heard in the setting by Thomas Tallis. 'O nata lux' is a hymn of praise to Jesus, the 'nata lux' – he who was born of light, recalling the opening of John's Gospel. 'God of God. Light of Light.'

But the hymn then goes on to contemplate the meaning of Christ's incarnation, and of course, that must include his death. For the unknown writer of the hymn, Jesus is the God who deigned to be hidden in flesh…the God who gives up his divinity, to become one of us, and to die as we might die. Why? The entire purpose of Jesus' incarnation is summed up in the final line of the hymn: Jesus came to rescue the lost, and to join us in one body.

That – for me – is a far more compelling notion than the notion of a wrathful God whose anger can only be appeased by his own death. Instead, Jesus comes to us, perhaps out of frustration that we have failed to listen to Moses and Elijah, perhaps frustrated that we have not even the faith of a mustard seed, and he reaches out to us. He reaches out, and draws us in. He rescues us from our own blindness and stupidity, and draws us into union with himself. By sharing in our humanity, he dies our death. By sharing with us his divinity, he transcends death and draws us into his own body.

'Listen,' says St Paul, ecstatically absorbing the glorious truth, 'I will tell you a mystery. We will not all sleep, but we will all be changed— in a flash, in the twinkling of an eye, at the last trumpet.' Like Jesus on the Mount of Transfiguration, we too will be changed and given glorious new existence in the kingdom of our father.

And all because of the event we will celebrate together, just a quinquegesima from now!

Stories

Four original short stories intended to fire the imagination

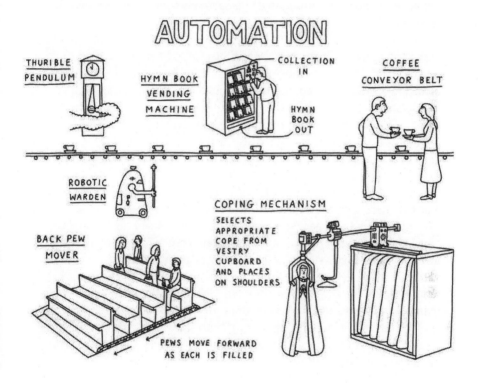

Charlie and the Toilet

Or: What's so amazing about Grace?

Reading: Ephesians 2

This is a story which shouldn't be taken literally (not least because it doesn't reflect modern good practice in schools, neither for the disciplining of aberrant behaviour, nor for personal relationships between teachers and students). Please read it as an allegory for the love of God.

Once upon a time there was a boy called Charlie. Charlie was one of those little boys whose behaviour was feared by all his teachers at school. Frankly, sometimes, he acted like a complete idiot. He would shout at his teachers. He would refuse to do what he was asked to do. His language was appalling. Perhaps worst of all, Charlie was a bully to his classmates.

One day, Charlie's teacher, Mr Browning, had had enough. He had just found Charlie in the boy's cloakroom - trying to flush another boy's head down the toilet. Mr Browning grabbed Charlie by the ear, and frogmarched him to the Headteacher's office.

The head-teacher, Mrs Sanderson, was a scary sort of person. Her hair was tied back in a very ferocious knot. She had a very loud voice, which could stop small children in their tracks at a hundred yards. And she wore some of those half-mooned glasses which she would look over at every child. Even Charlie, who wasn't scared of many people - even Charlie was afraid of Mrs Sanderson.

Charlie's teacher pulled him into Mrs Sanderson's office. "Yes?" said Mrs Sanderson, looking over her glasses. "What's Charlie been up to this time?".

"I just found him in the boy's wash-room trying to flush another boy's head down the toilet", said Mr Browning.

"Really?" said Mrs Sanderson. "Charlie - why were you doing that?"

"Dunno" said Charlie. "He looked at me".

"Thank you, Mr Browning", said Mrs Sanderson. "Leave this to me." Browning turned and left the room. "Now, let me get this straight, Charlie," said Mrs Sanderson. "He looked at you?"

"Yeh," replied Charlie. And then it all came tumbling out. "He was looking at me and I said to 'im 'wot you fink you're looking at?' and he said 'nofink' and I said 'liar' and he said 'I'm not' and I said 'you are!' and then I grabbed him and got him in a headlock and I flushed his head down the bog just to teach him a lesson".

"Right" said Mrs Sanderson, in that sarcastic tone that only head teachers really know how to use. "What do you think is going to happen now, Charlie"

"S'pose you're going to punish me."

"Actually," said Mrs Sanderson, "I'm not going to punish you."

"What?!" said Charlie - puzzled by this term of events.

"No, said Mrs Sanderson, "I'm not going to punish you - I'm going to teach you a lesson"

"That's just another word for 'punishment' isn't it?" asked Charlie.

"Sometimes," said Mrs Sanderson. "But today, I really am going to teach you something. Today, Charlie, you are going to learn about grace"

"Grace?" said Charlie. "What - you're going to teach me how to do that silly praying-thing before I eat my dinner?"

"No" Mrs Sanderson laughed. "No, this is another kind of grace altogether". Then to Charlie's surprise, Mrs Sanderson took off her half-mooned glasses, and laid them on her desk. Then, she reached up behind her head, and undid the knot in her hair, and let her hair fall softly over her shoulders.

"Charlie," she said, her normally hard voice now sounding very soft. "Come here"

Charlie was suspicious. 'I know what's going to happen,' he thought. 'She's just pretending to be nice so as she can catch me. If I go over there, she'll grab me, and batter me.' So he stayed rooted to the spot, staring at Mrs Sanderson.

"Charlie", said Mrs Sanderson, "In all the years you have been at this school, have you ever known me to tell a lie?"

Charlie thought for a moment. "Well, no" he replied, hesitantly.

"Well then," said Mrs Sanderson, "believe me when I say that nothing bad is going to happen if you come over here - if you let me teach you the lesson I want to teach you about grace"

Charlie was intrigued now. What was going to happen? What could Mrs Sanderson possibly teach him? Nervously, he put one foot forward.

"That's right," encouraged Mrs Sanderson. "Come to me"

Charlie figured that it might just be worth trying. It was better than getting battered, anyway. So gingerly he made his way across the head-teacher's office, until he was standing right in front of her desk. He thought to himself, 'At least the desk will protect me if she tries anything'. Mrs Sanderson smiled. It was a warm smile; a welcoming, friendly smile.

"Now come round the side of the desk, Charlie" said Mrs Sanderson. "Come round here to me."

Charlie was mesmerised. He didn't have a clue what was going on. But suddenly he felt drawn to do what Mrs Sanderson asked. Carefully, he made his way round the side of the desk and stood right in front of her, just one step away...just enough room to make a break for it if he needed to.

"Do you know what I'm going to do to you, Charlie", asked Mrs Sanderson.

"No."

"I'm going to give you a hug, Charlie"

"You're a loony," said Charlie.

"No, Charlie, I'm not. I'm going to give you a hug because I know that deep down inside, under all your bluster, and your violence, and your bullying there is a small boy who just needs to know that someone cares about him. Would you like a hug from someone who understands why you behave like you do...who understands that there are bits of your life that are out of your control...who understands that you behave the way you do because you can't help it? Something in you is trying to get control over some part of your life...and you use violence to try to get it." Mrs Sanderson opened her arms, as if to receive Charlie into them.

Charlie thought about it for a moment. He didn't really understand what Mrs Sanderson was talking about. All that stuff about trying to get control. All he knew was that he was angry all the time -

and that no-one seemed to care about him. A hug? Wouldn't be the end of the world, he supposed. Never really had a proper hug - not for a long time anyway.

Tentatively, Charlie took a final step, into the arms of this strange, enigmatic woman whom he didn't understand at all. She was weird. One minute she looked all ferocious and fierce, and then here she was offering him a hug.

Charlie let himself go. He relaxed into the hug. He put his head on Mrs Sanderson's chest, and he just let go.

Then the tears started. It's funny how a sudden change of mood can make the tears flow. Charlie hadn't cried for years. He was too tough for that. But now, here in this strange woman's arms, Charlie's eyes filled up, and the tears flowed like rivers down his cheeks.

Mrs Sanderson stroked Charlie's head. "It's alright Charlie. I understand. Let it all go. Let me take some of the pain. Because, you know what Charlie? I love you just as you are right now…and just as I hope you will be one day."

Charlie's life changed, from that day onward. Somehow, knowing that he was loved, seemed to make a difference. As the weeks and months went by, Charlie's violent outbursts became less and less. He started to focus on his work, and started to show kindness to his classmates, instead of hatred.

Sometimes, when he knew that all his friends were busy in another part of the school, he would creep into Mrs Sanderson's office - and they would talk about his plans, and his ideas for the future.

And occasionally, just occasionally, just so that he would know it was real, Mrs Sanderson would give Charlie a hug.

Sons of Thunder

Reading: Mark 10. 35-45

It was a lovely sunny afternoon, that day. The disciples and the crowds had been following Jesus all around the countryside, through Galilee and Judea, listening to his teaching, hanging on his every word. Towards sunset, as the crowd started to cast about for places to camp for the night, Jesus motioned to his disciples. Instantly, they stopped laying out their sleeping blankets, and clustered around him. What did the Master want? What did he need from them?

With a nod of his head, Jesus motioned for his closest friends to follow him. They moved off up a slope to a patch of shade under an olive tree. The disciples sat down, teasing Peter as he lowered his slightly arthritic hip onto the dirt. Matthew and Nathaniel leaned against the trunk of the tree. And then all 12 pairs of eyes focused on the Master. What was he going to say to them? This was going to be interesting.

Jesus seemed hesitant. What he was going to tell them was going to upsetting for them to hear. It was going to shatter some of them...they would not understand it. They would protest. Some might even decide that they didn't want to follow him anymore. Jesus took a deep breath, and began.

"We are going up to Jerusalem," he said. Judas and Andrew exchanged glances. Yes, their eyes communicated. We know. We're not stupid. Jesus went on, "And when we get there, the Son of Man is going to be betrayed to the Chief Priests and the Teachers of the Law."

Simon began to protest. "What?!" he said. "How can that happen? You've got all these crowds...." Jesus held up his hand, and Simon fell silent.

"And..." Jesus went on, "They will condemn him to death"

It was Andrew's turn now. "No, Lord!" he protested. "That's impossible. Look how everyone loves you! Everyone is following you". Jesus shook his head. That sad look the Disciples had been noticing all day clouded his eyes again.

"The Chief Priests and the Teachers of the Law will condemn him to death," Jesus repeated. "And then they will turn him over to the Gentiles - to the Romans - to be mocked and flogged and crucified."

The Disciples erupted. Each one tried to out-do the other with protestations. "No, Lord! We won't let that happen! It's impossible! No-one could do that to you".

Jesus stood back and watched. He let them rail their incomprehension at him for a while. And then, he started smiling. A smile crept into his eyes, and then made its way down to his mouth, until it took possession of his whole face. The Disciples' protests dropped to a low murmur, and then to silence. "Why is he smiling? Has he been winding us up?" Jesus fixed the Disciples with his eyes, and finished his speech,

"But on the third day, he will be raised to life!"

There was silence. Judas turned towards Thadeus and mouthed, "He's cracked!. Must be the sun. Go and get him some water". Thadeus, shook his head. This wasn't the first time that Jesus had said this kind of stuff. Though this time, it looked like Jesus really meant it. Besides, Thadeus wasn't Judas' slave. If Judas wanted to get Jesus some water he could do it himself. Thadeus wanted to stay and see what happened next.

But nothing happened. Having said what he wanted to say, Jesus turned away from the Disciples, and made his way down the slope to the rest of the crowd. The Disciples watched him leave...wondering what it all meant.

Simon was the first to speak. "Well, I believe him," he stated boldly. "Everything else he has ever told us has been completely trustworthy, hasn't it." He turned to James and John, the so called 'Sons of Thunder'. "Guys, do you remember how Jesus met with Moses and Elijah on that mountain the other day? When only the three of us with were him? If he can do that, I can certainly believe that he could rise from the dead."

"Yes," replied James. "But what happens then? Once he's been raised from the dead. What is he going to do after that?"

Matthew, the former civil servant, piped up. "Well, I reckon he'll start a new Government. I reckon he'll sort out the Romans, and then set up a new, holy Kingdom...you know, that 'Kingdom of God' that he's always been talking about. I wonder who he'll ask to be Chancellor?"

Matthew suddenly had a far-way look in his eye.

"And who will he make Prime Minister?" said Andrew. "Simon, that's going to be you!" Simon shook his head modestly - but he smiled as well. Everyone knew that Simon was Jesus' right hand man.

The Disciples continued to banter among themselves. Who would be minister in charge of the drains? Who would command the army? But James and John, the Sons of Thunder, went silent. They didn't like the way that their friends were talking. They were not at all happy about having posts in the new Kingdom of God being carved up by the other Disciples like this. James decided he'd had enough.

"See you later, guys." he said. "I'm off to bed. Come on John." John got up off the ground, and followed James down the slope towards the crowd. When they were a little way from the others, James stopped John with a hand on his arm.

"Listen", he said. "Why don't we go and see Jesus and ask him for jobs in the new government ourselves? If he says it, the others won't be able to stop us getting the best jobs"

"Do you think he won't mind?" asked John

James pondered for a moment. "Maybe", he concluded. But if you don't ask, you don't get!

John looked thoughtfully at James. There was a chance here. Perhaps they might just make it, and become Jesus' right hand men. John nodded at James, and together they looked at over at where Jesus was sitting, on a rock, alone on the edge of the camp. They walked carefully over to him, picking their way between sleeping bodies. They approached the Master.

"Um" said James, "Um...Rabbi? Can we bother you for a minute?"

Jesus looked up from his prayers, with a knowing look in his eyes. "Yes, boys. What is it?"

"Rabbi," said James, "We want you to do for us whatever you ask. Ok?"

Jesus wasn't going to make any promises. He was cannier than that – and quite used to people trying to trap him into saying something he might later regret. "What is it?" he said cautiously.

James got ready to make a well-considered plea, backed up with lots and lots of good reasons as to why they should be important officials in the new Government. But John couldn't contain himself. He was so nervous, that it all came tumbling out!

"We want you to grant for us to sit on your left and on your right when you come into your kingdom! Um...please...."

Jesus looked disappointed. He had hoped for better from these two. He had hoped that perhaps they had begun to understand that his Kingdom was not like that at all. He shook his head, and said, "You will indeed drink from my cup. But to sit at my right or left is not for me to grant. These places belong to those for whom they have been prepared by my Father."

James and John were a bit puzzled, but they were wise enough to know when to back down. What did Jesus mean? We will drink from his cup, but the places of honour are decided by God? That was typical of Jesus. He always talked in riddles.

Unbeknown to James and John, however, they had been followed. Judas, who had never quite trusted the Sons of Thunder, had trailed them from a distance, and had heard the whole conversation from behind a tree. As James and John turned away from Jesus, Judas slipped back through the darkness to the other Disciples.

"You'll never guess what James and John are up to!" he hissed, when he got back...and then proceeded to tell the whole story.

"That's not right!" "Who do they think they are?" The Disciples were livid! After a quick discussion together, they decided that this would just not do, and they all strutted over to where James and John were settling down dejectedly for the night.

Simon, ever the spokesperson, spoke first. "What's this we hear? Have you been up to Jesus to ask for a place on his right and on his left?"

James looked at the ground, and shuffled his feet nervously. "Well, erm...", he mumbled. "We did just have a chat...".

"That's not good enough" replied Simon. "Who do you think you are? Do you think you are better than the rest of us? Do you think Jesus is going to choose either of you over us?"

Jesus, in the meantime, had been sitting on his rock, looking over the camp. He wasn't surprised. Disappointed, but not surprised. He had smiled to himself as he saw Simon stride across the camp over to James and John with the other nine disciples in his wake. Jesus made a decision. It's time for me to intervene here, he thought.

Jesus climbed down from his rock, and wandered down the slope to where the ten disciples were gathered around the other two. As he approached, one of the Disciples, Philip, looked up from the argument, and saw Jesus approaching. He nudged Bartholomew in the ribs and pointed at the approaching Rabbi. Bartholomew nudged Matthew, Matthew nudged Andrew and in a few seconds, the little group of angry men had ceased shouting, and waited for Jesus to approach.

Jesus walked up to them and stopped. He looked around at them with love, but also a little disappointment in his eyes. Into the anger in the air around him, Jesus spoke gently.

"You know how the Gentiles do things, don't you? You know how their rulers lord it over the rest of the people, and how their high officials dominate everyone else?" A few of the Disciples grunted. They knew what Jesus meant - they had seen how the Romans bossed everyone else around. "Well", Jesus went on, "That is not how it shall be with you. Instead, whoever wants to be great among you must be your servant - not your Prime Minister," he said, looking knowingly at Peter, "and not your Chancellor", he said, smiling at Matthew. "Whoever wants to be first among you must be a slave to everyone else. This should not surprise you. The Son of Man did not come to be served, but to serve. The Son of Man came to give his life away, not to go lording it up over anyone."

And then, the Disciples noticed that Jesus' eyes seemed to become distant. He seemed to be staring off into the distance, over vast miles, and even through time itself.

And then, Jesus' voice was heard in a little church in the heart of Portsmouth; a little church named out of affection for another follower of Jesus, St Mark. A congregation of ordinary people were gathered that morning: people just like the Disciples and the other followers of Jesus. These were ordinary people - but people who had heard the call of Jesus, across the millennia. They'd heard the call to live in ways that were life-giving; the call to live in love with God, and with each other. These were people who longed to hear Jesus speak to them, and longed to hear from him how life could be even richer, deeper, more meaningful. And across time, and through the walls of the church that morning, the congregation of St Mark's heard Jesus speaking to them.

"In my service, there is perfect freedom. By serving me, in your homes, in your jobs, in your schools, in your church, in your community - you will find me. By serving me with your time, and with your talents and with your money, you will know me. When you serve others, you serve me. When you reach out to others, you reach out to me."

And all the people, in that little church in North End, said, "Amen".

PARISH LIFE

BEFORE THE INVENTION OF THE COMPUTER

THE NOTICE SHEET
WAS COPIED BY HAND

MESSAGES WERE DELIVERED
ON FOOT

A GREAT BIG BELL WAS RUNG
TO TELL PEOPLE THINGS

PEOPLE HAD HOBBIES, AND DRANK
AFTERNOON TEA, AND DID NOT SPEND
EVERY SPARE HOUR OF THE DAY
IN AN EXASPERATED STATE TRYING
TO MAKE THE WRETCHED THING WORK

Massacre in Norway

Reading: Romans 8. 26-39

I'm going to tell you a story. It's a fictional story, based on the 2011 events in Norway, and on a reading of Paul's letter to the Romans. I offer it as a thought...as a story...in the hope that it will open our imaginations to what might be possible in the love of God. Are you sitting comfortably? Then I shall begin...

Once upon a time, not very long ago, a young man called Anders lived in Norway, the land of the Norsemen, the Vikings. Anders was blond, and blue-eyed...a true Viking, descended from Vikings. In his history books he read about the time when the Vikings had ruled vast swathes of Europe, a time when blond and blue eyed people had been in complete control.

But looking around his own country now, he saw that Vikings were no longer in control. Instead, Norway was ruled by faceless bureaucrats in faraway Brussels. He saw that his country was being too kind, too welcoming to people from other countries. Foreigners were crowding his streets...people from Africa, people from Asia, people from parts of Europe which certainly weren't blond. And worse than that "these people are taking jobs from us Norwegians. They are claiming money from our Government, living in our houses, and stealing our jobs." thought Anders.

Slowly, day by day, anger started to grow within Anders. He couldn't understand that the world was a shrinking place, in which overpopulation, famine and war were driving desperate people across all sorts of borders, in search of a better life. No-one challenged his thinking. When he complained about black people in his city, friends and family members would just shrug their shoulders, and agree. It was easier to agree...even when they didn't agree. Anders always looked so angry about the issue. It was easier to just go along with him...not to challenge him.

Slowly, slowly, the hatred grew. Anders began to look around for someone to blame. Someone had to pay for this situation. It was impossible for him, alone, to attack all the foreigners in his country...there were too many of them. But perhaps he could attack those who had let them in? In his unchallenged, warped mind, his anger turned towards the leaders of Norway. It was the fault of the Government. It was the fault of the Prime Minister. It was the fault of the ruling Party of Norway.

A desperate, angry plan began to form. Anders gathered his resources. Guns, bullets, explosives. He built up a stock-pile, until one day, on the 22nd of July 2011, he was ready to show the Government that they were wrong to let so many foreigners into his country.

So, with deliberate care, and seething rage, Anders planted his bomb. The bomb would go off right outside the Prime Minister's office. Anders planted his bomb, and then waited for it to explode.

Boom! The bomb ripped a hole in the Government's main building. The Prime Minister's office was shattered. Anders had started his war. What next?

Anders knew that there was an island where the ruling party of Norway took its young people for training and indoctrination into their stupid beliefs about the equality of all human beings. That is where he would strike next. Gathering his many guns and bullets, Anders set off for the Island. He would strike a blow not just at the present Government, but at the next generation of politicians. He would teach them a lesson they would never forget.

Arriving at the island, Anders set to work at his grim task. He opened fire on hundreds of people, sending them scattering all over the island...they climbed trees, they tried to swim to the mainland, they barricaded themselves into log cabins. Terrified.

At the end of his day's work, 84 people – mainly young people – had been slain. Another seven had died in the earlier bomb blast. Anders was content. He had sent a message to the whole world...a message that no-one could ignore. He allowed himself to be taken...to be arrested...so that through his forthcoming trial, his message of "Norway for Norwegians" would have the maximum impact, as the press followed every twist and turn.

Then, one day, many years later, after spending the rest of his life in prison, Anders died. There were many who celebrated that day. Many of the parents of those children, the ones who were gunned down in their prime, believed that prison had been too kind a treatment for Anders. "Now, he'll get what's coming to him", they said to themselves. "Now, he'll burn in hell".

Anders himself had thought that would probably happen too. After years of thinking about his actions in jail, he had come to understand that he had taken the wrong course. But what could he do about it? What was done was done. And if there was a God...well, he'd just have to take the punishment, wouldn't he?

Anders' day of judgement had arrived. He stood, in the presence of God. An awesome light shone all around him...a light which pulsed with love, and yet also judgement. There was clarity in that light. Anders knew that everything he had done, everything he had thought, every warped impulse was seen, judged, weighed in the balance, by that light. And yet, there was love too...along with judgement.

Anders took his courage in his hands. He looked into the light. And said..."I suppose you're going to send me to hell now?"

"That's up to you", said the Voice of God.

"But I have done awful things," said Anders.

"Yes," said Jehovah, "you have".

"So, surely I deserve to rot in hell"

"Probably," said Jesus. "But then so do many of my children. Your crimes were particularly horrible...but you are not the only one. Many of my children have killed their brothers and sisters. It started with Cain and Abel...and it has never stopped. Many have lived lives of hate. Others have stood by, taking no action at all, while their brothers and sisters have died in famine and war. Many have carried on partying, taking massive bonuses and living on luxury yachts, while others around them were dying. Your hatred is great, Anders...but it's not all that unusual."

"So what's going to happen to me? What are you going to do to me?"

"I'm going to love you," said the Spirit.

"What?" said Anders, struggling to take it in.

"I'm going to love you," said God.

"How? How can you do that? After all I've done?"

"I can't do anything else." said Love. "That's what I am. Love. That's what I do. Love. I created you, and the whole Universe out of

182

love. It was love that brought you into being. And it is love which will bring you home."

Anders was speechless.

"Did you ever read the Bible, during the life I gave you?" asked Love.

"Well…" replied Anders, "bits of it".

"There's a passage in there that I am especially proud of", said God. "It was written by a child of mine called Paul. Now he was a mess…let me tell you. He actually started out by murdering followers of Jesus. But eventually, Love got to him…and he saw the light. He wised up, and got the message of Love. Fortunately, for other Christians, he did it while he was still on Earth. Paul ended up writing this, in a letter to some Roman Christians: 'I am convinced that neither death, nor life, nor angels, nor rulers, nor things present, nor things to come, nor powers, nor height, nor depth, nor anything else in all creation, will be able to separate us from the love of God in Christ Jesus our Lord'. Pretty good eh?" said God.

"Lovely," said Anders, "but what does it mean?"

God sighed, and said, "It means, Anders, that whatever you have done, whatever warped influences you gave into, whatever your weaknesses, whatever your thoughts, whatever you were driven by madness to do, I will never stop loving you. I will always keep on inviting you to give in to my love."

Anders didn't know how to respond to this. It was so far removed from what he had expected. He had spent years of seething anger in his cell, watching the little television that he was allowed. Over the years, countless journalists and commentators on his crimes had convinced him that he was at best, nothing. Or at worse, he was evil personified. Even if he believed in God, Anders had always thought that there could be no other outcome for him than death and destruction. In his heart, he had accepted destruction as inevitable. He had even started to embrace it as welcome. He looked up to God…

"What if I don't want to be loved?" he asked. "I'm not sure that I want it. I've kind of got used to who I am, and what I've done. I'm not sure I want to give that up."

"That," replied Love, "is why I said that the decision about whether or not you will go to hell is yours"

"What do you mean?" asked Anders

"I will never stop loving you, Anders. But I can't make you want my love. That's your choice. I give you free will to accept my love, or reject it. After all, I can't make you love me. That wouldn't be love…it would be manipulation."

"And what happens if I reject your love?"

"You'll die, forever. Remember what I told you…I created you out of Love. My love brought you into being. My love has sustained you and all people, even through the terrible things you have done. But now, you have a choice. If you refuse my love, you'll gradually wither up, and die. It's a bit like food. If you stop eating, eventually you will die. If you stop receiving my love, you'll fade away. My bible talks about those who reject my love being thrown into the fire, or thrown into the rubbish dump called Gehenna…where there will be weeping and gnashing of teeth. Those are pictures… metaphors that I have used to warn all my children of what happens when they reject my love. Fading away, becoming less and less real, wailing and crying in the pain of selfishness, until eventually, destruction takes place. Paul called it "the second death". Anders… don't choose that path. Despite all you've done, I still love you".

"But what about justice?" said Anders. "Surely there has to be some justice for the people I killed?"

"Yes," said God. "And for all the millions who have died through the selfishness of my other children. And for all those who lived lives of abject poverty because the people of the West would not share the world's resources. And for all those who died in leaky boats escaping wars over oil and gold. There has to be justice for all of them too."

"So…how?" said Anders. "If all the world is guilty of sin…can you punish everybody?"

"I could. But what kind of Father sends all his children to hell? All have sinned, Anders. All have fallen short of the glory of God. Love, Anders. Love is the only way. My justice is not like the justice of human beings. My justice is tempered with love. My judgement sees all that is wrong with the way humans chose to live…and then meets it with love."

"How?" asked Anders.

"Through a cross." said Jesus. "A cross where love and mercy meet. A cross where God and human beings have the chance to connect, through Love. A cross where the evil that all human beings are capable of doing is confronted with the force of my love."

"My Lord and my God!" said Anders. "Teach me more about this kind of Love!"

READING THE LESSON

ADVICE

SPEND TIME REHEARSING
AT HOME

WORK ON YOUR DICTION
AT EVERY OPPORTUNITY

TURN UP

ADJUST THE MICROPHONE
AND LECTERN LIGHT

TRY NOT TO RUSH

BE CONFIDENT-
RELAX AND ENJOY IT

Mary's Visitor

Reading: Luke 1.26-38

Mary plonked herself down onto her bed. "Crikey, I'm whacked!" she said. It had been a long day of household chores - chasing spiders out of corners, catching up with the laundry, sweeping, dusting, cooking. But now, Mary had one more important job do. She reached down, under her bed, and pulled out an old basket. Inside was her nearly-finished wedding robe...the one she had been working on for the past several weeks.

Mary was engaged to Joseph, the old carpenter in the village. No-one knew why Joseph had not been married before...perhaps he had been waiting for the right girl to come along. Mary's mind started to wander as she stitched along the hem. I wonder what it's going to be like - being married. Come to that - what's it going to be like to kiss him? He's got that great big bushy beard...I wonder whether it will tickle!

At that moment, unbeknown to Mary, something began to happen in the corner of her room - just over her shoulder. A twinkle in the air. Now a soft glow. Then, suddenly, a tall figure with wings on his back appeared in the corner.

"Greetings!" said the figure.

Mary jumped out of her skin! "Where did you come from?", she demanded. "You shouldn't creep up on people like that!"

The tall figure with the wings looked a little surprised at her reaction. People usually quaked in fear when he appeared. He wasn't used to being told off. "Sorry", he mumbled. "Didn't mean to startle you. Can I go on now?"

"Alright" said Mary, thinking that this tall fellow looked a little bit like one of Mrs Cohen's sons, from down the road. "What's this all about....and why have you got those, those feathers clipped onto your coat? Are you going to a fancy dress party?"

"They're not clipped onto my coat." said the tall man. "They're sticking out of my coat...they're my wings!"

"Oh," said Mary who was beginning to realise that this wasn't Mrs Cohen's boy after all. "Who are you?"

"I'm an Angel", said the Angel.

"Get away!" said Mary. "You're pulling my leg. What's this...some kind of prank?"

"No, really", said the Angel. "I'm an actual, real, Angel. Sent by God. The name's Gabriel. I've got a very important message for you. You are really very favoured you know. Not everyone gets a real Angel sent with a message from God."

Mary was distinctly puzzled by now. An Angel? Sent to her? Here in little Nazareth? What ever can it mean? Mary started to shake. "I'm sorry, Angel," she said, "I didn't mean any dis-respect. I thought you looked like Nathaniel from down the road...dressed up. Oh crickey! What have I done?"

The Angel looked kindly at Mary. "Don't worry about it, Mary. Don't be afraid. It was an easy mistake to make. Now listen..."

"Ok," said Mary. "I'm all ears!"

"Mary," the Angel started again, patiently, "I've got really good news for you. You are to be given the greatest gift that any woman has ever been given."

"Oh, my!" said Mary, agog.

"Yes," the Angel went on, "You are going to have a baby, sent from God. You are to name him Yeshua"

"What, like Yeshua who led the People of Israel into the Promised Land?" Mary enquired...trying to take in what the Angel was saying.

"Yes," said the Angel, "Just like that...although years from now people will change the way they pronounce it, and will call him Jesus." The Angel drew himself up to his full height, and started to proclaim, slightly pompously, "He will be great and will be called the Son of the Most High. The Lord God will give him the throne of his father David, and he will reign over the house of Jacob for ever." (The Angel was really working himself up to a climax now...the big finish.) "His kingdom will never end...and..."

"Erm...", said Mary, holding up a finger.

"What now?!" said the Angel - a little bit annoyed that he had been stopped in mid-flow.

"Tiny problem." said Mary.

"What?!" said the Angel

"Well, you see, I don't think I can have a baby. I'm not married yet. Haven't even kissed Joseph yet. Do you know whether beards tickle, by the way?" The Angel took a deep breath. A little pomposity crept into his voice again.

"Nothing is impossible for God. The Holy Spirit will come upon you, and the power of the Most High will overshadow you. So the holy baby that will be born will be the Son of God."

"Well," said Mary. "It all sounds very unlikely, I must say. I mean, why on earth would God choose a peasant like me to bear his son? The son of God will be born in the palace, surely? Are you sure those wings are real?"

"I'm completely sure. " said the Angel, " You see, God doesn't approve of the kind of people who lord it over others in palaces. His real passion is for those who are poor and humble"

"Incredible!" said Mary. "Well, they don't come much poorer than me. I've even got to make my own wedding dress!" she said, holding up her sewing for the Angel to see.

"It's always been God's way. Right back to the dawn of time."

"Hmm," said Mary, still not quite convinced. "Let me get this straight. I'm going to have a baby, right?"

"Yep" said the Angel

"Even though I haven't even kissed Joseph yet?"

"Even then"

"And my baby is going to be the Son of God...even though he will be born in this little hut?"

"Well," said the Angel cautiously, "He won't actually be born here..."

"Why not?" asked Mary, suspiciously

"It'll be a bit more rustic than this"

"A bit more rustic? How much more rustic do you want it?" said Mary, pointing at her surroundings.

"Umm" said the Angel, with a worried look in his eye, "Think donkeys. And cows"

"What!" exclaimed Mary. "My baby is going to be born in a field?!"

"Oh no!", said the Angel. "Nothing as bad as that. More like a stable"

"A stable!" said Mary.

"Mary..." said the Angel, a little sternly. "You've got to trust me. You've got to trust God. God knows what he is doing. Jesus has to be born somewhere that no-one would expect a king to be born. He's got to be born in utter poverty...so that God's love for the poor can be made clear. In years to come, people will help one another in his name, precisely because of his humble origins. He will be one of the people, born like the poorest of the people...so that the people will take him to their hearts and trust what he tells them."

Mary slid forward off her bed, until she was kneeling on the floor in front of the Angel. She could no longer deny what was happening to her. After all, here was an Angel, from God, telling her all about it!

"I am the Lord's servant", she said. "May it be to me as you have said."

The Angel smiled. Mary had accepted what he had told her. She had tasted something of her future, and the future that would be shaped by her Son. Satisfied that his task was complete, the Angel slowly faded from Mary's view.

In the corner of the room, the smile of an Angel hung in the air for a few seconds. And then was gone.

Ghana and Togo Journal

August and September 2012

During 2012, I spent 3 weeks in Ghana and Togo, establishing the basis of a link between my home deanery in Portsmouth and the Diocese of Ho in Ghana.

By visiting www.tomkennar.com it is possible to see many photos of the trip, and a short video. However, for those without access to the Internet, I hope that the following account will be interesting and thought provoking. Travel with me, from your armchair and in your imagination...

27th to 28th August 2012

After rather squashed flight (and a slightly sore bottom!) I arrived in Accra last night at around 8.30pm. It never ceases to amaze me that airlines seem unable to improve the standard of their seats. I travelled Economy class, of course. But even Economy class makes claims about the comfort of the seats, and the 'amazing' inflight entertainment. The seats are, frankly awful for someone of my size and weight. My head sticks over the top of the seat, making any kind of head-rest a mere illusion. The seats themselves are designed appallingly, resulting in constant shifting to try to find a more comfortable position. The in-flight entertainment was reasonable, in theory, containing a few very up to date movies...but the sound system is appalling. No matter how much I tweaked the volume controls, or fiddled with the headphones, it was impossible to hear any dialogue at all.

Rant over. Flying is a necessary evil for those who don't have time to take a leisurely boat-trip. I just wish the air-line companies would get their act together. (I wonder how often their executives travel in Economy class, just to understand the horror of the experience for their customers).

Anyway, having arrived at Kotoka (Accra), I was warmly greeted by Bishop Matthias, who had travelled by bus from to collect me. (His car had been in Accra for repairs...repairs which we were to discover on the journey back to Ho had not been completed).

I offered to drive because Matthias is suffering with immense neck pain at the moment, and finds driving very hard. We set off for Ho around 9.30pm, and arrived three hours later, in the middle of the night. It's been a long time since I've driven on country roads in the pitch black night, with cars and lorries coming in the opposite direction (mostly with their lights on full beam, while one's own lights are giving out only the power of a couple of candles). But we made it without any incidents, for which we thanked God on our arrival.

One real challenge of Ghanaian roads is that the majority of towns and villages along the route try to slow down the traffic by placing 'sleeping policemen' in the road. These are horizontal ridges, around 3 inches tall, which tend to shake the car to pieces if not spotted in time. Few of them are signposted, and only a very few are painted with white paint (and one is often being blinded by traffic coming from the other direction). So one tends to spend a fair percentage of the journey praying that the last 'sleeping policeman', just passed over at speed, has not shaken loose something vital to the car's operation!

Unfortunately, the Bishop's ancient Toyota Land-ranger has definitely seen better days. The engine makes a rather worrying knocking-sound if one tries to accelerate beyond a snail's-pace. In addition, the driver's window (needed for frequent toll-road payments) can only be opened by squeezing two bare wires together with one's fingers. I initially found the experience of electrical sparks between my fingers to be a bit disconcerting...but soon got used to getting a mild electric shock every time we needed to wind the window down!

On arrival at Ho, the Bishop directed me to a local Hotel, insisting that honoured guests stay in hotels, not in homes. I had said that I was more than happy to sleep on a floor in his home to save money, but Matthias insisted that this is the Ghanaian way. It is a matter of pride, he tells me; guests should be given every possible comfort and convenience.

The Hotel is a large complex, and even has a swimming pool. (I wish I'd brought my swimming trunks!). The rooms are clean and air-conditioned. So I spent a very pleasant first night. Looking to the future, when I hope to bring a group from my Deanery, the hotel would seem to have the makings of a very suitable base.

After a reasonable night's sleep, I breakfasted on egg, bacon, beans and 'butter-bread' - a Ghanaian sweet-bread which I am rather partial to. I then had a couple of hours to kill before the arranged meeting time with Matthias, so went for a stroll around the streets near the hotel, just to get a feel for Ho as a place.

Ho seems similar to other towns I have visited in Uganda and Ghana. Small enterprises line the streets, selling all manner of goods. Everything can be bought here, from second hand electrical items to food, clothes and hardware. Ho does strike me as slightly more ordered than some towns I've seen, at least in this quarter. The people are friendly, and tend to smile as they pass you on the street. The taxis are slightly less aggressive at trying to get you into their car than those I've encountered in Cape Coast.

Matthias arrived around 10am, and we made our way to his house via a tour of the major educational institutions of Ho.

The City is well known throughout Ghana for the high quality of its secondary and vocational education, including a large and successful polytechnic. The Roman Catholic Church has a vast complex of schools, as does the Presbyterian Church. Both have long, historic foundations in Ho, having been established during the colonial era when this part of the country was under German administration. As a consequence, the Catholic and Presbyterian churches are strong and powerful in the area.

In contrast, the Anglican Church is tiny. The Cathedral of Ho is a very small church indeed, in the grounds of a church-owned primary school. One is almost tempted to wonder why the Anglican Church does not simply retreat from Ho, and leave the task of the Gospel to the other, vastly stronger churches. However, as Bishop Matthias himself said this morning, "Our task is to preach the Gospel and we do it in partnership with the other churches". Matthias has also said that despite the size of the cathedral and congregation, it is very important for the Anglican Church to have an active presence in Ho. This is the administrative capital of the Volta region, and here is where all the politicians of influence in the area have their homes and offices. Matthias' engagement with such people and institutions means that the Anglican Church is well thought of in the area, and definitely 'punches above its weight'. Matthias has been the chair of the regional education committee, and is sought-after for many other influential committees. The Church, then, acts as salt and light to the secular institutions.

On arrival at Matthias' modest house (known as Bishopscourt) I set about unpacking my bulging suitcases. I had brought various electronic gadgets for Matthias, to aid him in his ministry – including a battery powered loudspeaker system which will help him to continue preaching even when the power goes off! We then spent a bit of time trying to sort out some of the knocking noises coming from Matthias' engine (without much success!), before having a tour of the Cathedral and surrounding school.

This afternoon, after a lunch of delicious home-cooked food from Lucy (Matthias' wife) we headed off to Worawora, and to the retreat centre where I would be leading the pre-ordination retreat for Ho's new ordinands.

Our journey to the retreat house took around three hours. We have definitely 'retreated' from civilization as I know it! The last hour of the journey was over unmade roads, made treacherous by recent rains, with giant pot-holes ready to swallow our vehicle's tyres! I now understand, without any difficulty whatsoever, why a large '4 by 4' car is essential for Matthias' ministry. Some of the roads I have driven along today could simply not have been passed in a normal car!

The Retreat Centre is called the 'Foyer de Charitie'. It is a Roman Catholic establishment, which nestles in the middle of a valley, surrounded by tall mountains, and with a rushing stream flowing through the centre and then over a dramatic waterfall. The Sisters who live here gave us a very warm welcome, despite the fact that the electricity has failed. This journal is being typed by candle-light, using my computer's battery! A charming mixture of the old world and the new.

I confess to having felt a little nervous about meeting the ordinands, and leading their retreat. Coming from another culture altogether, I wonder what I can offer them by way of inspiration. It was also rather interesting to meet four young men with whom I'm going to spend the next four/five days in the dark (as there is only the occasional hour or two of power from the National Grid!). However, they are a charming bunch, and they have quickly made me feel at home. We sat in the light of a single candle, sharing brief life-stories with each other. I won't share their stories here, because what passed

193

between us is confidential. Suffice to say that I have met Selin, Macarphuy, Angelo and Dennis and already think of them as friends.

I go to bed, by candlelight, looking forward to celebrating the Mass with my new friends in the morning, and to spending more time listening to their stories and sharing mine.

29th August to 1st September 2012

The last few days have had a gentle and predictable rhythm which has been very soothing for the soul. We have lived, effectively, as a monastic community. We have had five services per day (morning, midday, evening and night prayers, plus a Mass every mid-morning). Around that structure, plus meals of traditional Ghanaian food, we have met to talk about the life and role of deacons and priests. Together we have considered strategies for mission, and how to sustain the ordinands' ministries, and their membership of the worldwide church. It's been a wonderful few days, of deepening friendships and sustaining patterns of worship. One could almost wish to live like this every day. But, the 'real world' calls us back.

Sunday 2nd September 2012

We left at 6.30am this morning, just after sunrise and 'departure photos', in the hope of getting to Worawora (pronounced 'Raa-raa') in time for the Bishop to give his 'Charge' to the ordinands before the service would begin at 8.30am. Unfortunately, we had car-trouble along the way. One of the brakes on the Bishop's car (which I had borrowed to get us to and from the Retreat) started to 'bind' on the wheel...causing some rather distressing screeches! The car was fully loaded – because three of the ordinands' wives (and one child) had joined us yesterday. There were therefore nine of us, with all our luggage, jammed into the Land-ranger. For about 40 minutes we were forced to travel extremely slowly, over what I dubbed, in Jeremy Clarkson-style, 'the Worst road in the *Wooorld*!' I think that all the use of brakes to negotiate gaping potholes had probably heated-up the brake pads so much that one of them got stuck on the wheel.

Just at that point, the heavens opened, and the rain came falling in sheets out of the sky. I got out of the car to see if I could detect what was making the horrible noise. I got drenched to the skin, but to no avail. After a phone-call to the Bishop (to see if he had heard such screeching before and might know what the cause was) we decided to try to try to reverse back up the road to a house we had seen, to see if they might know a local mechanic. With just a few feet of reverse motion, the brake mercifully came free and we were able to make our way on to Worawora.

The Bishop's car, by the way, really is a death-trap! The engine bangs loudly at anything over a couple of thousand revs, and it has no power to climb up hills. Every hill is encountered with a mixture of hope, prayer, and very gentle footwork! The tyres are nearly bald, and the suspension makes some truly horrendous noises. The headlights are like candles, and point in all the wrong directions; the difference between full and dipped beam is frankly laughable – as I have discovered on numerous night driving occasions. (It is impossible to avoid driving at night, given the vast distances that the Bishop has to travel to be seen and to support his parishes). The car is about 12 years old, and has done over 170,000 miles. But without it, the Bishop quite simply could not do his job. His territory is far too vast and far too remote in places to consider any other form of transport.

We arrived at Worawora only about 40 minutes late, which no-one seemed to mind very much. Transport difficulties are a fact of life in Ghana, and everyone is very sanguine about them. A congregation had gathered in the church, and under surrounding canopies, made up of Synod members from all over the Diocese. (They had been meeting as a Synod while we were on retreat). As we pulled up into the churchyard, we could hear the sound of people already singing and praising God. The 'Diocesan Choir' (made up of choristers from all around the area) was practicing in another house next door. There was music and laughter and chaos all around. Wonderful!

Another Diocesan Priest, Fr Prosper, grabbed the ordinands for prayer around the car bonnet as soon as we arrived. He grasped them in a fatherly bear-hug, and together they prayed with arms around each other's shoulders. I wondered whether Fr Prosper was worried that this foreigner had not done enough praying with his friends already during the retreat!

The Bishop took us into a private room and gave his charge to the ordinands and their wives. By convention, the Bishop's charge is confidential to the ordinands, so suffice to say he spoke to them of John 15 v 16, reminding them that Christ had called them and appointed them to go and bear fruit in his name.

We then took part in an enormous procession into the church. The procession included the Diocesan Choir (about 50 choristers I would guess) followed by the 'Knights of the Order of St Jude' (a ceremonial Order inherited from the Roman Catholic Church) with swords drawn. Then came the clergy of the Diocese (around 10) and the Altar Party (Crucifer and Acolytes), and finally the ordinands, myself, the Archdeacon, and the Bishop. A guard of honour was provided by the Guild of the Good Shepherd (a fellowship of mainly women who pray together and care for the sick and disabled in the parish). Each of them held a wooden Shepherd's crook which they formed into an arch over the Procession. At the West door of the church, the Bishop knelt in prayer, and then 'censed' the congregation with the thurible. Then a slow and stately procession took place down the centre aisle, while holy water was splashed by the Archdeacon on the congregation.

This was the grand commencement of a service which lasted for five and a half hours! If I start to recount all the service at the same level of detail I've just used for the opening procession, this will become a very long account indeed! So, I'll confine myself to a few observations.

Like other Ghanaian services I've taken part in, the service was an eclectic blend of (to me) very old fashioned Anglo-Catholic worship, combined with sudden explosions of loud and energetic local music and customs. Very ancient Anglican hymns and chants are sung very slowly, and there is a great deal of choreography used to celebrate the Eucharistic elements of the service. In such a setting, however, which is unbelievably hot, with an odd assortment of vestments and worship paraphernalia, and an almost casual regard for the choreography itself, the whole thing has a unique and yet slightly wonderful 'haphazard' feel about it.

A few key images stick in my mind. The church itself has a rusty tin roof, which bounces the sound around all the time. There is never silence, because the noise of rusty old ceiling fans combines with the chatter of people outside the open windows and doors.

Visually, the Altar and Sanctuary were rather interesting. The east end of the church is dominated by a five-foot tall picture of a very European-looking Jesus, exposing his Sacred Heart. It is surrounded by coloured light bulbs which are lit during the service at the Eucharistic prayer. The picture itself is notable for the number of paint drips which are all over it! It appears that the last time someone painted the East wall, they didn't bother to take down the picture; they just tried to paint around it and didn't seem to care very much that Jesus was covered in emulsion!

The rest of the Sanctuary was largely empty, except for a proliferation of plastic patio chairs, in various colours, which served as stalls for the clergy.

Services tend to be long in Ghana for a number of reasons. The first is the speed of singing, especially of old Anglican hymns and chants. I imagine that this is because English (especially prayer-book English) is not the native tongue of anyone present, so it takes time to get one's lips around unfamiliar words. (English serves as the National Language because there are so many other tribal languages in use. It is helpful for the country as a whole to have an external language as a National one. If any of the native tribal tongues were chosen for this role, there would naturally be uproar from the other tribes!).

When traditional liturgies and ancient hymns are in use, the only people who seem to be genuinely engaged are the choir and clergy. The rest of the congregation seems to use these moments for chat. They seem clearly not to be engaged to any great extent – quite probably because most of the language being used is only barely understandable. I can't blame them at all! On the other hand, as soon as a local language is used, or a tribal dance rhythm is employed, the congregation transforms itself from bored and listless to being joyously praise-centred.

There is a dilemma for the church here. Its theology is communicated through the liturgy, to a great extent. Simple praise songs, however enthusiastically sung, cannot give congregations the depth of meaning offered by the liturgy. And yet, at present, there is a 'disconnect'. The full depth of theology in play is not actually getting through. I don't know what the answer to this dilemma is. This is not my country, nor my context. But I suspect that an offering of more modern English liturgies, and some more modern hymns and songs, would be appreciated by the majority of Ghanaian Anglicans. (16th Century English is tough…even for an Englishman!) There is also, perhaps, a chance of re-interpreting traditional tribal forms of worship – 'Christianising' them, as the church has done for centuries in other places. The imposition of a restrained English liturgy (with all its solemnity) on a naturally joyous and vivacious population seems to be a very difficult trick to pull off. That very difficulty might account for the proliferation of independent churches (with their sometimes highly dubious interpretations of the Bible) all around the country. Churches which offer a good 'song and dance' that is close to local culture tend to gain more traction in communities than those, like the Anglican Church, which essentially imports a culture from elsewhere.

The second factor in the length of services is the need to translate sermons and other important speeches into at least two other languages. In our case today, my sermon was translated into Ewe (roughly-pronounced 'Ébey') and 'Akan' (also known as Twi). This takes time, and significantly reduces the amount that can be said by a preacher (and the depth to which he or she is able to go).

A third factor is the length of time given to offertories and processions. There were two offertories today (one for the training of future ordinands, and one for the general needs of the Diocese). In both cases, a long and complicated dance takes place as each worshipper 'jiggles' their way to the front of the church along a long procession, to give their gift. The offertories today were accompanied by a frankly deafening blast of trumpets, trombones and drums from a sort of local marching band which had everyone up and dancing energetically.

Some other notable features of the service, included the extremely, and wonderfully, emotional way in which the newly ordained Deacons and Priest were greeted by the congregation and by their now fellow clergy. To an Englishman, used to a stiff handshake and muttered compliment in such circumstances, it was quite humbling to see the absolute outpouring of joy for each of the newly ordained. Each one was enthusiastically hugged and touched. In one case, an older priest knelt in front of the newest priest to receive that priest's first blessing. Tears flowed easily and without apology. It was truly sight to see.

At the end of the service, five and half hours later, the congregation poured out into the churchyard and compound to share food and fellowship together. However, such celebrations did not last long. Within an hour or so, people began to pack up and make their way to the various minibuses and cars which were lined up to take them home. No doubt many had very long journeys ahead of them, and on Ghanaian roads, those are even longer! Minibuses poured out of the compound, packed solid with passengers. Windows were opened, and handkerchiefs waved, while singing continued all the way up the road.

In due course, with a farewells said, we made our way off the Bishop's car – hoping to get at least some of our journey completed in daylight. (Evening falls around 6pm, every day of the year in Ghana). The car was once again loaded to capacity. Not only did it contain the Bishop, his wife Lucy and me, we also gave a lift to the Bishop's son and his son-in law – plus our entire luggage! In addition, the Bishop had to take back the robes of the Diocesan choir, and all the office equipment he had had to bring to run basic administration of the Synod (laser printer, computer, and so on). The poor old car was packed to the gunnels once again! I had a rather anxious moment when I realized that my laptop was buried under three suitcases and assorted choir robes, but it was quickly rescued by Prosper, the Bishop's son.

On the way home, we encountered a priest on a motorcycle, who had broken down. Fr Simon, like many of the priests of the Diocese, is the fortunate beneficiary of a motor-bike to get around his parish and wider Diocese. These motorcycles can be bought for around £700, and they make a huge difference to the ability of priests to get around their mainly rural parishes. Motor-bikes are by far the best way of navigating the endless potholes of Ghanaian road (although riding them in the torrential rain and the mud is no fun). Fr Simon had a loose chain, which no matter how many times he refitted it, would keep coming off. Unfortunately, having no tools with us or him, there was nothing we could do to help him, so had to leave him in the hands of some other priests who had also stopped to help. (Later in, in the city of Kpando, I learned that they had managed to purloin a pick-up truck from somewhere, and had transported him and his motorbike to the Archdeacon's house for repairs. Ghanaians are nothing if not creative when it comes to finding solutions to problems).

I took over the driving of the car from the Bishop, just before darkness fell. His on-going problems with neck, shoulder and arm-pain are quite severe, and he needs to rest whenever possible. I then had the challenge of getting us back to Ho...

a) without damaging the car in a giant pothole (or by running over a sleeping policeman at speed)

b) while largely having to guess where the road was in the face of oncoming headlights (many of which stayed on full-beam no matter how much they were flashed),

c) and at the same time hoping not to kill one of the many pedestrians lining the edges of the roads!

It was terrifying, but exhilarating all at the same time. Driving around the well-lit streets of Portsmouth at night will never be the same again!

4th September 2012

Last night was quite an adventure. I went to bed around ten o'clock, but was woken at one in the morning by some loud door-banging on the part of another hotel resident. Not being able to get back to sleep, I did some diary-writing; then went back to bed around half past three. But I still couldn't sleep. The national grid power was turned off. National electricity rationing, or 'load sharing' as it is known, means that this is a frequent occurrence in Ghana. The hotel generator is not large enough (I assume) to run the air conditioning. It was a hot sticky night, and I slept very badly. (Some Ghanaians complain that the problem is caused by the Government selling its adequate hydro-electric power to neighbouring countries. Ghana, apparently, has enough generating capacity for its own population, but the frequent need for hard currency for other national projects results in electricity being sold across the border. This leads to frequent black-outs all around the country).

I had, however, just about managed to get an hour or so of sleep, when I was woken at a quarter to six in the morning by the loud noise of a television, coming through my bedroom wall. I got up to discover that the early morning cleaner had put the television on in the Reception area, next to my room, and left the door open to the corridor. I stomped into reception, and found that she was not even watching it! She was outside the Reception door, sweeping up. I turned off the TV, at which point her quizzical face appeared at the doorway, wondering what I was doing.

Switching on a TV seems to be a sort of divine right in Ghana. Everywhere you go, in restaurants, waiting rooms, bars and hotel Receptions, the TV is on...either showing football, Nigerian and Ghanaian soap operas, or some of the most awful religious broadcasting I have seen. A certain Christian TV station, for example, is said to regularly ask its viewers to put their hands on the TV to receive God's blessing. Or they are asked to put a jug of water on the TV, which will then be made holy by the TV Pastor, and can be used for healing miracles. The schedule is packed with apparent testimonies of healings received in this way and appeals for the faithful to send money for the station's on-going ministry. I leave the reader to draw their own conclusions about how much of this enterprise is truly holy, and how much of it is done for profit in a theologically illiterate society.

I explained to the young cleaner that I had been hoping to sleep until seven o'clock, after an exhausting previous day. She looked very puzzled, as if the idea of sleeping beyond sunrise was incomprehensible to her. (Perhaps it was. She is clearly an early riser herself!). "But," she said, "You have to get up for breakfast". I then reminded her that the hotel served breakfast until 9am, and that I certainly didn't need three and a half hours to get up and dressed! I explained as kindly as I could (through gritted teeth) that I was a guest of the hotel, and had paid good money for a quiet night's peace.

I went back to my room, but was now fully awake. I decided that this room was not working for me. I been disturbed in my sleep by other guests and the staff member. Worse still, I had tried to work in the room on the previous day, but found it impossible. The part of the hotel in which my room was situated is currently under construction, and all through the day, overhead, came the noise of banging and scraping. It was very difficult to work in the room at all.

Being now fully awake, I therefore determined to ask for another room in the hotel (having also noticed some more private chalets in one corner of the compound). I therefore went to the main Reception, and asked for a chalet. The Receptionist kindly obliged and we went to view a chalet room. Unfortunately, (although these are the most expensive rooms in the hotel), none of the chalets had a working shower-head-holder—so I have had to choose between a better night's rest (hopefully) and the inconvenience of having to wash with one hand while holding the shower with the other.

I have written to the Manageress of the hotel. Hopefully, she will accept that the inconveniences I have so far encountered will merit a discount on the chalet room-hire rate. She hasn't spoken to me yet about it...but I did have some satisfaction (during my breakfast) in observing her holding my letter in one hand, while railing at some of the staff! I will see what, if anything, she offers later.

Around 9am I set off with the Bishop to take his car to the mechanic. First, I dropped him at the hospital, so that he could get some more medication. The poor fellow is clearly in some real pain. Having dropped him off, I drove to the garage, and then set about waiting for the car to be fixed.

2.30pm.

After a stroll round the market, a short nap at the hotel (to make up for last night!) some lunch and a chat with the Bishop in the mechanic's waiting room...we are still waiting for the car to be fixed. The mechanic has been unable to diagnose the problem with the engine. It still bangs and knocks at anything over tick-over speed. We are going to have to go to the Toyota main dealer in Accra to use their diagnostic machine. The mechanic did manage to fix a wiring problem with two of the car's headlights, but now two other lights have stopped working! The Bishop and I are therefore patiently waiting for the newest problem to be fixed.

The manageress of the hotel has, by the way, now spoken to me and graciously offered a discount on my chalet room.

4pm. The car's lights are all working! Halleluiah! We are now leaving in search of a switch (for the bare wires currently used to operate the driver's window) and to find a car-wash and fuel to prepare the car for tomorrow's trip to Kpando

6pm. Our efforts to find a suitable switch failed. There is very little in the way of auto-electric shops in Ho. Our only present alternative to mild electric shocks when we operate the window is a complete new switch unit from Toyota, at a cost of £200! We are going to continue to try to find an alternative solution!

However, we did find a car wash, where the car was enthusiastically jet-washed by a young man. He clearly didn't know much about how cars actually operate, not least because of his enthusiasm to jet-wash the engine (with all its delicate electronics). I managed to persuade him that this was not a good idea. He also jetted water up the exhaust pipe at one point, but he had done it before I could stop him. I just hope the water doesn't collect for too long in the silencer, and rust the thing solid!

At the end of the procedure, the young man charged us eight Ghana Cedis (about two pounds and fifty pence, in Sterling) for his efforts, but then had the cheek to then ask if he could keep the change from the ten Cedi note we gave him. The Bishop patiently explained that he had been about to let the young man keep the change anyway, but that it was not polite to ask to keep it. Begging in such a way, the Bishop explained to the man, demeaned the young man, and the gift. In the end, though, the soft-hearted Bishop relented and gave him the extra two Cedis.

Later. We made our way back to the Bishop's house, where after doing battle with a few nasty bugs on his computers, I managed to successfully install a back-up service on the Bishop's two computers. He has an ancient laptop for general administration and a little (equally ancient) netbook which he uses for administration on the road. Neither had any kind of backup system, and the Bishop has been fearing for a long time that, given the age of both machines, a lot of important Diocesan documents will be lost one day.

I went back to the hotel for an early night, around 9.30pm, ready for tomorrow's 6am start.

5th September 2012

Today has been the first of a series of 'parish visits' - the main reason for my being in Ghana in the first place (apart from strengthening ties with, and offering support to, Bishop Matthias). We left at about 7.15am for the journey to Kpando—about 2 hours' drive from Ho. The roads were much as before: stretches of smooth tarmac, punctuated by sudden and unexpected craters in the road.

It is impossible to miss every pot-hole on Ghanaian roads. Sometimes I find myself swerving to avoid one, only to clonk the car over another. (The Bishop has his own saying about these pot-holes: "miss one, get two or three free". Once again, the vital need for the Bishop to have a rugged vehicle was underlined, and the urgent need for it to be functioning more adequately was re-enforced). Nevertheless, I find that I quite enjoy driving these roads. There is a level of challenge that is no longer available on the well-lit, well-maintained roads of the UK. One finds all one's senses are alert in way that is often missing on safe roads!

Arriving in Kpando at around 9.30am, we first made our way to the 'Mission House' - the home of the local Vicar, The Venerable Joseph Kingsley Bentum. As well as being the local parish priest for Kpando, Fr Joseph also serves as Archdeacon for the Diocese, Rural Dean for the Kpando area, and Vicar General at any time when the Bishop (as Presiding Bishop of Ghana) is out of the country. He is also a teacher at the Anglican School! All of these roles are carried out from a very modest little house, and on the back of a 125cc motorcycle, which he rides in all weathers all around the Diocese. (I noticed that for security, the poor man has to keep his motorcycle in his living room!)

Motorcycles are a really vital tool for Ghanaian priests. Unable to afford more than one aged car (for the Bishop), £700 motorcycles provide a basic means of getting around the Diocese, and of course the large rural parishes being supported here. In some ways they may even be preferable to a car, because it is easier to navigate pot-holes on a motorcycle. But, on the other hand, there is very little carrying capacity (for vestments, books and the like) and one is exposed to all kinds of weather (including the torrential rains which fall from time to time).

The Archdeacon is currently in a poor state of health. His doctor is not sure what is causing his extreme fatigue, but the common view (including that of the Bishop) is that the poor man has simply been overworked. During the last two years, while the Bishop has been Presiding Bishop, Fr Joseph has been carrying a great deal of the burden of administering and supporting the Diocese, including pastoral support for Worawora following the death of their priest. The Synod which finished last Sunday seems to have finished him off as well! So, after serving us some breakfast, Fr Joseph stayed at home for some rest, while we went on to visit St Patrick's Anglican Village.

Before describing the visit to St Patrick's, a little background to the area might be useful. In colonial times, the Volta Region was a German protectorate (while the rest of Ghana was held by the British). A lasting legacy of those days is the strength of the Roman Catholic (RC) Church. All over the area (as I've previous mentioned with regard to Ho) one finds substantial RC facilities—churches, schools and hospitals in the main. The RC Church is to be congratulated for their on-going commitment to the people of this area—it is truly an impressive legacy. The lives of millions of people in the area are substantially improved as a result. However, the local view seems to be that with such a large infrastructure to maintain, the RC Church has become a bureaucracy in many ways. Some of the personal touches made possible in a smaller, more relational context are missing. As a result, some RC worshippers apparently feel disconnected from the church; some are turning to other churches, including the Anglican church, for a sense of community.

Around 30 years ago, there was a violent uprising against what was perceived as 'heavy-handed' bureaucracy from the RC hierarchy, and a significant number of worshippers left the church en masse. For a while they formed an informal break-away church, but still considered themselves Catholics. They were known as the 'No-Fathers' (in contrast to the 'Yes-Fathers' who remained within the Church). After a while, the 'No-Fathers' did some research into other churches and found that the Anglican Church was Catholic in its traditions but democratic in its governance. They approached the then Bishop of the Anglican Diocese with a request to be formed into a new Anglican Parish. It was a difficult decision for the then Bishop to make. Disaffected worshippers from another Church do not always make ideal new members. They have a tendency to want to do things their own way. But the then Bishop decided that this was a pastoral need which he could fulfil, and so agreed to form a new Anglican Parish in Kpando.

The result of this history is that Kpando has a substantial body of Anglican worshippers, who have set about the task of building a new Parish with enthusiasm. Relationships between the Anglican and RC Churches have been a bit strained over the last couple of decades, but there are increasing signs that the two churches are beginning to work together in the common work of the Gospel. The present Anglican and RC Bishops have a good working relationship.

In Kpando itself, the Anglican Church has acquired a large plot of land, known as 'The Anglican Village'. It essentially comprises a school (with about 380 pupils), with some ancillary buildings. Worship takes place in long school classroom block (and is therefore a multi-function space). Work is underway on a new Vicarage, being built brick by brick as money becomes available. The eventual intention is that Fr Joseph (or whoever may be the Vicar at that time) will move into the Anglican Village, and have a daily presence there. In time, other homes and infrastructure may be built to truly create a feeling of a Village. The Parish has already benefited from financial support from the Portsmouth Diocese, especially through the parish of Clanfield.

Our morning worship (an Episcopal Mass) started at around ten o'clock. At around seventy in number, the congregation was not large (although significantly larger than one might expect for a Wednesday morning Mass in the UK!). I'm told that on Sundays, the church is packed solid with around five hundred worshippers. It is the largest congregation in the Diocese. The congregation was made up of older students from the school, and about 20 core members of the Parish. Given the presence of the School children, we had some fun together—including my taking photos of them from the pulpit (explaining that I wanted to show some pictures in the UK). I had to explain that smiles and waves would be appreciated. Ghanaians have a habit of not smiling in photographs, and of deliberately looking formal and dignified.

Here are a few other observations about the Service:

The music was led by a small but very proficient choir; a small selection of the five choirs currently ministering in the parish. Most of their music was unaccompanied, because the organist (a Diocesan Catechist) was not really up to giving more than the occasional supporting note. As a result, the choir sang really beautifully, in close harmony.

On our way into church (in the traditional long, slow, procession) I noticed a group of ladies sat in a circle outside the church, apparently in prayer. The Bishop explained that this is group of Anglicans who have been somewhat influenced by some of the more Pentecostal churches in the area. As a result, they have a tendency to want to focus on intercessory prayer—'naming and claiming the Victory'- rather than participating in the worship of the rest of the community. They are a little bit of a challenge for the local congregation, as they tend to look critically on the rest of the church, and tend to undermine the practice of the rest of the community. Certainly by positioning themselves for prayer just at the West door of the church where the Bishop was passing, they certainly seemed to be trying to make a 'political' statement. I was reminded of UK churches where such splinter groups sometimes form around the teachings of an external pastor to the church (or after small group visits to 'mountain-top' experiences like Greenbelt, Soul Survivor or Walsingham). Such groups are capable of breathing new life into churches, if the new insight they bring can be incorporated wisely into the life of a church. But they can also sow dissent and cause splits. It's a tricky situation, common to churches in Ghana and the UK (and something the New Testament writers knew only too well).

The service was short by comparison with other Ghanaian services I have attended...only about an hour and a half including the translated sermon. My translator was Father Fred, a former Roman Catholic priest from the area, now an Anglican. Fr Fred has in fact lived in the UK for more than 20 years. (He was in Ghana for the funeral of his late Mother). As a result, he understood me easily, and was able to inject humour into his translations of what I was saying, interpreting my weird British humour in a way that was accepted by the congregation! Together in this way (and adapting to the presence of a large body of students) we talked about the importance of

Teachers—and especially focusing on the Teacher of Teachers and Lord of Lords, Jesus Christ.

After the service, the Bishop and I went for a tour of the school. It was break-time for the students, and many were deployed in cutting the grass in the school playing field. Even very small children were wielding 2-foot long machetes (i.e. flat-bladed swords!) for cutting the grass. Health and Safety officials in the UK would have had heart-attacks, but in Ghana these are essential tools for clearing ground, and their use is therefore taught to even the youngest children.

We looked into a couple of class-rooms out of curiosity. With the children at play, and the teachers on break, there was not a great deal to see. However, I was struck by two things: first, the lack of resources. Other than simple desks and a blackboard, there were no other visible resources to aid with teaching. No text books, no paper, no computers, nothing. Secondly I was struck by seeing one student asleep on a bench, while the rest of her friends were playing. Clearly the child was exhausted. But what was the cause? The Bishop offered two distinct possibilities: perhaps the child had had an early start to do farm chores, or to sell goods in the market before even starting school. Or perhaps she was suffering from malaria, which is the cause of much misery and extreme fatigue in the area.

Following our tour of the school, and a chat with the Head teacher and his Deputy, we made our way over to inspect the new Vicarage.

The Vicarage is very much a 'work in progress'. To look round it, we had to walk between a forest of bamboo poles which were used to form and support the concrete super-structure of the building. When finished, the building will comprise about eight rooms, built in a square around a large central living space. After an office, kitchen, pantry, bathroom and toilet are installed, the building will have about four modest bedrooms for the Vicar and his family. In due course, it is hoped to build a second story which will act as a Mission House for various guests, trainees and needy folks to stay.

After our tour, we returned to the Archdeacon's house for some lunch, and for the Bishop and I to have little nap in our chairs! After an early start, a long morning's drive, a service and tour in the heat of Ghana, followed by a meal, we were both in need of 40 winks!

However, we managed to do so separately; so each of us got a cheeky photo of the other having our naps!

After taking our rest, we went out to visit another part of the area. First we went to a distant rural village, Bame, where an 'out-station' church has been in operation for the last 30 years. However, the community there is so poor that the church building (dedicated to St Thomas) is just a few palm branches spread over a wooden frame, with a rudimentary altar at one end. Unfortunately, heavy rains on the previous night had destroyed the roof, so all that greeted the Bishop and I on our arrival was a collapsed structure. The local Catechist (Gabriel) explained that he had planned to re-build the roof today, using the labour of his local parishioners. Unfortunately, however, a 'community labour' edict had been issued this morning, to which all his parishioners were compelled to respond.

It was really very humbling to see the facilities of these fellow-Anglicans. In my Deanery we have beautiful worship spaces, with soaring roof-lines, and well equipped churches. (We also, though, sometimes struggle to find people who can maintain our buildings!). But this new church, formed in the middle of nowhere, up a dusty track from Kpando, really did feel like missionary work on the edge. There is real excitement here about what God is doing: binding communities together in a common endeavour. The Bishop does his very best to support these rural and desperately poor churches. Whenever both the condition of his car and his purse allow he travels for miles and miles to support such parishes. On Palm Sunday 2011, for example, he came to visit at this church, and lead an Episcopal Palm procession, through the street of the village to the site of the out-station church.

Humbled by seeing this church, and meeting its Catechist, we went on to our third church of the day. This turned out to be a brand new church building, designated St Mark's—so I was immediately attracted to the place (because St Mark is the patron of one of the three churches I serve as Team Rector in Portsmouth). It was about 4.30pm by the time we arrived, and the local congregation had begun to gather. There were only about 40 people in attendance (again, it was, for them a midweek service) though a number of others trickled in throughout the service. The church is built out of a concrete frame, with breeze-block in-fills. It has a tin roof, and as yet no electricity.

But it is a large structure which, I guess, could hold about 120 worshippers when full. The local congregation is already thinking about how to expand the building—even before this one is finished!

We took the opportunity of this service to test out a new battery-powered PA system I had brought from the UK for the Bishop. After a few adjustments, the system worked really well, and allowed both me and the Bishop to be heard by even the deafest among the somewhat elderly congregation. I had learned something of the history of this particular congregation before arriving, so was able to use my sermon to congratulate them on being the one congregation in the entire Diocese which has been responsible in recent years for supplying four new priests/deacons to the church. This has been a sacrifice for them, because all four talented men have been sent to serve elsewhere in the Diocese. But, it was also a mark of their commitment to sharing Good News of God's Kingdom 'to the four corners of the Earth'.

This congregation is clearly very close to the Bishop's heart. It is one that he has particularly nourished, and the first of the many 'out-stations' of his various parishes to have built their own church during his period in office. (Out-stations are generally the kind of congregations which worship under a shady tree, or as I saw earlier, under a simple palm-covered wooden frame.) St Mark's is a significant achievement for this very much missionary Diocese. It puts a new church building, redolent of a community working together, into the very heart of village. It stands as a sign of new life and new hope for all the people of that village.

The Bishop was really excited to be able to tell the congregation that new funds for their building project were on their way. Through a process known as Indaba, the Bishop has been linked to a Diocese in South Africa. They have sent money as a gift to the St Mark's congregation which will enable them to complete their church; plastering the walls and installing doors and electricity. It is then hoped that they will be able to at least build the foundations of a Mission House/Vicarage, which will eventually enable a Parish Priest to be appointed and housed in the community. There was much rejoicing at this news. The congregation were also very excited when I explained that St Mark's was close to my own heart, and that I hoped that in due course a link could be established with St Mark's

Portsmouth—subject to the agreement of both church committees of course.

Darkness was falling as we set off for home after the service, and after the presentation of a gift of some traditional Ghanaian clothes for me and my wife. The new lights on the car proved to be a significant improvement on the 'candle-power' of previous night journeys. But there is still more that could be done. Tomorrow we head for Accra to get a computer diagnosis of the engine problems on the car, and also to track down some used spare parts for other issues. We are to be accompanied by a mechanic from the Toyota garage in Ho, who has asked if we can leave at 6am. So another early night is definitely called for!

6th September 2012

Today has been quite an adventure. We started at 6am for Accra, the car being driven on the first leg by our mechanic from Ho. He quickly realised that the knocking and rattling we had been hearing from the engine was a result of imminent drive-shaft failure. So he drove as carefully as we have been doing for the entire journey. That meant, unfortunately, that over-taking was a near impossibility (as there was no additional power in the engine, and the damage to the drive-shaft could be catastrophic if pressed!). So much of the journey was made behind slower vehicles, usually belching out diesel smoke.

Right at the start of the journey, the mechanic attempted to raise the driver's window by squeezing together the wires hanging out of the door. But unfortunately, the wrong wires touched each other, resulting in a shower of sparks, and the complete failure of the entire window system, along with the air conditioning. So the whole journey to Accra (about 3 hours) was conducted with no air conditioning, and all but the driver's window shut. Through the open driver's window, however, came all the diesel fumes of the aforementioned slower vehicles, and the dust from the various dirt-roads we had to traverse. I cannot say that this was the most pleasant car journey I've ever had...but at least I've sweated-off a couple of pounds of excess weight!

Arriving in Accra, we made our way to the main Toyota dealer, and to a friend of our mechanic. He put a diagnostic computer onto the car and quickly established that there appears to be no immediate problem with the mechanical or electrical essentials of the engine. He told us that he believed the lack of power to be a problem with either the fuel pump, or the fuel line—so that when extra fuel was called for by the engine (for example when accelerating) insufficient fuel was being received. This at least gives our mechanic something to focus on back in Ho.

We then made our way to the spare parts market in Accra. It is an incredible place. It is a huge market, crammed with stalls selling just about any car part desired. Think of something the size of Camden Market in London, but with every stall piled high with batteries, drive-shafts, tyres and lights! As well as the stall-holders there are a number of young men who act as self-employed 'runners' around the market. They try to persuade customers to commission them to go and find the part required. They then set off around the market to locate the said part and bring it back to the customer. Obviously they charge a commission to both the customer and the stall holder for this service; the amount of which is the subject of noisy and protracted haggling.

The trick with haggling, I have discovered, is to offer about 10% of the price original asked for by the seller. You then haggle away until the seller or the buyer walks off saying that the price is either too high or too low (depending on the point of view). At this point, the remaining party shouts after the other that they may be prepared to adjust their price a little. Sometimes an agreement is reached, but often not. Sometimes the buyer or seller will find the other out some times later (as much as an hour or so later) once tempers have cooled. More negotiations can then take place. But the gap between what a seller wants and what a buyer is prepared to pay is sometimes unbridgeable.

On one occasion, for example, we were approached by some 'runners' who wanted to sell us some used tyres. We are sorely in need of tyres, as the Bishop's tyres are smooth and have no visible tread! But the tyres on offer were of a very low quality indeed. They were made of a very soft rubber; so soft that one could pick little pieces off the tyre with a finger-nail. So whilst I was interested in principle, for the right price, I could see that these tyres would not last long on the Bishop's punishing schedules. So I offered a very low price...around £50 per tyre. The seller wanted about £150 per tyre. But the gap between his expectation and mine was simply unbridgeable, so in the end he gave up and walked away. Later on, on a separate foray into the market, the Bishop was offered the self-same tyres by another seller, but again no reasonable price could be achieved.

Eventually, one of the local runners located the new electric-control unit we urgently needed to repair the window system on the car. We already knew (from Toyota) that a brand new unit would cost £200, so we were reasonably happy to haggle down to £50 for the used one we had located in the market. It was fitted and tested for us, there and then, by a local electrician. We also managed to locate two used drive-shafts in good condition, which the mechanic will fit back in Ho tomorrow. Unfortunately, the air conditioning system was still not working (the earlier shower of sparks had done something very weird to the system). In the end we were unable to locate any tyres within our available budget. By the end of tomorrow, the Ho Toyota garage will have done three days' work on the car, so we need to keep some funds in reserve to meet their bill.

Having had a reasonably successful trip to Accra, we set off for home around 4.30pm. Unfortunately, this meant catching the Accra rush-hour. I've driven in some pretty hairy situations in my life, but let me tell you, rush-hour in Accra is something else entirely. The whole system operates on the basis of 'every man for himself'. Every road junction is a little bit like driving around the Arc de Triumph in Paris, with cars coming from every direction. However, in addition one has to contend with pedestrians, motorcycles and traders' hand-carts being pushed in entirely the opposite direction! The total madness of driving in Accra is perhaps best illustrated by the following episode along the way:

Approaching one particular junction on a two-lane road, we found that the traffic was piling up. At first, the jam was caused by a lorry which had tried to join the traffic, by turning onto the road from the verge across both lanes, but then stalling and blocking them both. While he tried to get started again, the two lanes of traffic suddenly became four, as cars and lorries used the hard shoulder and the verge to go around the blocking vehicle. Unfortunately, by the time the lorry had got himself moving again, the road had become well and truly a four carriage-way road. This might have been ok, except for the fact that about 50 metres later on, there was a side road of cars who wanted to join the main flow. They were already blocking the hard shoulder, so suddenly, all the cars in the newly formed 'hard-shoulder lane' then tried to make their way back into the central lanes.

But, remember, the rule here is 'every man for himself' - so no-one was going to let the 'hard shoulder cheaters' (the outside-verge drivers) back into the flow of traffic. Quickly, the whole jam became solid. Cars were literally inching themselves into other lanes. Any sign of weakness (or moment of hesitation) from a driver in a legitimate lane was instantly exploited by the 'cheaters', who would wedge a corner of their bumper into the available six inches and then force their way into the lane. As a result, the attitude of 'legitimate lane' drivers was to drive virtually bumper to bumper, not leaving as much as a hair's breadth of space between cars. Drivers with passengers, like me, were goaded all the time by a chorus of approval from their passengers. "Go on...go on...don't let that cheater in! Closer...get closer to the car in front".

This of course was intolerable for the "hard-shoulder" and "outside verge" drivers, who then, following one of their number, employed a new strategy. Seeing that the side road, 50 metres ahead, was relatively free, the hard-shoulder drivers set off across an intervening field to attempt to get back onto the main road legitimately—by wedging themselves into the cars already queuing on the side road. They were not greeted with any warmer welcome there either. So now the road was entirely blocked, with cars inching their way forward and around each other from about four different directions. Some cars were still heading enthusiastically across the field, while others were just as determined to stop 'those cheaters' from getting ahead.

It was chaos. Utter chaos. I'm not entirely sure how I managed to manoeuvre the Bishop's rather large Toyota Land Cruiser through the middle of it unscathed! In order to edge the vehicle forward, bumper to bumper (goaded on by my enthusiastic passengers!) it was necessary to give little bursts of acceleration, followed immediately by sharp stabs of the brake pedal. My right foot was doing a sort of tap dance from accelerator to brake, over and over again! The real challenge, however, was to judge by how far the Bishop's car's rather spongy suspension would rock the car forward once a sharp stop had been executed. On more than one occasion, I was convinced that I had misjudged, and that the bull bars on the front of the Toyota would smash into the car in front. But, mercifully, we escaped from the melee unscathed!

I was, however, by then a little grumpy. I longed for a more British approach to such traffic chaos. 'Every man for himself' simply doesn't work as a collective strategy for solving such log-jams. In Britain, generally, there is an acceptance that when, say, four lanes reduce down to two, cars will merge 'in turn' into the reduced space. It's not a perfect solution (and I've sat in plenty of frustrating jams in the UK) but there is at least a sense of shared misery and a shared acceptance of the solution when the 'merge in turn' technique is applied.

Next came another bit of frustration. Through a mis-communication by my passengers, or a lack of attentiveness on my part, I tried to inch my way to the wrong exit on the roundabout. I believed that I had one more junction to go...millimetre by millimetre, and was attempting to position myself accordingly. But suddenly, my passengers told me to take the next exit, not the one after. So I then had to cross three lanes of traffic, wedging myself into gaps (doing just what I had been trying to stop others doing only minutes before!) to get off at the right exit. There was then a somewhat heated exchange between me, the mechanic and the Bishop each of us trying to repeat again what we had said, or what had been misunderstood by the other! Fortunately, we all realised that the issue was caused by way the English language is deployed by different nations and so no-one held on to any lasting grudges. After a few minutes of grumpy silence, we were quickly friends again!

The rest of the journey home was reasonably uneventful by comparison. There were a few tussles with 'cheaters' at various junctions, but we eventually got on the much quieter road to Ho. We now had only to contend with the appallingly adjusted headlights of oncoming vehicles for the next couple of hours. The only significant problem was that for some reason the new lights on the car were nowhere near as bright as one might have expected. Once again, I felt like I was driving with a couple of candles on the front of the car—a situation not helped by a shower of rain which fell on my dust-covered

215

windscreen. It was only when we finally arrived safely back at Ho that I realised why this had been. Three of the new light bulbs, fitted by some apprentices at the Ho garage, had come loose from their housings, and were dangling uselessly under the engine!!

As I conclude this portion of my Ghana Saga, I truly understand why Ghanaians (and Africans in general) routinely pray for 'journey mercies' and usually give thanks audibly at the end of a journey. African roads, and the standard of work of some local mechanics, are awesomely awful! Divine Protection is about the only safety-system on offer!

7th September 2012

Most of today was spent catching up with some essential tasks. I completed and uploaded the latest edition of this diary, and then spent the rest of the day with the Bishop and his family at their house. We reviewed the diary together, and then set about doing some more repairs to the Bishop's aging computer (always a time consuming process, but essential for his administrative needs). At the same time, the Bishop's car was back at the mechanic's shop, in the hope that he would be able to trace the diagnosed problem with the fuel system. Unfortunately, despite working on well beyond dark, they were unable to do so. The engine performance is now worse, if anything. It is extremely sluggish and a badly fitted fan-belt is now shrieking loudly. It will have to go back to the garage on Wednesday, when the mechanic says he will take it to Accra for another go with Toyota's diagnostic machine! I retired to bed relatively early (around 9.30pm) in anticipation of a four o'clock wake-up tomorrow.

8th September 2012

Having borrowed the car to get back to the hotel last night, I picked the Bishop up at five-thirty this morning, to begin our 'tour of the South'. We then coaxed the car for the three-hour trip to the outskirts of Accra, where we collected one of the Bishop's daughters who wanted to join us for the Diocese of Accra's ordination service. Unfortunately, we got a little lost after that! Outside of the mainly orderly centre, Accra is a vast jumble of bumpy dirt roads, and has no road-signs!

It took us about two hours of weaving through traffic, exploring various possible roads, and asking for (usually totally ineffective) directions. Eventually we arrived at "St Joseph's Maxi-Cathedral" around half past ten, where the service was already in full swing. We arrived just in time for the ordination of Deacons. Having been driving for five hours, I elected not to robe, but to loiter on the outskirts of the service (principally in the hope of being able to rest a little before we had to leave for our next engagement).

The Bishop however, joined a large number of other visiting Bishops in the Sanctuary. Accra is clearly the most influential and powerful diocese in the country at present. Unlike Bishop Matthias' own ordinations on the previous Sunday, there were episcopal visitors from all over Ghana to this service. In many cases (including Matthias') this was because Bishops had come to support ordinands whom they knew and previously supported for ordination. Being based in the capital city, Accra Diocese acts like a magnet for ordinands from all over the country. Many of them will serve as non-stipendiary priests while continuing in relatively well-paid Accra-based jobs. It was good to see and be able to greet both Bishop Daniel (Cape Coast) and Bishop Edmund (Dunkwa) whose brother was being ordained.

I was struck by a number of things both in and around the service, including:

First, although St Joseph's Maxi-Cathedral (as it is called) was large, it was not big enough for the immense number of folks who had assembled. Common to other large and lengthy Ghanaian services, this meant the erection of canopies all around the church. TV screens were provided for those who were outside.

Secondly, I managed to get a place inside the Cathedral (by flashing my clerical collar). I was struck by the sheer volume of the singing, which was frankly deafening. I sat among other priests, many of whom seemed to be competing with each other for the volume of noise they could make! A large choir and the assembled Bishops were also singing with gusto; and the congregation followed suit. The overall volume was actually very uncomfortable! Matthias commented later that singing very loudly is a feature of worship in Accra.

Thirdly, I was struck by the immense length of the service. We only stayed for a couple of hours (essentially for the ordinations which took place in the centre of the whole service). However, by keeping in touch with the Bishop's son, Prosper (who was also in attendance) by phone, we later learned that the whole service didn't finish until around three in the afternoon; which makes the whole thing a six and a half hour marathon!

I found myself wondering out-loud to the Bishop whether such long services would perhaps be off-putting to worshippers in the longer term. As prosperity increases, and people have more to do with their days, will they be put off from joining churches if they fear having to give up their whole day for a service? Matthias explained that this was very much Ghanaian culture. People feel free to come for the whole service, or just to drop in and out (as we had done). He also commented that for many of the poorer people of Ghana, Church was their home on a Sunday. They usually have no TV, no land to farm, and only few chores to attend to in their homes. They enjoyed being in church because it gives them a sense of community and family. Short services, he believed, would in fact be less popular! I'm realising just how different our cultures are and how much I still have to learn.

We left around one o'clock to make our way back into the Diocese of Ho and to start our tour-proper of the southern parishes. After driving along the coast for some way, we dropped Imelda (the Bishop's daughter) at her home and then proceeded to the South-East highway towards Togo.

The highway was a horrible thing to drive on, especially with a failing engine. It is a simple two-way road, with long straight stretches for overtaking. Unfortunately, it is also a very busy road and so it is very difficult indeed to find somewhere to pass slower vehicles (especially when one's engine has no extra power available). On a few occasions, we encountered Government vehicles heading in the opposite direction. Their technique for navigating the slow roads is simply to sit in the lane of the oncoming traffic (i.e. our lane!) going in the opposite direction, with sirens and blue lights; thereby forcing us off the road onto the hard shoulder. On one occasion, while being thus forced off the road, I narrowly avoided a boulder which some careless soul had left on the hard shoulder!

About two hours later, we arrived at our destination for the day: St Anthony's Anglican Church and Schools in Penyi. It was dusk as we arrived for a service of Confirmation for 13 young people. Unfortunately, few of the normal congregation were present on our arrival, but as before a number of them trickled in once word of the Bishop's arrival had got around the area.

I think that another long description of another long Ghanaian service will probably bore my readers, so I will confine myself to a few comments. First, it was wonderful to see 13 young people being confirmed from just this one parish. The Bishop says that each of his congregations have around two confirmation services per year, and with similar numbers. So there is real hope that a new generation of Anglicans is being fostered. However, the Bishop was very keen during his remarks to remind these newest members that they took on a solemn duty to belong to the church. He finds, like churches in the West, that confirmation can be a 'rite of passage' rather than a commitment to a life of faith.

Secondly, St Anthony's has similarities to the 'Anglican Village' in Kpando—with the school, Vicarage and Church all sharing the same (somewhat smaller) site. However, in St Anthony's case, the church building is an impressive construction—built in cruciform shape, with capacity for hundreds of worshippers. It is a testament to Bishop Matthias himself who was the driving force behind the building when he was parish priest at St Anthony's. He was clearly (and rightly) proud of the achievement.

Third, the church site has a strange addition: namely a 'fetish shrine' on the edge of the property. It is an ancient idol, built to give protection to the surrounding town. It is still clearly in use by fetish worshippers (there were signs of recent sacrifices all around the idol). The church is forced to live with this uncomfortable imposition next to its land. The local Fetish religions are very strong in members and any attempt to remove the Shrine would no doubt be met with great hostility, and, probably, violence. The Church's strategy, instead, has been to let the surrounding bush grow thick around the Shrine. The Church then teaches its own congregation and school children about the dangers of worshipping idols.

219

In some ways, this uncomfortable juxtaposition of religions has parallels in the UK. We live alongside stone circles (from Druidism); our ancient church buildings are often built on former pagan sites. Pagan symbols (like the Green Man) are often woven into church architecture and thereby 'Christianised'. Pagans tie ribbons and other tokens in our Yew trees and Wiccans sometimes hold rites in our churchyards. To put a positive spin on this, one can be glad that even in our technological and scientific age, people are still interested in spiritual things.

From all I've heard so far about Fetishism, though, it sounds a worrying religion indeed. Matthias clearly believes that there are real, evil spirits abroad in the land, and that Fetish priests (especially those who practice Voodoo) have the power to invoke the activity, help or retribution of such evil spirits. His belief arises out of real experience, which I respect. But theologically I struggle with how a loving, omnipotent God could permit any evil spirits to exist; especially any who would turn God's people away from God's love. If God is omnipotent, almighty and loving (as we declare and believe) the existence of demonic powers is surely a contradiction in terms. Belief in the existence of such powers verges on 'Dualism' - the theological premis that God and Satan are equal powers, battling it out across history (a 'heresy' which was discarded by the Early Church). If that was indeed the case, we would have to dramatically change our language about God.

Nevertheless, belief in such evil spirits (whether they are real or not) is very strong in this area. Fetish shrines can be seen all over the place, as can Fetish priests. For the local people, this religion is very real, and very powerful. They live in fear of upsetting one of the local deities, whom they believe have the power to wreck their lives. The curse of a Voodoo priest is something to be greatly feared. For my part, I am not wise enough to even suggest how the Church can combat this phenomenon. Their present strategy is peaceful co-existence. Despite there being a majority of Christians, the old ways still have great power among the people. Instead, the Churches preach a God of Love, who provides schools for local children, (and other community services) and they pray for repentance and the movement of the Holy Spirit in people's lives.

I have asked for the opportunity to meet a Fetish priest in the next couple of days; the Bishop has set this in motion. I would very much like to understand more of what they believe. I am reminded of a book called 'Christianity Rediscovered' by Vincent Donavan, a Catholic priest who brought the Christian Gospel to the people of the Massai in the 1950s and '60s. He found that he first needed to understand the Massai's own beliefs before he could communicate the added insights of the Christian gospel to them. I wonder whether a similar approach might be needed here.

Anyway, back to St Anthony's. We had a very pleasant service together, and I very much enjoyed preaching to the youngsters about the sacrifices of faith. We were then taken to a guest house, for the night (and a cold shower!) before having breakfast with Fr Ablorh the following morning.

9th September 2012

After breakfast we made our way a few miles down the road towards the Togo border (but with a detour back onto the Accra road) to the parish of St Paul, Agbozume. On our arrival we noticed that the Church/School compound was being prepared for a major event—canopies were being erected, and chairs brought from the four corners of the town. It turned out that this was graduation day for a group of tailoring apprentices, and the whole compound, except the church, would soon be flooded with noisy and exuberant apprentices and their families.

The church congregation itself was somewhat depleted. Around 70 worshippers, I suppose, had gathered in an impressive building which could easily accommodate 400+. Matthias explained that two factors were in play. First, the celebration about to take place in the compound would naturally draw worshippers away (because they would have family members who were graduating). Secondly, this is 'school fees' week—in which families who are desperate to find the fees for their children are either visiting friends and relatives in the hope of some financial help, or sitting depressed at home because their endeavours have already failed. Schools cost money in Ghana. There is no free education (as I understand it). Rather, the Government has a programme called fcube (free, compulsory, universal basic education). However, the running of schools costs more than the Government provides, and PTAs (parent/teacher associations) have sort of quasi-ownership of schools. If a PTA decides that it wants to improve a school, it can levy a fee for each student. When parents are too poor to pay such a fee, they prefer to withdraw their children from school, rather than face the embarrassment and indignity of having to admit that they cannot pay. So, whether or not a child gets an education depends very much on the resources of its parents.

Another long service took place (about 3 hours), during which I preached on the way Jesus sometimes has to take us out of our comfort zones in order the bless us (based on the Mark 7 story of the deaf and dumb man's healing). I talked about how I was out of my comfort zone at the moment, visiting a 'strange land'...but that I was being blessed constantly by new friends, and stimulating thought. I encouraged the congregation—which appeared a little lack-lustre to me— to think about which of their comfort zones God might be calling them out of.

I said in the last paragraph that the congregation at St Paul's appeared to be a little lack-lustre. Now that I am beginning to get used to Anglican worship Ghanaian-style, it's a pattern I'm beginning to see elsewhere. Initially, Ghanaian worship struck me as vibrant and exciting (and there are certainly great examples of that around). But the elements that first surprised and delighted me, are becoming familiar. So, for example, the first time I saw people dancing up the aisle to give their offering, I was astounded. But when 'dancing up the aisle' is the norm, every week, every service, one can't help noticing that the demeanour of the worshippers is less than truly joyous. There's a sort of resignation in their faces, and in their dancing...which communicates a sense of 'here we go again'.

I can't help but wonder whether the church in Ghana, as much as the church in the UK, needs to think creatively about how its traditions can be re-formed, and re-imagined from time to time.

I was very pleased indeed to be able to spend a little time with Rev Canon Prosper Deh, the local parish priest. At 35, Fr Prosper is one of the youngest priests in the Diocese, and a protégé of Bishop Matthias. He clearly has great energy and vision, and I'm looking forward to hearing about his football project in the morning.

After lunch at the Vicarage (3 rooms which used to be a school house), the Bishop and I set off with Prosper and a few other local folks to view two potential houses for the parish's new Curate, Fr Dennis (who was one of the ordinands I led on retreat). A local family have recently lost both their father and mother, and two houses in the town are currently available to the church for no rent. The mother, in particular, was a pillar of the church, and her family believe that she would be very happy to know that her house was to be used by a Curate. Both houses require some essential maintenance to be habitable (including the installation of toilets!). But the church is embracing the offer enthusiastically, and Fr Prosper seems confident that one of the houses can be made habitable by the time Fr Dennis and his wife arrive in January.

Agbozume, and a neighbouring town are the Bishop and his wife's original homes. So, we could not pass through without a visit to his, and Lucy's mothers. We passed a couple of pleasant hours visiting both ladies, and their various family members, including Matthias' youngest sister Theresa and her children (who live with Matthias' mother). Matthias was able to give each family a small amount of money, and for his own mother, some bags of produce which she could sell at the market for more funds. (Some of these had been donated by church members during 'The Great Entrance' - for the use of priests and their families). I was struck by the relatively poor conditions of both families, and by how much help they clearly needed. I wonder how many Bishops' mothers in the UK live in such reduced circumstances?

As dusk fell we made our way to a local hotel, where food was kindly brought to us by Fr Prosper. Strangely, he refused a fulsome invitation to stay with us to chat and share a drink...but we speculated afterwards that he might have felt that he would have been gate-crashing his Bishop's conversation. I am hoping for the chance to meet with him again in the morning.

Went to bed around 9pm, with the intention of rising early to write this diary!

10th September 2012

After a couple of hours of diary-writing in the early morning, we made our way to Fr Prosper's house for some breakfast. There, over a breakfast of Milo (fortified hot-chocolate) and butter-bread (delicious!) I was able to discuss some of the queries that had arisen in my mind during the morning's reflective blogging. In particular, I wondered whether Prosper agreed with me that worship in Ghana could appear lack-lustre at times. He agreed that it could, but that a service without dancing and drumming would be totally alien to Ghanaian culture. In much the same way that traditional Anglicans in the UK could not do without their traditional hymns, Ghanaians can't easily imagine their services being conducted in any other way. 'Re-imagining' is a challenge for both churches.

It seems I was right about Prosper's refusal of my invitation for him to sit and chat with us at the hotel. As a young Ghanaian (he is 35), it would be the height of rudeness for him to take a place at a discussion by an older man, let alone his Bishop. Once again, I have much to learn! However, in his house, at his breakfast table, he was much more relaxed and willing to chat.

Prosper told me about his football initiative in the town, which sounds very promising. Essentially he organises an Anglican football team which competes against the teams of other churches in the Town. He chatted around some possibilities for how this bit of ecumenical and fitness-based activity could be expanded, and some other broader ideas about ministry among young people. The most significant need in this community (as in every other I have encountered) is for school fees. This is not an overly poor country (although of course pockets of real poverty exist, as in the UK). But every family struggles weekly to find the fees needed to educate their children. Without an education, young people have few prospects of being able to raise themselves about the level of basic subsistence and market-trading.

I have observed, by the way, that the main form of commerce in Ghana seems to be in the market place. This stands in contrast to Uganda (which I visited some years ago) where agriculture and subsistence farming seems to dominate. Ghanaian land-plots are smaller than those in Ghana, so home-farming is not as practical a money-making tool. Ghanaians are traders...buyers and sellers, all trying to make a little profit along the way. Ugandans are farmers.

Prosper, the Bishop and I discussed whether the establishment of some sort of bursary fund for students might be a possibility. There would be real challenges in doing so—not least because as soon as everyone in the community found out about it, everyone would apply to the fund! Without personal accounting or tax-returns (and in a cash-based economy anyway) it is very difficult to establish the truth of anyone's claim to be poor. The only way of attempting some sort of bursary fund would be in secret—perhaps a 'Vicar's Discretionary Fund', which clergy could use to give help to those families whose circumstances are well known and understood.

One other interesting topic of conversation revolved around an observation I had made in the church yesterday. I saw that a new wall painting of Jesus was underway in the Sanctuary of St Paul's, and that in line with all other pictures of Jesus I have seen in West Africa, the picture was very much that of a long-blond-haired, white-skinned Jesus. We talked around the possibility of this picture perhaps breaking the mould, and perhaps an African (or at least Middle Eastern) Jesus might be contemplated. For a while, this idea intrigued both the Bishop and Prosper, but then on further reflection, their position began to shift. The Bishop, in particular, reflected that despite all their pride about Independence, Ghanaians still tend to look to the West for inspiration and support. A white Jesus epitomises this relationship: God is seen as a potential source of support and succour, and the fact that Jesus comes from somewhere other than Africa is a positive thing.

I found this a really interesting comment, and it chimed with what I have observed generally in the country. Ghanaians are rightly proud of their beautiful country and culture, but there is a general malaise which seems to infect everyone here. Nothing is done quickly...everyone walks slowly from place to place, dragging their feet. Nothing is maintained well (evidenced by the dilapidated state of most of the hotels we have stayed in). Even in the churches, attention to maintenance and high quality is lacking—things happen when they happen, and nothing seems particularly planned— including maintenance schedules and the like. While they are not generally starving, daily grinding poverty (and the constant search for

225

a little profit) is endemic. Many Ghanaians move abroad, as soon as they have the chance to do so—in the hope of a better life. In such a context, it should perhaps not be surprising that a 'foreign' Jesus might be preferred as a symbol of hope.

After a pleasant morning of discussion and debate, the Bishop and I set off for the border with Togo, where we planned to visit the congregation of the Resurrection at Lome. Getting through the border was a bit of a palaver! First it was necessary to pack a small suitcase, because we needed to leave the Bishop's car on the Ghana side of the border. (There is a tax for bringing in a vehicle—plus a pile of paperwork— which the Bishop wanted to avoid). Exit and Entrance visas were required for me, plus an entry visa fee at the Togo border...but we got through without any problems.

We were met at the border by Fr Ernest Uche, Priest in Charge of the Resurrection church, who drove us to his house for refreshment. Driving in Togo is even more of a challenge than in Ghana! Rules of the road seem to be entirely non-existent! Overtaking happens on whichever side of the car one feels like, and there are even more motorcycles on the road than in Ghana—weaving dangerously in and out of the traffic. If the motto for driving in Ghana is 'every man for himself', I think the Togo motto should be something like 'Kill or be killed'!

The Church of the Resurrection is currently the only formally-recognised Anglican congregation in Togo, although there are plans afoot to include some new congregations which have been formed in the north of the country. The Bishop plans to travel to northern Togo in October to welcome these new churches into the fold of the Diocese. The Resurrection is housed in an old industrial unit, which the members have converted into a church (having been previously expelled from a former church building by the owner of the land on which it was built). They have also built a new Vicarage on the site, and have plans to extend it upwards to form a mission house.

The congregation is made up, mainly, of Ibos—most of which have a strong connection with Nigeria. Fr Uche is himself a Nigerian, sent from the Nigerian Anglican church as a mission priest. As a result, the culture of the church is somewhat different from that of Ghanaian churches. For a start, they use an order of service which has been imported from Nigeria. Decoration of the church—and the

Sanctuary in particular, is somewhat garish to English tastes - with frilly altar cloth, multi-coloured curtains, and domestic arm-chairs for the clergy to sit in. They also have some organisations within the church which owe much to their Nigerian roots—including some ceremonial Knights (who carry ceremonial swords during special occasions).

After some refreshing fruit at his home, Fr Uche delivered us to our hotel for a rest before the evening's service. The hotel was called the 'Max-Doss'! (I've managed a few doss-houses in my time, but I've never stayed in one!). It was a pleasant, if somewhat decaying hotel. (Cold showers again!). But the staff were welcoming, and the beds were clean, so we were content.

We were collected just after sunset for the short ride back to the church, along largely empty streets. The Togolese seem to have adopted a French approach to commerce, which stands in marked contrast to that of Ghanaians. In Ghana, stalls and shops stay open late into the night—in the hope of that last minute bargain or few cedis of profit. Many traders live at their stall or shop—staying open as late as possible, and opening again before dawn. The Togolese, however, seem to pack up and go home to be with their families. Ghanaians have, it seems, adopted the 'work-ethic' of their former colonial masters, the British. Togolese have adopted the 'laise-faire' attitude of the French, who were their colonists.

The service was not brilliantly attended—only around 40 people. Again, I'm neither surprised nor offended—it was a far larger congregation than would have turned out in England on a Monday evening to listen to a foreigner preach a sermon. The church of the Resurrection had an interesting approach to music and sound. A public address system was essential to overcome the noise of a surfeit of ceiling fans, but it was not an especially helpful system. The budget-priced microphone popped noisily at the use of every verbal consonant, which made hearing what was being said rather difficult. Musically, the congregation was served by a band, an organist and a choir. But the choir (about 9 young men) only sang in unison (not especially loudly), and the band was unfortunately out of tune with the organist! Hymn singing was led mainly by Fr Uche, using the popping microphone: but strangely, he usually sang the bass line of the hymn, rather than the melody—so anyone searching for a tune amidst the general cacophony was likely to find it rather a challenge. The whole effect was really quite marvellous!

It was lovely to be welcomed at the church door by the newly ordained Fr Dennis (one of the ordinands from my retreat of week one). He was beaming and happy; yesterday (Sunday) had been his 'thanksgiving service' for his ordination, and the Church had been packed and joyful. He was still, clearly, on 'a high', and his usually sombre, serious expression had been replaced by a broad smile!

The service lasted for just under an hour and three quarters...positively short by West African standards! I preached again on 'comfort zones' - which fitted the Gospel reading of the day rather well (and thereby saved me having to prepare another sermon!). Afterwards we retired to the courtyard of the Vicarage, where Fr Uche's wife (known to everyone as 'Mama') had prepared a little surprise for me in the form of chips! Halleluiah!

Conversation revolved around the very real problems that the Bishop has in running the Diocesan finances. Very few churches in the Diocese take seriously the payment of 'Assessment' (what we call 'parish share' or 'quota'), resulting in the Bishop having to spend a great deal of his time raising funds for the work of the Diocese. He was at pains to point out that when we say 'Diocese' in the UK, we refer to a bureaucracy of secretaries and 'Directors of Mission' and the like. In the Diocese of Ho, the only staff-member is the Bishop, and he is expected by the churches of the Diocese to keep the whole show on the road without them paying their 'assessment', in an old, dying car, and with no staff support.

I think the poor fellow gets a bit depressed about the situation! Priests need stipends, conferences need organising and paying-for, ecumenical and inter-Anglican relationships need fostering, finances need accounting-for, and pastoral support needs to be given to a very wide range of priests, deacons and lay-people. Unfortunately, some of his priests don't really understand the pressure of his role, and tend to complain loudly about what 'the Diocese' should or shouldn't have done in various projects at various times. The Bishop, on the other hand, is intensely frustrated that he often delegates roles to various priests, who then appear to do nothing to pro-actively drive-forward the area of responsibility they have been given.

The problems which the Bishop has identified with the Diocesan structures seem to me to be indicative of Ghanaian society in general. The whole society operates with very 'flat' management structures, which I think may have their roots in tribal cultures. Each organisation has a 'Big Man' - the Chief, the Bishop, the Government Minister or the Chief Executive. But then there is very little in the way of a support structure beneath them (often because there are simply not enough funds available to pay such staff). As a result, everything goes through the 'Big Man', and he is feted as the source of help, advice, direction and, crucially, funding for everyone in his care. Conversely, the 'Big Man' is inevitably blamed when anything goes wrong!).

To illustrate this, I have one Ghanaian friend who passed up the opportunity to become Chief of his tribe. He did not want to have to occupy such a position of leadership, which he knew would result in having to manage (and often fund) the minutiae of every problem he was presented with by members of his tribe. There is, as a result, very little in the way of self-management or pro-active work in the community. Everything goes through the 'Big Man', and if he doesn't have time to engage with, bless, fund or organise a project, then the project doesn't happen.

The amount of authority invested in these 'Big Men' results in a culture of apprehension. People won't act on their own initiative, for fear of being told off (or worse, demoted) by the Big Man. Instead, they wait to be told precisely what to do. The 'Big Man' then gets frustrated with his minions, who appear to him to be lazy or indolent—and he ends up replacing them anyway. The whole cycle then starts all over again.

It is difficult to see how this system could be easily improved, given the economic circumstances which drive it. In an ideal world, one would want to encourage the use of devolved powers, through effective delegation. Job descriptions would be agreed, clearly outlining the responsibilities being passed on, and the outcomes expected. But this is a culture in which there are frequently not even printers or computers—let alone the training and travelling-resources necessary for effective delegation and on-going work-review. (For example, I was staggered to learn that the Education Office of the Anglican Board of Education in Ho does not even have printer in their office! All letters and reports are saved to a memory card, and then printed at a local shop, for a fee!)

On top of these issues is a more fundamental issue of the stewardship of personal resources.   In a culture where everyone is scrambling around for enough money for food and school fees, it is very difficult to get people to part with cash for any other project. Collections in many of the churches are very small indeed, and without help from outside sources, much of the work of the Diocese would simply not happen. Similarly, it is hard for people to think beyond their local context and needs.   A fundraising drive for improvements to a local church building will, eventually, succeed. Church members can also be relied on for generosity to support a struggling church family. But fundraising appeals for issues beyond the life of the congregation are rarely if ever successful. There is not a culture of 'giving to charity' such as we have the luxury of affording in the UK.

Churches in the UK, of course, suffer from a similar parochialism from time to time. However, in the Portsmouth Diocese we have nearly a 100% record of paying parish share/quota/assessment, and congregations are generally highly inventive about fundraising strategies. In this part of the world, there is no particular culture of running table-top sales or social events to raise funds. Fundraising is done largely through collections, and highly emotional appeals. (During some fundraising collections, the organiser will encourage wealthier donors to come forward first, using the style of an auctioneer. "Who will give 50 cedis for this project? Who will give 40 cedis, 30 cedis" and so on. Rounds of applause are given to anyone who feels moved (or able) to give the larger amounts, and then the whole congregation dances up to give whatever few pennies they can afford at the end.)

Some congregations are experimenting with raising funds through commerce (in a typically Ghanaian fashion!). Some corn mills have been donated by the Diocese of Fredericton, Canada, and it is planned to use these to grind corn for local people, to generate some income.

I do wonder whether commerce might be the most natural, Ghanaian-way-forward for churches. There are lots of 'services' which Ghanaians are happy to buy from each other, and the more that churches can engage with this culture, the better. A good example is that of Lucy, the wife of the Bishop. She runs a stall, just outside her house in Ho, selling sweets and basic education tools (pencils, pens, pads of paper) to students at the school. She also has a small hair-dressing salon. These bits of commerce serve to supplement her income, and that of the Bishop, and enable them to be very generous indeed to a number of local young people who they have informally 'adopted' - paying their school fees, for example.

After this interesting and thought-provoking discussion, Fr Uche drove us back to the hotel (in his ancient Rover, complete with cracked windscreen and clapped-out suspension). He's lucky...he is the only priest I have met so far to even have an old banger to run around in!

11th September 2012

I had a reasonable night's sleep in yet another new bed (I'm reminded of the song from 'Evita': "Another Suitcase, Another Hall"). I woke before dawn, and with no obvious prospect of being able to get back to sleep, decided to go and sit in the hotel foyer, and write my blog (Part Four). I rather enjoyed the company of a cheeky parrot, kept in a cage in the Foyer, who chirped and chatted to me all the time I was there. Interestingly he showed no sign of wanting to escape....one of the hotel staff left his cage door open for ages during a cleaning and feeding operation, but although the parrot put his head out of the door, he made no effort to leave the cage whatsoever. They say that prisoners can become accustomed to their incarceration, and actual fear release. (Is that Stockholm Syndrome? I think so). It was graphically demonstrated to me by the parrot this morning.

The Bishop and I were collected by Fr Uche around 9am, and then given a splendid breakfast at his house, thanks to his wife. Then, after some more conversation with Fr Uche and Fr Dennis (who joined us) we made our way to the market in Lome, to buy a few essentials. (The Bishop had promised to find some particular clothes for his wife). Fr Uche delivered us to the market, where he parked his car in a dubious spot. Initially, a young man came over and angrily told him to move his car, but as soon as Fr Uche got out of the car, and was recognised as a 'Father', the young man's attitude changed dramatically. "Oh, Sorry Father. No problem, no problem!". I'm not sure what the roots of this deference are...it would be nice to have such deference in the UK from time to time! I suspect that it arises out of mixture of genuine respect for the church (which still has much influence in the country) but also perhaps a superstition about not upsetting one of 'God's servants', for fear of upsetting God himself!

At the market we were met by a woman called Favour who is a member of the Lome church, and a trader in the market. She took us through the labyrinth of market stalls to her own small lock-up unit, from where she deals in wholesale clothing. We heard a little about her trade, and then prayed for her and her business, while the Bishop prayed a blessing. She then walked us through the rest of the market to find the clothing the Bishop needed, and a pair of sandals for me. (I'm not usually one to wear sandals, but in the heat of Ghana, I have found shoes to be too uncomfortable.)

The market was an amazing place. The streets were heaving with people, and motorcycles and hand-carts were all over the place. The motorcycles drive as fast as they can through the crowds, and it is a wonder to me that I didn't see one of the apparently frequent collisions between motorcyclists and pedestrians!

After getting our provisions, we went back to Fr Uche, who had stayed with his car, and said farewell to Favour. Fr Uche then drove us to the border with Ghana, where after the obligatory stamping of exit and entry visas, we collected the Bishop's car for the journey back to Ho.

Along the way, we stopped at Penyi, where it had been arranged that we could meet a Fetish Priestess, as I had requested a few days ago. After a stop for refreshment at Fr Simon Ablorh's Vicarage, we made our way through some backstreets of Penyi to the home of the Priestess (who happened to be a sister of one of the congregation at Penyi).

We were warmly greeted by the Priestess, who welcomed us to her home and the surrounding compound in which there were a number of Fetish shrines. We then sat down in the shade of a canopy outside her home, and began a fascinating conversation. Unfortunately, neither of us could speak the other's language, so our conversation had to be interpreted both ways by the Bishop. Nevertheless, it was a fascinating exchange.

As I now understand it, Fetishism is a mixture of Christianity and native superstition and ancestor worship. They believe that the world is inhabited by Spirits, many of which are the spirits of ancestors. These spirits have power to bless or to curse—to support life or take it away. Fetishism is designed to ameliorate the harsh side of these spirits, appeasing them through sacrifices and prayers, and hoping to seek their blessing. Underpinning all this is a basic belief in God, and an acceptance that Jesus Christ is at least a very significant Spirit, so should also receive sacrifices.

Fetish worshippers (at least as they appeared through this Priestess) are basically good people, who seek a peaceful co-existence with the Spirits and their local community. In many ways they are not so far from Christianity (they have a rudimentary concept of sacrifice, and they seek to do good). They have a less developed sense of the 'sacrifice of self' that is at the heart of the Christian gospel—which Matthias tells me can be an issue for new converts to Christianity. When a Fetish worshipper gains something, they believe it comes as a gift from God or from a Spirit, and that they should hold on to it. Asking them to sacrifice it to the greater good of the community (e.g. through a collection of money) is a difficult concept for them to get their heads around.

It was, as I say, a fascinating encounter, and I'm glad I had the chance to do it. Clearly there is a huge distinction between Fetish and Voodoo forms of the religion...Voodoo having more to do with harnessing the power of spirits for revenge or other petty motives.

It may be hard for Europeans to understand how Fetishism can co-exist alongside Christianity. Many families have believers from both sides, who still manage to get along and love each other. (Even the Bishop himself was brought up as a Fetishist in his childhood. His mother-in-law remains one, despite the Christian faith of her own daughter and her Episcopal son-in-law!). However, for us Europeans, it is important to recognise how we too live in peaceful co-existence with more ancient belief-systems. Over UK doors, one will often find a horse-shoe, nailed up with its points heavenward, (so that the luck will not 'run out'). The Christian marriage tradition is full of references to older religious practices (e.g. "something old, something new, something borrowed, something blue") and we routinely wish each other 'Good Luck' even though the Christian religion has no concept of luck.

After this fascinating encounter, we drove back to Ho, where I am to spend my last couple of days before heading off to Cape Coast. On our arrival in Ho we unfortunately found out that a Receptionist at the Bob Coffie Hotel had not noted my booking for this evening (though I was very clear about it when we left on Saturday). I have therefore moved to another Hotel—the Hotel Stevens—which is very pleasant.

The Bishop and I spent the evening in his office, catching up with some admin, answering a few emails and uploading my diary to the internet, before I made my way back to the Hotel for the night.

12th September 2012

I drove back to the Bishop's house around 7.45am, in time for an 8 o'clock assembly and morning prayer with pupils of the Junior High School. I spoke to the children, got them laughing, and generally had a very good visit. Worship was led by Fr Ibeto, one of the two priests assigned to the Cathedral. The tiny Cathedral was packed solid (about 80 students, I would guess, plus some teachers.) Morning Prayer was from the Book of Common prayer, and I was once again struck by the inappropriateness of the language for modern young people. They seemed to know the words by heart (which was impressive in itself), but I wonder how much they really understood. Their unaccompanied singing was loud and enthusiastic.

After Assembly, leaving the Bishop to catch up on some long over-due administration, I went on a visit round the school. I sat at the open window of a few classes, and observed the way that teaching is done. To a UK teacher, the techniques employed would be archaic, I guess. But given the resources available, it is difficult to see how else it could be done. Information is communicated in lecture form, with notes written on a blackboard for the students to copy. Much chanting takes place, as teachers attempt to get key concepts and ideas into young heads.

I was struck by the apparent differences in ages between students. Some were (I learned later) as old as 17. Advancement through the school system is based on attainment, not age. Therefore, some classes have a wide mixture of ages, all learning together.

I found my way to the administration office, and there had the pleasure of meeting Headmaster Boniface. He kindly took some time to explain a little more about the funding of the Ghanaian school system to me. (I've already discussed this at a previous point in the blog, so won't repeat too much here). He explained that, after paying teachers' salaries and buying text books, the Government gives only 4.50 Ghana Cedis per child per year to the school (roughly £1.30) to pay all the administrative costs of the school and its buildings. From this tiny budget, each school is expected to pay electricity, administration and maintenance bills. This further explains the need to charge school fees to parents, despite the Government's trumpeting of 'free, compulsory, universal, basic education' (known by the acronym 'fcube').

I thanked Headmaster Boniface for his time, and promised to do what I could (without making any promises) to see whether a link could be established with a school in the UK in due course.

Arriving back at Bishopscourt (on the edge of the School compound) I was delighted to discover that three out of four of 'my' ordinands had arrived, with their wives, to meet with the Bishop. It was great to see Selin, Macaphuy and Angelo again, along with Rose and Yvonne.

The rest of the afternoon was taken up with conversations between these newly ordained ministers and their Bishop and me. The Bishop was keen to give them certain warnings, messages and encouragements as they set about starting their new ministries. After a good lunch, prepared by one of the Bishop's daughters, Angela, sitting in a warm room, listening to the Bishop talk at significant length about his ideas, concerns and hopes, I confess that I might have dozed off on a couple of occasions!

We had hoped to have the presence of Fr Dennis (the fourth of 'my' ordinands) as well, but unfortunately a domestic emergency delayed his arrival until much later in the evening.

At around 4pm, I offered to drop the ministers and their families to the Bus Station, and then made my way back to the Cathedral for a specially arranged 5pm service. Arriving at about 4.55pm, I was cutting it fine, and then was surprised to be told by the Bishop that he would prefer me to celebrate and Mass, as well as preach! I was initially a little nervous, because I am not terribly familiar with the Old Roman Rite which is still used in the Cathedral. Thankfully Fr Ibeto was on hand to point at the right places in the missal for me!

It was quite a privilege to celebrate Mass in the Bishop's Cathedral. He stayed in normal dress, and sat at the back of the congregation, leading the unaccompanied singing with gusto. I preached on the topic of the day—the Beatitudes— focusing on the phrases 'Blessed are the poor' and 'Woe to the rich'. I ruminated on the fact that for all its wealth, the UK is not a happy place, compared to Ghana. Wealth brings acquisitiveness; TV and shopping-centre consumerism have taken the place of family and community activities. Absolute poverty (and hunger) are of course to be resisted at all times. But, as monastic communities have lived and taught for centuries, modest poverty—being poor—is a state of being which fosters interdependence, rather than independence. Communities grow through mutual dependence, whereas people who believe they don't need anything will only rarely lift a finger to 'love their neighbour'. It is these kinds of comparisons I hope that our deanery link with Ho will help other UK Christians to begin to understand.

After the Mass, and a lovely presentation to me of a traditional Ghanaian costume, we returned to Bishopscourt to find that Fr Dennis (and his wife Antonia) had finally arrived from Togo. It was late, and the power went off (thanks to 'load sharing') so we decided to adjourn any meeting about Dennis' future ministry until the morning.

I went back to the hotel, for a reasonable night's sleep on what is undoubtedly the hardest bed I've ever encountered! Ghanaians are great believers in hard beds...which are supposedly good for back-pain. My own experience (having given up an orthopaedic bed some years ago) is that the opposite is true! Unfortunately, we needed to leave the Bishop's car at his house tonight (because it is to be collected in the early hours for another trip to Accra by the mechanic), so the Bishop (now only just awake, poor fellow) had to drive me back to the hotel.

13th September 2012

My last day in Ho. Mainly set aside as a day for administration, for agreeing priorities for the Link we are establishing, and catching up with the blog. However, the morning was given over to meeting with Fr Dennis and Antonia. The Bishop asked me to take charge of the meeting so that he could focus on the urgent and over-due task of sending out monthly clergy stipends. I gladly did so, and re-iterated to Dennis many of the messages that the Bishop had shared with the other new deacons yesterday. These included the Bishop's stated desire for clergy to pray together daily, and a general message about the importance of not being lazy in ministry. (The Bishop is very concerned that all his priests should not tend towards laziness...becoming essentially 'service-takers' without engaging in the pastoral, leadership and missionary tasks necessary to develop the church). I have no doubt that Fr Dennis is a man of great integrity, and that laziness is the last idea in his mind! He is fired up with enthusiasm for what God will accomplish through his ministry. Coming from the more evangelical background of Lome, he hopes to add some evangelical zeal to the already impressive and well-established high churchmanship of Agbozume. He has worked with Canon Prosper in the past, and is confident that they will quickly establish a good working relationship, drawing from the best of both their traditions.

The Bishop was able to join us near the end of the morning, just to re-enforce some of the ideas we had already been developing, and to pray for God's blessing on Dennis and Antonia. They left, soon afterwards, to travel back to Togo (where they currently live) hoping to stop off along the way at Agbozume, to view the clergy house now being developed there.

After their departure, the Bishop and I set about some essential administration. We had some really excellent news, two days ago: namely that I've managed to secure some funding from the Anglican Communion for an operation he urgently needs on his neck. We therefore set about arranging for him to come to the UK in late October for the said operation, in the hope that he can be pain-free by Christmas.

The afternoon was taken up with mundane admin, like settling hotel bills, paying clergy stipends, catching up with emails and the like. We then sat down to think through the priorities for the Link we have now established between the Diocese of Ho and the Portsmouth Deanery.

We agreed a set of priorities, which are divided into categories of 'urgent' and then 'long term', which I will be sharing with the Portsmouth Deanery on Tuesday (the evening of my return to the UK!).

In the evening, we ate together with the whole family—a rare event. Delicious food (including yam-fries for me!) was prepared by Imelda, one of the Bishop's daughters who was visiting from Accra. The Bishop and I then walked back to my hotel (the car still being with the mechanic) along dark lanes. We managed not to kill ourselves by falling down a pot-hole, despite the fact that neither of us thought to bring a torch! I passed another reasonable night on the slab of granite which served as a bed!

Tomorrow, I leave for Cape Coast, to catch up with friends there before heading back to the UK.

That concludes my journal of a visit to Ho. I hope the reader has found it interesting and stimulating – perhaps even opening up some ideas about how the people of the Diocese of Ho can be helped in their ministry and mission.

The Last Word
Pithy reflections from weekly news-sheets

The following pages are a re-printing of some of the 'thoughts for the week' which I have offered on the rear of our regular news-sheet. They started as an attempt to offer something of my own thinking to the parish, at a time when with a surfeit of (wonderful!) preachers in the parish, I found that I wasn't getting the chance to offer such thoughts from the pulpit very often. But, when read in sequence, they also offer a semi-autobiographical journal (of a sort). In many cases, these are 'passing thoughts' tapped-out quickly with a publication deadline looming.

But nevertheless, I hope that they offer a few nuggets of wisdom, or at least something to challenge and encourage critical thought about our faith and the way we live it out.

239

The next generation. (15 July 2018)

Clare and I have been greatly touched by the many messages of congratulation from parish members, received after the announcement of the birth of our first grandchild (Lucas John Ashworth). (I was also delightfully amused by those older members of our parish who have delighted in saying things like, "Pah! One grandchild is nothing! Wait until you've got 17 great-children, like me!")

It is nevertheless a sobering moment when the next generation comes along. I can only speak for myself, but I have felt a mixture of emotions, ranging from joy at having lived long enough to see my family-line continue, through to a rather darker sense that perhaps there's nothing more for me to do - now that the next generation is here! After all, as scientists like Richard Dawkins would have us believe, our biological reason for living is simply to perpetuate our 'selfish genes' (from the title of one of his books).

The Christian perspective is rather different, however. Each of us is a uniquely prized, loved and regarded child of God. Not a grandchild...but an actual child. Our reason for living is far more than the perpetuation of our family line; rather it is that we live to love our parent God, and God's other children. That is our purpose. That is our calling. That is what we are here for.

Being where you need to be... (22 July 2018)

I'm anticipating a rather strange feeling this Sunday. With our Flower Festival reaching its conclusion after a week of huge community co-operation, many delighted faces, musical extravaganzas and the like, I find that I can't actually be in two places at once on Sunday morning! Instead of glorying with you all in the beauty of our florally-beautified building, I shall, instead be at St John's Purbrook - a parish which is currently in vacancy, and in urgent need of our help.

Many of us experience that frustration, of course, at many points in our lives. How many of our service-men and women find themselves removed from important family occasions by their duty? How many of us are torn, week by week, between the desire to come to church, and the need to attend to family or neighbour's needs?

A life lived in service to God is rarely predictable or simple. There are always more needs to be met than any one of us can hope to meet on our own. But one of the really excellent bits of 'good news' which we share is that we are all members of a much larger community - the one that Jesus calls his 'body'. In such a body, each one of us has an important role to play - and everyone's role is different. God's task of building a Kingdom is accomplished through us - his hands and feet to a world in need (as I preached only last week!). Just as an eye is not a foot, so each of us can be used by God just as required, and when required. All we have to do is remain open to the Spirit's prompting as to where we can be most usefully employed. Perhaps we are needed to set up an incredible Flower Festival...but perhaps we are called to simply and deliberately pray for others.

But let us not become anxious about whether we have heard God's voice for today. 'Where should I be?' is always a valid question, but it is not the only one. A better question is, perhaps, 'whom shall I be?'. For God calls us first into relationship with God. Whether I am, today, God's eyes or God's hands is less important a question than whether I am God's child. That is God's desire for us, above all else - that we might be children of heaven; loved, regarded and enfolded in God's love. Above all else, that's where I need to be today.

Flowery words... (29 July 2018)

I'm certain that every reader of this weekly column would agree with me that our Flower Festival was magnificent! A huge thank you must go to all of our flower artists for their energy, skill and sheer hard work over so many days. Thank you, as well, to all the musicians who performed whether in concert, or as 'background music' throughout the weekend; and let us not forget the army of cake-makers and refreshment-servers. Big thanks also goes to our staff team who supported the Festival with practical help, promotions, rainbow-hanging, scaffolding moving, and compost deliveries. There really are too many people to thank by name...though I think we can all agree that Sandra Haggan deserves a special mention, for being the 'Ringmaster' for the entire 'circus', as well as inspiring and driving everyone else to such enormous creativity and passion.

Thanking people is one of the biggest traps in a church leader's life. There will always be a danger of missing the name of some kind person who has given either money or time to make an event extra-special (but who will then feel that their gift was not recognised or noticed). What about the diligent cleaner, who was the last to leave the building after all the high profile people had left? What about the dear soul who poured their heart into making the Rector's favourite cake (it's Lemon Drizzle, by the way!)? So, in general, (as you will probably have noticed) I tend to avoid the trap of naming individuals.

But there's another reason, as well. Whilst simple politeness demands that thanks should properly be given wherever it is due, there is something rather different about service given as worship to God. Service to God is its own reward, for it is our way of expressing our gratitude to God for all the gifts we have been given...even our very lives. That's why, for example, we only rarely clap after performances by our choir and organist. Silence is a way of acknowledging that we have just been blessed by witnessing another person declaring their love for God. That might be worthy of praise, but it isn't done in the expectation of praise. Instead, in appreciative silence, perhaps we might take a moment to think how we too can express our praise of God? No flowery words. But instead, the action of lives poured out in loving, grateful, service of God and others.

Be yourself... (5 August 2018)

Once upon a time, a character called 'Tubby the Tuba' sang these words (at least, he did on a record I possessed as a child...):

"Be yourself: you can't be anybody else
Be yourself: that's my advice to you
Because you'll always be yourself,
no-one else."

Decades later, I still hear these words resounding in my sub-conscious, especially when I'm feeling under pressure to do something I don't feel called to do, or behave in a certain way to meet other people's expectations of what a Rector should be. It's still good advice - just as it was to my five-year-old self. Psychologists have taught us that we all have natural strengths and weaknesses...and when we spend too much time and effort trying to be what we are not, we can make ourselves ill and stressed. Who I am, who you are, is very precious to God - just as we are.

That's why I was delighted when I heard what (former Rector) David Gibbons preached to you all, during my sabbatical. I'm told that he said "We must not forget to be the church that we already are". Very wise words indeed, for there is much for us to celebrate about who we are. We are a congregation which is pressing forward to show God's love to our neighbours in Havant, through the creative use of our buildings and human resources. We are a traditionally-worshipping community, which also wants to discover and embrace other forms of worship, and to be creative about including non-traditional worshippers in our midst. We are an aging community; and yet through schools' ministry, the Play Café, Dynamo Youth Theatre, Christmas services, baptism ministry and other initiatives, we are constantly demonstrating God's love for young people and families.

The one person who is supremely 'himself' is, of course, God. God is the very essence of all being. Indeed, God is 'Being' itself, and he does not change. God is the same yesterday, today and forever. While loving us completely as we are, the one thing that God asks of us is that we discover more and more of who we are by going deeper into God.

Talk, talk, talk… (12 August 2018)

I like writing things down. Those of you who know me well will know that I generally prefer email to spoken conversations (because I'm less likely to forget what was said to me). I also quite enjoy spending time carefully-crafting written documents. They may be policy documents, letters and papers to the Diocese about our current renovations, minutes for the PCC and so forth.

However, I am often reminded how little that people take in the written word - or at least, how few of us go back and read papers more than once. The simple fact is that life moves on; the next email or policy document arrives, and the previous one becomes only so much recycling material. (It's the same for this weekly newsletter, which I usually find lurking in the church recycling bin only days after it was published!). The old saying that "today's news is tomorrow's fish and chip wrapping" still has power.

Here's a little fact about Jesus which is often missed: he never wrote anything down. This is all the more surprising when one considers that he could clearly read (he read aloud from the synagogue scrolls). Surely, someone seeking to completely and radically change human-kind's understanding of God would have written down his thoughts and teachings? It's certainly what other rabbis and teachers did. But perhaps Jesus had another idea.

Perhaps he believed that the spoken word actually has more power than the written one. Perhaps he chose to let people hear his heart, expressed 'live', through his mouth, rather than carefully edited on paper. Perhaps Jesus preferred to live dangerously, and let his words take on their own life in the ears (and hearts) of his followers. Certainly the different ways in which his words were reported to us by the Gospel writers bears witness to the sense of dynamism he created. Compare, for example, the different ways in which the Sermon on the Mount was reported by Matthew (Ch.5) and Luke (Ch.6). Both ways have power. Both contain truth. But neither, perhaps, contains every detail of what Jesus actually said that day. There is space between the two accounts for the Spirit to continue his work of 'leading us into all truth'.

"It's good to talk", after all.

Jesus loves to party!   (26 August 2018)

I've been getting a few puzzled looks ever since we announced that the famous 'Wurzels' were coming to give last Saturday's concert in the Pallant Centre. Surely, some have wondered, church-owned buildings are not the place for songs about cider-drinking and (let's be frank) a sometimes dubious sexual morality?

Truthfully, I have been a Wurzels fan since my early teenage years – long before I understood some of the double-meanings of some of their lyrics! (For those who wonder whether sex is a suitable topic for a Christian, check out the 'Song of Songs' in the Bible.) So for me, I confess, Saturday's concert was a particularly personal pleasure. But there was more to it than that.

I'm reminded of the time when Jesus himself was challenged by the religious people around him. They demanded to know why he chose to cavort with sinners. Why did he go to parties instead of the synagogue? Why talk with ordinary people instead of scholars? It seems that he wanted to be alongside people from every walk of life, not just the religious ones.

Jesus first public miracle (according to John's Gospel) was the changing of water into wine at a wedding. Jesus seemed to enjoy a good community celebration – so much so that the wine he miraculously made was the best of the whole night. Jesus' ministry was always abundant and generous. Miraculous wedding wine, miraculous bread and fishes for 5000 people, miraculous nets so full of fish that they broke. Jesus' message was one of abundance, community and joy, as well as forgiveness, healing and learning.

Gathering-together, joyfully, is always worth doing. It reminds us that we belong together, in community. Jesus knew that, and we follow his example.

An army of ordinary people... (23 September 2018)

It was a rather dreary afternoon at the Rectory, two Saturdays ago, when we invited all our volunteers and staff to a BBQ...but the company was great, we Brits (and friends) know how to enjoy ourselves in the gloom!

Perhaps the most surprising aspect of the afternoon was to realise just how much of the work of this parish is done by volunteers. We had around 70 of you in the garden last week. But I estimate that at least that many again were not able to be present.

What is the collective noun for a group of volunteers? Perhaps the most frequently-used is 'army'. There's some truth in it - because an army, like a group of volunteers, needs good leadership to thrive. My thanks therefore must go to our paid staff too - who without exception always go far and beyond the call of paid duty to make this parish the amazing place it is.

The hymn writer Graham Kendrick once developed the idea to write a song about 'An army of ordinary people, a kingdom where Love is the key...'. I rather like that metaphor - we are 'ordinary people', after all. There's nothing especially exceptional about us as individuals...though each one of us brings our unique talents and perspectives to the whole.

The point is that as an 'army of ordinary people', we find that by coming together we can do something transformative (for ourselves and for the parish we serve). Together, we have the capacity to touch and even to transform the lives of those around us. That might be by the offering of a kind word, or just the giving of the gift of conversation to a church or charity shop visitor who may speak to no-one else that day. But it might also be by leading the whole community to celebrate God in our midst (through the provision of community events, worship services and civic celebrations).

We truly are a 'kingdom where Love is the key' - for above all, it is Love which binds us together, Love which motivates our actions, and Love which guides us.

Praise be to God, the source of all Love, for all that we accomplish in his name together!

Growing-up in our faith. (7 October 2018)

A few weeks ago, I preached on a topic which Dr Mike Fluck had introduced at our Parish Conference in August - the topic of growing up in our faith. Subsequent conversations suggest that many of the congregation would value a brief summary of the ideas which Mike originally shared, from the work of Gerard Hughes. I'm very happy to oblige!

Hughes suggests that there three distinct stages of growth in faith, moving from a 'childlike' simple acceptance through to a 'grown up' faith which can embrace the mystery and deeper insights of a thoughtful faith. Here is a summary of the stages:

Institutional: analogous to a healthy childhood, this stage characterised by movement and sensory impressions. The needs of an 'institutional' believer are nurturance, belonging, affection – often provided through liturgy, fellowship and pastoral care.

Critical: analogous to healthy adolescence: critical believers begin to question and search for a sense of meaning in life. Without a movement towards the critical stage of spiritual growth, "our religion risks being just a harmless eccentricity or hobby". (Hughes)

Mystical: analogous to healthy adulthood, as life events cause us to reflect, we become aware of our inner life. It is here that we often encounter God, amid our memories and insights, at a level beyond conscious reflection (e.g. rather than simply through set prayers, written down for us to repeat together).

My invitation to you all, this week, is to spend time thinking about where you personally find yourself among these stages of Faith. Are you still at the beginning - when the familiarity of set words, familiar hymns, and the cosy feeling of the church 'club' are all you need from religion. Or have you moved beyond such 'institutional' faith into something more open to challenge, or which embraces the mystical aspects of life? Sometimes, I find that I can be at all three stages on the same day! What about you?

247

"Rest in peace...and rise in glory". (14 October 2018)

One of the most common ideas in Christian thought is the notion that when we die, we go to heaven (or to Paradise as Jesus called it to a repentant thief on the cross). And for most believers, that's as far as our understanding goes. In the popular imagination, the notion of Heaven is essentially that of an ethereal realm, where we will float around, perhaps chatting about music with Beethoven, or catching up with our deceased relatives and friends, or worshipping God for eternity. For some of us, these ideas might well provoke a sort of panic. Chatting with Beethoven and our deceased relatives could well become tedious after a while—like a sort of never-ending drinks party!

But an eternity in heaven is not what Christianity actually teaches, at all. Rather, the consistent message of Jesus, and those who followed him, is that heaven is no more than a temporary state, which will be followed in God's time by resurrection. The Scriptures promise us re-birth on an Earth which has been 'made new', over which a new heaven reigns.

How will Earth be 'made new' (as Jesus says in Revelation 21)? We don't know. Perhaps he will miraculously transform the world by a sweep of his mighty arm. Or perhaps (as seems more likely to me) he will work through us (as he usually does) to re-make the world through determined, just and holy action— because changing the Earth will not be enough. Our hearts and minds will need to change too, if any transformation of the Earth is to last.

Regardless of how the re-making of Earth is to be accomplished, it is vital that we should understand the importance of our planet, and of God's call on humanity to take care of it (see Genesis 1 & 2). The international climate change conference which took place last week has underlined once again how responsible we all are for that sacred duty. Perhaps God will indeed miraculously set right all the things we've done to our planet. But that doesn't mean that our duty to care for it is any the less real, right now.

So what part have you and I played this week, in the task of caring for our planet? After-all, we are destined to spend eternity here one day, after we have rested in peace, and then risen in glory.

Be your Present.   (21 October 2018)

It's that time of year, when many of us will rush from shop to shop, in earnest search for a gift (not too shabby, not too expensive) to give to our loved ones and friends. Many of us feel compelled to buy presents out of a sense of dread that we might be given a present by someone else, and then have nothing to give in return.

It's the same with Christmas cards. "Should I send one to Mrs Smith...because she might send me one, and then I'd feel awful if I hadn't sent one to her!"

I don't know about you, but I find that when I ask the question "What would you like for Christmas?" I very rarely receive the reply "Oh, I'd really love a £5 toiletries pack from Marks and Spencer". No-one to whom I have posed the question has ever responded "well, what I'd really love is a tin of Scottish shortbread, or a pair of comical socks".

Some years ago, my family and I decided to give up the fight to find presents for each other. As a result, our Christmases have been much more relaxed, much less frantic. We now have time to sink into the round of Christmas services and family gatherings, without feeling exhausted before they even start. No longer do we sing carols while mentally ticking off in our heads how many more presents we need to buy!

Our extended family and friends thought we were barking mad, at first. But in recent years, they have also stopped sending us packages of socks and shortbread. We have, instead, given each other the gift of time. We have freed one another from the assumed obligation of buying un-needed gifts. Now, our present to each other is to be present.

Obviously, I don't presume to tell you how to spend your money or indeed your Christmas. But I do encourage you to spend a little less time in the shops this year, and a little more time either in church or with your families. Let the joy of Christmas take you over...not the stressful panic of present-buying for people who are more than capable of buying whatever they need themselves. Fill up a charity shoe-box, instead. Or give to a charity which will make a real difference to lives which are not already full of socks, shortbread and soap. I think you'll be glad if you do.

The best laid plans... (25th November 2018)

Some religious thinkers invite us to see God as intimately involved with every human decision, and every act of nature on the planet - in other words that God has laid detailed plans for every person's life, and every natural occurrence...as if God is like some super-puppet master. This is where phrases like 'It's the will of God' come from. I don't think that can be right.

At the other end of the spectrum, some thinkers see God as a sort of Watchmaker - who has created the earth (and all of us) then sets it going on its own, subject to its own internal laws and processes. I don't think that's right either.

My own picture of God (which I offer to you to accept, reject or debate) is somewhere in between these two extremes. I see God as intimately involved with creation (and our lives) but not directing them, or interfering with them. God is the inspiration for all the great good in life - the power behind love, great art and great beauty. God walks beside us through all the trials of life, helping us and encouraging us to grow to become even more fully human.

God does have a plan for my life (and yours) - but it is not a specific set of steps that we must first discover, then choose to take. Rather, his plan for our lives is that we grow in love and faith, and that we bend our wills, our love, towards God (such as through worship). In that endeavour, he offers each of us a road to follow. Not a specific set of pre-determined steps, but a 'Way'. It's a way of life, a way of loving extravagantly. It's a way of learning to let go and learning to forgive. It's a way of looking outwards from ourselves - concerning ourselves more with the needs of others than even our own needs.

So God's best laid plan for my life (and yours) is ultimately a spiritual journey. The earliest disciples were not called 'Christians', but followers of 'The Way'.

Will you come along the Way with me? Will you seek to uncover God's best laid plan for your life?

Learning to say YES!   (2 December 2018)

There is, I detect, a tide of cynicism sweeping our nation. We are cynical about our politicians (and the Brexit crisis doesn't help!). We are cynical about our great institutions (fuelled by the seemingly endless scandals over mal-practice or horrific abuse in our banks, schools, churches, youth-organisations and the like).

The atmosphere of cynicism is propelled by the news-media and comedians - all of which are quick to point out the very worst about us and our society. As human beings, programmed to 'fight or fly', we cling like moths to a flame to any hint of danger, or bad news.

What are we to do, in the face of such relentless cynicism. Shall we pull the duvet over our heads? Shall we lock our doors, and never go out? NO! We must not do this.

We are followers of the God who expresses his Love for us by stepping into the cynicism, into the hate, into the fear - as a tiny, fragile, baby. Faced with the evil of the world, God did not crawl under his heavenly duvet! God did not lock the gates of paradise, and refuse to go out. Instead, God said 'Yes!' to the obvious need to sow the seeds of love, community and co-operation.

He could have chosen to be a distant God, watching from the mountain (as indeed the old Greek and Roman gods were believed to do). But this was not what God did. He entered fully into the human experience - even to the point of being born as a mewling infant, in a smelly stable, to a family who were about to become refugees from the persecution of their own Government. You don't get much more involved than that!

So what should our response be...we who are made in the image of God? My invitation to us all (myself included) is to resist the tide of cynicism, and learn to say 'Yes!' to every opportunity that is offered to us - especially every opportunity to grow spiritually, to deepen our love for God and for one another.

Perhaps, if we all learn to say 'Yes!' to just one new opportunity this next month, we all might have the chance to grow closer to God.

A nation divided? (9 December 2018)

As I write this, the Government of our United Kingdom has been defeated in a parliamentary vote (related to Brexit). Parliament and the Government are at loggerheads over the best way forward in these difficult times. These divisions reflect the strongly-voiced, opposing views of ordinary voters up and down the land - often manipulated by 'fake news' and mischievous social media.

At the same time, hate-filled rhetoric and violence are being ramped up all around the world, over a wide variety of issues. These are worrying times, are they not? But as Christians, we should not be surprised. The peaceful years we have enjoyed (more or less) since the Second World War were actually an unusual state of affairs. The Scriptures tell us that warfare is a normal state for human beings. We just can't seem to help ourselves. Nation makes war upon nation. Man's inhumanity to man is unfettered. And this is exactly what the prophets, and then Jesus himself, predicted would happen as history draws to its conclusion - not least because the evidence of their own history (set out in the history sections of the Bible).

Amid this chaos, and division, and warfare, let us hear again the proclamation of the Angels: "Glory to God in the highest heaven, and peace to his people on earth". By God's grace, we have learned the value of first giving glory to God in the highest heaven (by our regular, sustained, worship of God). And then we, with all our divisions and opinions, somehow find a way to live at peace with one another. Let us take some comfort from the fact that in our own congregation, there exists a wide variety of views about all the problems of the world. There are both Brexiteers and Leavers here. There are both supporters of Israel, and supporters of Palestine. There are both capitalists, socialists and communists in our pews. Catholics and Protestants, Evangelicals and Liberals.

The Church is God's gift to the world. It shows the world that peace is possible - even in the face of massive differences. May we continue to live out that calling - to be the House of Peace in a world of division. Shalom.

Living at the centre. (16 December 2018)

Tonight is one of those 'big civic events' of the year, when members of the Havant Rotary Club invite the Mayor, our local Member of Parliament, and various other dignitaries to celebrate Christmas at St Faith's. It's always a joyous occasion - and the St Faith's Choir has been practicing madly for weeks to be ready for their big anthems of the year! It's also going to be fantastic to welcome back two of our former young members, Archie McKeown and Emily Frost to entertain us with their vocal chords.

These occasions (and others like the annual Remembrance Service) remind me that we have a very privileged position - as the oldest continually-used public building in the Borough, a physically-central place in the life of our community, and the privilege of being able to speak and sing the Good News of Jesus Christ to a wider constituency than just our own members. We owe much to our predecessors who have left us this fantastic building, and a legacy of other buildings and funds which we can use to generate on-going income for parish ministry.

We must not sit on our laurels, though. The hard reality is that the centre of Havant (in the minds of many people) has now shifted to the West. For many local people, Tescos' supermarket is at the centre of Havant. Instead of an ecclesial building of stone and stained glass, a new 'cathedral' of steel and plate glass has been erected. Once upon a time, the residents of Havant came to lay their offerings on the altar of St Faith's, seeking wisdom for living from its priests. Today's priests (for so many people) are the marketing managers, who tell us how to find happiness by owning more stuff. And we lay our offerings on new altars now...altars with tills and tabarded shop assistants.

Against this background, we happy few who remain faithful to Christ are called to keep on proclaiming that God has a different plan for humanity. God has taught us that happiness is found in shedding the stuff that we accumulate...something which Clare keeps reminding me, every time she spies some languishing possession of mine which she thinks she can sell at the Charity Shop! Our task is to tread lightly upon the planet - the over-riding imperative being to 'take care of it' - as God said to Adam.

It's no yolk! (13 January 2020)

Some eagle-eyed parishioners noticed my deliberate (ahem) mistake of last week, when it seems that I suggested that Jesus invites his followers to carry a light egg-yolk around with them!   Of course, I meant to type 'my yoke is light' - but I rightly deserved the good-natured teasing that has been a topic of the last few days.

Co-incidentally, eggs have been rather a feature of the Rectory household in the last couple of weeks. The first occasion was when I tried to show off my cooking skills to Bishop Matthias (my Ghanaian friend who is visiting for a few weeks), by poaching some eggs. After many fruitless minutes of trying to get water to boil (and being told by my wife that I had used the wrong saucepan, so how could I expect the water to boil?) I only managed to achieve the cooking of eggs that were barely beyond the salmonella threshold. (The Bishop and I have now been formally banned from the kitchen).

The second occasion arose when I cheerfully presented the Bishop with a packet of Cadbury's mini-eggs last Sunday, and wished him a 'happy Easter'. He was singularly unimpressed by both my sense of humour, and the British habit of selling Easter eggs during the 12 days of Christmas. (Mind you, his protests didn't stop him from eating the said eggs during the subsequent days!).

Easter is still a long way off—in fact it is almost as late as it can-be, this year. But it does us no harm to be reminded of the Easter message throughout the year. For we are 'Easter-people' - we live in the light of the resurrection of Christ all year round.

Every time I encounter a real egg, I am reminded of the Sunday School lesson, in which I learned that the three elements of yolk, white and shell are a crude analogy for the Trinity (three distinct elements, working together as one). And, of course, the new life which is contained within every fertilised egg reminds us that we too have been offered the gift of new life.

Today, as we commemorate the Baptism of Christ, we will think about how that new life of the Spirit was demonstrated, through Jesus, by the spectacle of the Holy Spirit descending on him, 'like a dove'. That promise—of new life through the Spirit—is available for all of us too. Whether or not we enjoy a good yolk, from time to time!

The very last word? (20 January 2019)

I confess there was a moment, last week, when I wondered whether the previous week's 'Last Word' would really be The Last...as I clutched my chest while authorising some parish expenditure. A nearby member of staff, who shall remain nameless, promptly grassed me up to my dear Clare - who then insisted that I spend the rest of my day being poked and prodded by the NHS. As I write this (from a prone position on my couch), further tests are expected and I hope to update you all soon.

I'm not telling you all this in order to elicit the sympathy vote (though your prayers are always appreciated). I know that I am my own worst enemy, and that a combination of poor diet and insufficient exercise might well be contributing factors to my current condition. No doubt 'work-a-holism' and stress are areas that I will need to address too. I confess you to, my brothers and sisters, that I have sinned in all these areas. By God's grace, and no doubt your continued encouragement, I will try to do better in the future.

There is an irony about our faith, isn't there? The irony is that whilst few of us would want to hasten our own death, we hold the belief that what lies beyond this 'mortal coil' is promised to be infinitely better than that which we experience now. Last week, among some whimsical ruminations about eggs, I was reminded that we are Easter people - we are those who live in the light of the promise of life-without-end in the close presence of God.

What we perhaps forget, is that Jesus didn't just come to offer us 'life-after-death', but rather 'life in all its fullness' now. We shall explore something of that theme during today's service, when we find ourselves confronted by the Lord who turns perfectly good water into wonderful wine. The Christian faith is much more than a 'passport to eternity' - but rather, it is a way of living life to the full right now.

It may be suggested that in certain respects, I have so far lived life a little too fully - and that some adjustments are clearly necessary. But, while making such adjustments, I aim to hold on to a central theme of our faith, that a life lived with God means a life of fullness, meaning, community, hope and love.

Brexit...do I dare tell you what I think? (27 January 2019)

I have rather deliberately avoided the topic of Brexit over the last couple of years. My reluctance to address the issue more publicly, or regularly, has been partly because I know that within our congregation there will be people who voted on opposite sides of the Referendum question. I want to be a focus for unity within the parish, and so I tend to keep my political views largely to myself. As everyone knows, there is an old adage that 'politics and religion do not mix'...which is nonsense, of course. Jesus frequently addressed the political issues of his day, and religious people are citizens just as much as anyone else. But in the light of the great schism of public opinion over Brexit, what can we actually say that does not make us appear partisan?

What I think we can do is point to the underlying causes of the current Brexit battle. We live at a time when there are more people alive today than have ever lived - in total. We are destroying our environment at an ever-increasing rate. There are too many mouths to feed, and more mouths are on their way (2 billion more mouths are expected by 2050). Poverty, around the world, drives poor families to have as many children as possible - in the hope that at least one child will be talented, or lucky, enough to support the rest of the family. Family members are sent far and wide in search of resources.

These pressures, which we clearly cannot control as a species, lead to a fear of change in general. We look around us, and we do not like what we see. We either retreat, instinctively, to an imagined past, when Britain was 'Great', every one left their door unlocked, and the Vicar (and local Bobby) knew everyone's name. Or, we look to international alliances (like the European Union) with hope that they will be able to solve the World's problems, by working together. Both views are, of course, utopian.

The Bible has taught us that human beings are inherently flawed...the Bible's word is 'sinful'. Only God can rescue us from the mess we are in. Not Brexit, and not Remain either. There is no hope for us, unless we put our hope and trust in God. THAT is our task - to never give up trusting in God, following God's ways, and inviting our brother and sister humans to do the same.

Spring hope. (7 April 2019)

Easter is nearly upon us - though let us not wish away our days. Jesus encourages us to live in the moment. "Let tomorrow take care of itself," he says.

I was reminded of this while standing in the churchyard with our Churchyard Development Team, this week. All around us were promising signs of the spring and summer to come. Tiny flowers were pushing up tentatively through the sward.   Blue tits were making a nest in the bird box we've fixed to the tree directly in line with the West Door. (Go and watch them, why don't you?). Up in the tower, noisy jackdaws (at least 20 of them) were competing for nesting space in the 'putlog' holes...chasing away naughty pigeons.

I reminded myself that all these were signs of a spring yet to fully come. Daffodils have come and are now going. Primroses too. But much of Mother Nature is still only now stirring into life. Just like the Kingdom of God, there is a 'now, and not yet' quality of this moment in the year.

All around us, we see signs of the Kingdom. Wherever there is generosity, kindness, self-sacrifice, joy and love, the Kingdom comes into view. But, it is 'not yet' here, as well. And it will not fully be until we rid ourselves of xenophobia, the politics of division, extreme profiteering, knife-crime, vandalism, domestic violence...and all the rest. But, like a Rector standing hopefully in his proto-spring churchyard, we can all carry around with us the theology of hope. The Kingdom IS coming...and it is already among us.

On the passing of a centenarian. (23 June 2019)

This week, we shall lay to rest our oldest and dear member, and former Parish Secretary, Audrey Currie, on what would have been her 100th birthday. God bless her. A hundred years is long time to live. Her long life encompassed the rise and then fall of Soviet communism, the Great Depression, a world war, three monarchs (or four if you count Edward VIII!), the Falklands, Churchill, Thatcher, Reagan, Gorbachev, Cameron, the establishment of a European Community, as well as our current national attempt to leave it again.

And yet, like most of us, Audrey had nothing to do with any of these great events. Like most of us, she lived her life as faithfully as she could, serving God, her family, her church and her community. Is her life, or our lives, any less important than those of the great people who shaped world events? I think not.

Jesus never led an army, or a political party. He never built a ship, or ran a bank. He just faithfully followed the path he was shown. And yet nothing in the history of the world has affected the life of humankind as much as that one, solitary life.

May we too, like Audrey, have the grace to follow the path we are shown.

POLITICS

EVENTS OBSERVED FOLLOWING THE CHURCH COUNCIL ELECTIONS

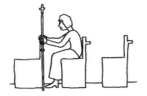

THE OUTGOING CHURCHWARDEN STILL OCCUPYING THE CHURCHWARDEN'S PEW

A COALITION BETWEEN THE FLOWER LADIES AND THE YOUTH GROUP

THE RECTOR BEING GIVEN A MANDATE TO RULE (I DID NOT KNOW WHAT A MANDATE LOOKED LIKE, SO I HAVE DRAWN A PINEAPPLE)

THE BELL RINGERS ATTEMPTING TO FORM A MINORITY PCC

Peter-tide reflections. (30 June 2019)

Yesterday (Saturday) the annual ordinations of new deacons and priests took place at our cathedral—this time including Hugo Deadman who, by dint of being Hilary and David's son, we can rightly claim as one of our own. It was also the 14th anniversary of my own ordination; so it was a day of minor note in my personal calendar.

Next week, on Thursday, we will joyfully witness the progression of Fr David Morgan from curate to incumbent.

And while we rightly celebrate all these new 'ministers' being created and affirmed in their callings, we do well if we remember this: all ordained ministries are mere icons. In other words, each ordained or licensed ministry is presented to us, by the church, as an example, or a model, of the Christian ministry to which we are all called, in our different ways. Like a painted icon represents something of the holy person it depicts, all ministers should (by their words and actions) represent the God whom they are called to serve. And should call the rest of us to do the same.

The danger, to the church, comes when congregations forget this, and leave the whole task of presenting the Gospel to their ordained ministers. That is the road to burn-out (for the ministers) and death (for the life of the church).

Each of us has our own callings under God. Some of us are ordained (or 'set-apart') for specific ministries...such as bishop, priest, or deacon. But we cannot, and rightly do-not, attempt to shoulder the joyful burden of the Gospel alone. We are in this together, folks! We are the Body of Christ—quite literally God's hands and feet to a dying world.

On the baptism of a grandson. (7 July 2019)

It is a rare pleasure for us to baptize a youngster in our main Sunday Service, as we will today. For most families, these days, the prospect of standing up in public to make promises is too nerve-wracking...especially when they are not regular church goers. So we bend, and we welcome them into a more private arrangement, with which they can cope. Some might wonder at this. Certainly, I know of some clergy who consider 'private baptism' to be close to heresy!

My own change of heart was precipitated by a baptism (in my last parish) during which the attending family members were SO noisy that I had to give up trying to preach even the family-friendly sermon I had prepared. When a group of children starting playing 'ring-a-ring-a-roses' down the central aisle, I knew that we had lost any semblance of an act of worship!

For me, the central point of baptism is this: baptism is a gift of God, given out of his loving kindness. It does not rely on us even being conscious that it is happening (my own baptism took place in hospital when I was only days old).

Baptism doesn't rely on us; it relies on God. On this point, the traditional Churches are at variance with our 'Baptist' (or strictly-speaking 'Anabaptist') friends, who hold that an adult confession of faith is required. We don't require that - though we encourage it via confirmation. But for us, baptism is about God's response to us, not our response to God. So, that's why private baptisms, when necessary, are OK for me. I'll offer God's love and grace, and spiritual power to anyone who asks for it!

The long view of history. (14th July 2019)

So...by the time the next 'Weekly News' is published, our country will have a new prime minister. Whether they will prove better able to solve the current constitutional crisis remains to be seen.

One of the things I like most about belonging to the church is that it tends to give one a very long view of history. The stories of the Hebrew Bible which we have inherited (and which we call the 'Old Testament') stretch back in time something like 6,000 years. The stories of the last 2,000 years of church history are similar. They give us a perspective on world events which can often be illuminating, and which can often help us to make sense of what is going on now.

Brexit, for example, is by no means the first time that the UK has wrestled with what it means to belong to a bigger family of nations. In many ways, the European Union is just the latest iteration of the same political drive to unify nations which drove the Roman Empire, and the empire of the Roman Catholic Church. The Roman Empire broke from us in around 400AD. Then we broke from the Roman Catholic church at the time of Henry VIII. The Hebrew Bible shows us that falling in and out of alliances with bigger nations, or groups of nations, has always been part of human history.

So, whichever way Brexit finally goes, I draw comfort from the fact that this is just the latest expression of the restlessness of human beings - always hoping that things will be better if they could be different.

God, of course, shows us another way. God's vision of how the world should be - God's 'Kingdom of Heaven' - is so radically different from any politician's short-term plan. Ultimately, whatever we think of the Brexit question, we are called to keep on talking about God's plan. It will definitely be different, and undoubtedly better, in every conceivable way!

Being a free thinker… (25 August 2019)

I had an interesting 'spat' on the internet this week. In response to a comment I made on a Facebook post on a political issue, a person I don't know said critically "everyone knows you're a Socialist". (It was intended as an insult). "Actually," I responded, "I'm neither a Socialist, nor a Conservative, nor a Liberal...I'm a free thinker who likes to make up his own mind rather than follow any party line".

It would probably have been even more true to have said that I'm just confused! Even having worked in Westminster for five years (as I did at the turn of the Millennium) I am utterly incapable of nailing my colours to any one political mast. There is much that I find attractive about Socialism (especially the notion of sharing a nation's wealth as equally as possible between all its citizens). But I also see the benefits that a regulated free market and low taxation brings to national economies. As a theological liberal, I'm somewhat inclined towards political liberalism too...but, I'm also a traditionalist (a 'conservative' with a small 'c') who is wary of jumping on every liberal band-wagon too quickly.

Ultimately, my affiliation is to a higher political idea - the Kingdom of Heaven (or Kingdom of God). That is a Kingdom which operates on principles that none of our current political parties really understand...the principles of humility, meekness, and prayerfulness. Our current politicians have to operate in a media-driven culture of celebrity and bombast. Only the loudest and most controversial voices get an airing. The quiet, thoughtful voices have nothing of interest to say to a media which is thirsty for headlines. And that's a challenge for all of us who want to see the world change. We, however, are called to continue praying 'thy Kingdom come'...and, in face of all provocation and political temptation, perhaps that is the best thing we can do, after all.

On being defined by frailty. (1 September 2019)

I've been feeling a bit frail this week. It all started when saving my motorbike from toppling over on an adverse camber (and wrenching my foot in the process). Then I managed to put my back out over-night (how does one do that while asleep?!). These two accidents come on top of a recently-diagnosed arthritic knee, and were topped off by the act of tumbling to the ground while making a fool of myself at this week's Tuesday concert! I was demonstrating the Morecombe & Wise dance at the time, and ever since I've been singing "Give me codeine" (instead of sunshine!)

Feeling temporarily frail has served to remind me of the frailty that I know many of you live with every day. I can only imagine the frustration of being dependent on others for a long period of time. All those who have to do so routinely have my sympathy and my prayers.

But I also offer this thought…it is far too easy for us to define each other by our frailties. I know I've done it (and I guess most of us have). I've certainly described people to others by their disability or their frailty. (Oh you know, "the woman who uses a wheelchair"… or the "man with the two hearing aids"). It's never meant in malice...but sometimes, a person's frailty can be the most obvious descriptor of them. When we do so, though, we miss the opportunity to describe them as God sees them...as God's beautiful child, rich in wisdom and experience, or as the one who gives of their time (and even their frailty) to others.

I hope, selfishly, that my current physical frailty is a passing thing. But should it not be, I hope I'll have the wisdom (that many of you show me) to re-direct my energies into new ways of serving God, even in frailty. Perhaps if I wasn't charging about the parish at a thousand miles an hour, I'd have more time to write, or pray, or sit and share with friends (or the lonely).

Belong, believe, behave. 15 September 2019

We don't half-do social events at St Faith's! I've just got back from our weekly lunchtime concerts, and have once again rejoiced in the sheer number of non-church members who attend. Our monthly coffee morning, and now daily gatherings of friends in church are hugely successful. We have our new social group, TAT (Thursday at Two), on the last Thursday of every month, and we're looking forward to our Harvest Supper, and then the Variety Show. Some people might question why we do so many social things...and not spend our time on our knees, instead.

My answer is that belonging to a church like St Faith's is something that usually happens gradually...especially for folks who don't yet feel comfortable with calling themselves followers of Jesus Christ. So, quite deliberately, we say 'belong first'. Then, as God draws you closer, you might choose to 'believe'. That's a massive step for many people, and those of us who already believe need to give our neighbours the space to explore belief at their own pace.

The final step along this simple road is to choose to 'behave' like a follower of Christ. That's something we all struggle with. I certainly know how often I fail at behaving as I should. I could certainly be more mindful of God and others. I could certainly learn to be more generous. I could certainly learn to love more, and criticize less.

But as a general maxim for the kind of journey we offer at St Faith's, Belong, Believe, Behave will do nicely for now!

Rector or Dictator?   22 September 2019

In these days of supreme court hearings (over Government decisions regarding the proroguing of Parliament) we have been reminded of the balance which the British constitution affords. The power of Government, Parliament and the Judiciary are each held in check by the other, and all under the ultimate authority of the Crown.

This 'balance of power' is mirrored, somewhat, in the parish system. Under the Church of England's legal framework, the Parochial Church Council has a similar in-built balance of power. Clergy, churchwardens and elected members each hold power from different sources.

Churchwardens are technically elected by the whole community, (although in reality few non-church members exercise that right). Elected members are appointed by the annual meeting, and clergy are appointed by the Bishop. Legal cover is provided by the Diocese, through the Chancellor, who though appointed by the Bishop and Queen, is not beholden to either. And of course, like the organs of the state, the Church of England sits under the titular authority of the Crown (which is why we pray for the Queen every Thursday at our mid-week mass, and often on Sundays too).

Such a balance of power is a healthy thing. It acts as a brake on a Rector (or indeed a PCC) who might suddenly go bonkers and decide to knock down a church, or paint it with pink polka-dots. It also reminds us that power to change anything in our society is a shared thing.

As members of the body of Christ, each with our own ideas, talents and abilities, we all have a part to play in shaping the future, and advancing the Kingdom. The work of the Kingdom in Havant is not mine alone...it belongs to all of us!

Amid the chaos... (29 September 2019)

For news addicts (like me), or those with any interest in Brexit, it's been an anxious and fascinating week. It's notable how words which once struck fear into the heart have begun to lose their impact... the phrase 'constitutional crisis' no longer has us running for the hills. Nor do the words 'traitor' or 'law-breaker' hit us with the force that such words have had in times gone past.

Human beings have an in-built 'flight or fight' response to conflict. It's what drove us out of the woods and fields into cities, and ultimately what taught us to co-operate with each other to build relatively safe communities. It's also what feeds our 'fear of the other', which some politicians use very skilfully to make us look to the wrong causes of society's problems.

In the world of sport, this week's 'derby' between Portsmouth and Southampton prompted some extreme behaviour on the part of fans, who hate each other with an entirely unreasonable passion. After-all, both sets of fans love the 'beautiful game'. Why can't they also love one another?

Amidst all the conflict and chaos, we do well to remember the eternal perspective of God. There is 'nothing new under the sun' (as the writer of Ecclesiastes teaches us). For God, all human conflict is symptomatic of a child-like race, which is yet to grow into its full maturity as a saved and redeemed people. Amid the chaos, our task is to keep on loving, and keep on teaching the ways of love to our community, our neighbours and our families.

It may seem 'ostrich-like' to carry on singing services, attending lunchtime concerts, running 'Little Seeds' and 'TAT' amid the chaos all around. But this is what we do. We keep on declaring that there is more to life, even than Brexit or football! We keep on calling the world to a life of love, community and sacrifice.

Finding God amidst the pain… (6 October 2019)

Many of you will have heard by now of the sad situation being faced by my family this week. Clare's mother, Jan (a regular worshipper with us at St Faith's) suffered a severe stroke on Tuesday morning. As I write this (on Wednesday), we await further news from her medical team. Thank you to those of you who have held us (and especially Jan) in your thoughts and prayers over these days.

Sudden and life-changing illness is, of course, a risk that we all face - just by being human, and apparently in spite of our very best efforts to live healthily. (Until yesterday, Jan was fit, active and ate very healthily). Others in our congregation face slower, creeping illnesses, such as Parkinsons or dementia. I never cease to be amazed at what a work of wonder is the human body. Ironically, only last weekend I was reflecting with Jan at the difference between a 20 year man-made machine (ready for the scrap-yard) and a 20 year old human machine (at the peak of health and efficiency). And yet, amid such wonder and complexity, the introduction of a tiny virus, or (as in Jan's case) a blood-clot can upset the delicate balance so easily.

The challenge for followers of Jesus is to look for signs of God, even in our frailties (as I've reflected in this column before). In the last 48 hours, we have indeed experienced God at work, even through the tragedy of a severe stroke. There has been the kindness of strangers (especially the fantastic medical staff) and the love of family. There have been many moments of great tenderness towards Jan from her family (as they have come together from all over the country around her bedside). There has been the sense of loving prayerful support from all at St Faith's who were aware.

These, and many more, are signs that God continues to work, even through our pain and suffering. Through the example of Jesus, God shows us how he enters into our suffering with us, constantly redeeming even the worst circumstances into something that can speak of his continuing and passionate love.

Can you read my mind? (13th October 2019)

It is a feature of all organisations, perhaps especially churches, that members assume the power of telepathy. I made that mistake last month when I assumed that everyone would know that, as usual on third Saturdays, I would be in the church for FaithTalk at 11.00am. As a result, only three of us showed up! My fault entirely.... for not reminding folks (though we had a great discussion!)

Sometimes, some congregation members make a similar error in judgment, when they assume that I have the power of telepathy about them. 150 members, and a wide number of other parishioners all seem to think that their parish priest should just know that they need a visit, or a chat about something on their mind. And when the parish priest doesn't call, or forgets (on meeting them) to ask about the progress of their illness or life-challenge, there's a real danger that they feel unloved or unregarded; though nothing could be further from the truth. (I simply have a crazy schedule, and a useless memory!)

If we struggle to read each other's minds, how then can we read the mind of God? Scripture can certainly help, and (read with care and intelligence) it can point us accurately towards God's mind on the whole of our existence. So too can the fellowship of all believers, coming together in humility to listen to what God may be saying to us all. Being a church is actually an exercise in reading, together, the mind of God. By our conversations, sermons, prayers, committee meetings and fellowship we begin to discern together what the Spirit is saying to the church.

Your PCC is soon to begin the task of reviewing our five-year Mission Development Plan, and gazing into God's future for us. We need to read God's mind together, about what he has next in store for St Faith's. So please join in the conversation, and help us to read the mind of God!

Quizzical eyebrows at Hallowe'en. (27th October 2019)

A few quizzical eyebrows have been raised, of late, about St Faith's approach to Hallowe'en. Some other churches (notably St John's, Rowlands Castle) have 'Light Parties', which are designed to offer a complete alternative to the modern propensity for scaring people on that night of the year. I think such initiatives are great! (In former years, I well remember spending a previous Hallowe'en with youngsters at a swimming pool...completely ignoring the way others chose to commemorate the festival.)

In our case, this year, eyebrows have been raised at our choice to read 'spooky' Dickens' stories in the church, and to display 'Harry Potter'-themed goods in the Charity Shop. The underlying motivation for these events is mine: I posit that ignoring Hallowe'en can make the church appear to claim superiority over popular culture...whereas I want us to engage with it and transform it.

Hallowe'en is of course the eve of All 'Hallows', or All Saints. It's a festival in which we especially remember and give thanks for the lives of those who now reside on another shore, and in a greater light. And that means that we are forced to confront the reality of death—something that most of us would prefer to forget, after all. Hallowe'en also has deep roots in the Celtic festival of Samhain (literally 'end of summer') when the ancient peoples believed that the gods and spirits came out to play tricks on the living, as the winter took hold.

By reading Dickens' ghost stories, and permitting the metaphor-rich Harry Potter stories to be depicted in the Charity Shop, my aim is to awaken us to the eternal struggle between life and death, and between good and evil. Dickens' stories always call us to higher moral action, as do the tales of J.K.Rowling. You may well still raise a quizzical eyebrow in my direction, but I hope you'll at least understand my point of view.

A better form of government... (8 December 2019)

By the time the next 'Fortnightly News' is published, the latest General Election will have come and gone. I wonder what state of excitement (or misery) we will feel at that time. I've been a bit naughty recently. I've been deliberately poking fun, or sending challenging social-media messages, to people on all sides of the political divide. You see, I'm convinced that most people simply do not understand even the most basic of political language. After all, what is the difference between 'trickle-down economics' and 'tax and spend'? Or, still more opaque, what do we mean by 'fiscal drag' or 'quantitive easing'? What is the difference between the Government deficit, and the Government debt? I'm sure that these are just simple questions for the well-educated people of St Faiths!

There have of course been many attempts across the centuries to design and run an effective system of Government. Democracy (in the sense of every person over 18 getting a vote) is still in its infancy...barely 100 years old in its present form. Before that, we've tried being an Absolute Monarchy and a Constitutional one (we still are, to an extent). We've had a 'Theocracy' (when the church ran pretty-much everything). We've tried building Empires, and we've been subject to the Empire-building of others (not least the Romans, and perhaps the European Union). We've even been a Republic, under Oliver Cromwell.

According to Plato, Socrates had an interesting notion (outlined in 'The Republic'). He suggested that the political class should be educated simply and only to govern. They should then been given basic housing and all their necessities of life, and forbidden from earning any money beyond those basics. Then, Socrates suggested, politicians would be free from the corruption of money. An intriguing idea - but I think Socrates may have mis-understood the effect that power can have on a politician. Regardless of personal wealth, power alone can be a dangerous drug.

Democracy, therefore, seems to be about the best system we've come up with yet. But it is full of flaws...not least that it gives the power to people who barely understand how to calculate their own household budget, let alone have a qualified opinion on the macro-financing of Government ambitions. As Winston Churchill famously said, 'Democracy is the worst form of Government...except for all the other forms of Government!'.

God holds out a still greater offer of effective Government, which Jesus called the Kingdom of God, or of Heaven - which we are invited during Advent to glimpse as a possibility. Unless Jesus suddenly returns 'on the clouds' (as the poetic language of the Gospels suggest) we still have a lot of waiting to do.

But our task, as Jesus' royal ambassadors, is to keep on reminding our families, friends, and yes, social media contacts, that there is a yet still greater vision held before us. Whatever the result of the General Election, it will be only a pale shadow of the Kingdom yet to come.

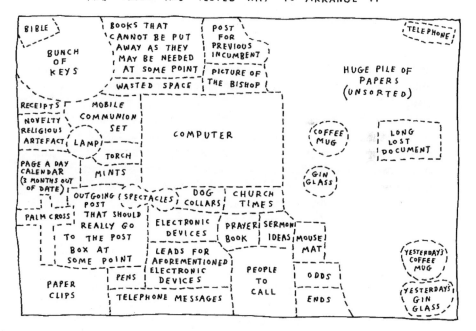

THE CLERGY DESK
THE TRIED AND TESTED WAY TO ARRANGE IT

The end of the decade? (5 January 2020)

A spirited argument takes place at the end of every decade. Is a year ending in '0' the end of a decade, or the beginning of the new one? Of course, the answer depends on where we count from. It's a startling fact that there is no year zero in the Christian calendar. There was the year before Christ, and then there was the year of Christ (Anno Domini) - year 1. On that basis, I'd have to say that I agree with those pedants who argue that 2021 will be the start of the next decade.

Nevertheless, as the calendar rolled over to 2020 at our Watchnight Mass, I felt a deep sense of God doing something new among us. In February I will mark the first five years of being your Rector - an honour and privilege I continue to cherish. In those five years, we've spent a lot of time worshipping among scaffolding, ladders, half-working electrics and the like. But together, we've achieved a great deal of physical progress in all of our parish buildings - providing a firm foundation for the spiritual road that I believe God is now calling us to travel together.

What our future may look like, I don't yet know. There is no doubt in my mind that God calls us to be a spiritual centre for the town of Havant - literally 'Faith in the Heart of Havant'. We are undoubtedly called to provide a welcome to people of all faiths and none, and an opportunity to find friends and seek counsel. But what else?

Through the gospels, Jesus calls us clearly to announce his coming Kingdom, and to call all humanity to embrace his 'Way' - 'to make disciples of all people'. As I look around our gorgeous, faithful, congregation, I nevertheless have to draw the conclusion that none of us is getting any younger. If the mission of St Faith's is to continue beyond our own stewardship, a new generation of disciples will be needed to carry on God's mission in this place.

So my invitation to you at the beginning of this new year is to start praying for guidance about how we might rise to the challenge of offering the life of faith to more and more of our neighbours - especially in a culture that increasingly views religion as an odd thing to do!

O death, where is thy victory? (2 February 2020)

Praying for the dead is a contentious thing to do in church circles. There are some who believe that a decision to follow Christ must be made in this life only, and that heaven is only granted to those who have made that decision before death. Such believers therefore argue that prayers for the dead are superfluous and theologically incorrect (remember last Sunday's sermon about correctness!).

For liberals (like me) a wider, more generous picture of God is uppermost in our minds, perhaps summed up best by C.S. Lewis, when he wrote to the effect that whilst Christians maintain that it is only through Jesus that we can be saved, we don't know (from Scripture) whether it is essential to have chosen Jesus in this life. Lewis holds out for our consideration the idea that God offers a welcome, through Jesus, to all his children. Most of us would surely run into his arms...though there may well be a few totally self-absorbed, malignant souls who would shrink from such love.

It is this more liberal view that gives me immense hope for the future, even for those of our families and friends who never set foot in a church, or picked up a bible. But whatever the correctness of this view may be, I live in firm confidence of a God whose whole being is characterised by Love. I simply cannot conceive of a God who would not give every opportunity—in life and after it—for his children to bathe in his love, and be drawn into eternity by it. It is for that reason that I delete a single word from the traditional prayer said by choirs and altar parties as a dismissal in the vestry: "May the souls of all the faithful departed rest in peace and rise in glory"

I trust in a God who is described in Scripture as a Father, and who acts in so many ways like a Mother (bringing forth life, guiding and shepherding through life, nurturing and sustaining us). The cross, for me, is a powerful symbol of that parental Love, but it is not (for me) the singular mechanism by which a Loving God reaches out to his/her children. This belief gives me confidence that death, indeed, has no sting. For the balm of God's Love heals all.

Discuss!

273

Epilogue

A collection of writings such as this will inevitably be somewhat of a 'curate's egg' – good in places. Among these pages, you will have gleaned *some* of my personal story, and *something* of what I think on a broad range of religious, theological, societal and political topics. The task of writing a more comprehensive, even scholarly work on these topics must, of necessity, wait until the time to focus on such a monumental task presents itself. The best I can hope for is that by reading them, you will have at least had your imagination tickled, and perhaps your own thinking shaped a little.

In drawing these 'scribblings' together, I have been surprised at the topics I find I have *not* addressed (or only obliquely addressed) within the general medium of sermons and talks. These are topics on which I certainly have passionate views, and they would include gender identity in Christianity, parish management & governance, Christian socialism, the use of music in worship, the art of leadership, the fundamental unity of all religions, and colonial Christianity (to name but a few). Perhaps some of these may form the basis of future publications.

As I said in the prologue, the decision to publish these 'scribblings' arose out of a desire to offer these ideas for debate and challenge. Indeed, I rather hope that some of the sermons, or 'last words' contained in this collection *might* form the basis of some discussions within my parish, in the future. If, however, you would enjoy engaging with me directly, I have created an email address specifically for the task. I warmly welcome you to write to me, challenge or encourage me about anything you have read here. I promise to try to respond as soon as the limited time I have available permits (while working as a parish priest).

Emails can be sent to: scribblingsoftom@gmail.com. I very much look forward to hearing your thoughts!

Tom Kennar
May 2020

Scriptural Index

Note: These references are intended to point the reader to places where such Scriptures are directly referenced. Often, this occurs at the beginning of a sermon or thought-flow, where they form a back-drop to the topic under discussion. New Testament scriptures are definitely in the majority, because most of my sermons tend to focus on the Gospel reading of the day.